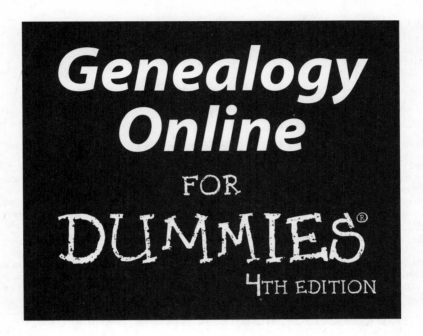

Genealogy Online
FOR
DUMMIES®
4TH EDITION

by Matthew L. Helm and April Leigh Helm

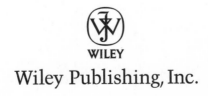

WILEY

Wiley Publishing, Inc.

Genealogy Online For Dummies,® **4th Edition**

Published by
Wiley Publishing, Inc.
111 River Street
Hoboken, NJ 07030-5774

Copyright © 2004 by Wiley Publishing, Inc., Indianapolis, Indiana

Published by Wiley Publishing, Inc., Indianapolis, Indiana

Published simultaneously in Canada

For general information on our other products and services or to obtain technical support, please contact our Customer Care Department within the U.S. at 800-762-2974, outside the U.S. at 317-572-3993, or fax 317-572-4002.

Wiley also publishes its books in a variety of electronic formats. Some content that appears in print may not be available in electronic books.

Library of Congress Control Number: 2004101428

ISBN: 0-7645-5964-8

Manufactured in the United States of America

10 9 8 7 6 5 4 3 2

4B/RZ/QS/QU/IN

WILEY

Genealogy Online For Dummies, 4th Edition

Cheat Sheet

How to Use Helm's Genealogy Toolbox

You can use Helm's Genealogy Toolbox to identify genealogical resources on the Internet in two different ways: using the Global Search engine or browsing through categories. To do either, go to Helm's Genealogy Toolbox at www.genealogytoolbox.com.

Using the Global Search engine

1. **In the left column, you find a blue box with a Global Search graphic.**

2. **Type the keyword that you're looking for in the box, or type the first and/or last names that you're looking for, and click the Search button.**

   The Search Results page contains several areas. The top section lists the Helm's Genealogy Toolbox categories that match your search terms. The second section lists the links on the Toolbox that contain your search terms. The third section shows the results of a full-text search using the Toolbox with your terms.

3. **Choose a link that appears to have information on your topic.**

Browsing by category in the directory

On the home page for Helm's Genealogy Toolbox is a gray box labeled Site Categories. Each category has a small description to help you figure out which category contains the information that you're looking for. These categories include:

- Computers
- How-To and Help
- Media
- People
- Places
- Supplies and Services

1. **Click the category that interests you.**

2. **If a listing of subcategories appears, browse through it and click the subcategory that interests you.**

   On subcategory pages, you find lists of hand-picked links relating to that topic, a list of URLs generated from the Toolbox's full-text search, queries, and software related to the topic (if appropriate). For each link to another site, you're provided with the name and a brief abstract of the link's content.

Here are a couple of hints to remember when you browse through categories:

- **Looking for information about a surname?** Click the People category in the main directory.
- **Looking for information about a geographic location?** Click the Places category in the main directory.

For Dummies: Bestselling Book Series for Beginners

Genealogy Online For Dummies, 4th Edition

Cheat Sheet

Some Genealogical Web Sites to Remember

For news and information about developments in genealogy

Eastman's Online Genealogy Newsletter	eogn.com/home/
National Genealogical Society News	www.ngsgenealogy.org/newnews.htm

For links to lots of other genealogical sites

Genealogy Home Page	www.genhomepage.com
Helm's Genealogy Toolbox	www.genealogytoolbox.com

For surname resources

Genealogy Resources on the Internet Mailing List	www.rootsweb.com/~jfuller/gen_mail.html
Roots Surname List search page	rsl.rootsweb.com/cgi-bin/rslsql.cgi

To post queries and share genealogical research success

Ancestry Message Boards	boards.ancestry.com
GenCircles	www.gencircles.com
FamilyHistory.com	www.familyhistory.com
USGenweb	usgenweb.org
GenForum	genforum.genealogy.com

For United States government resources

Citizenship and Naturalization Service (formerly the Immigration and Naturalization Service)	www.uscis.gov
Library of Congress	www.loc.gov
National Archives and Records Administration	www.nara.gov

For Dummies: Bestselling Book Series for Beginners

About the Authors

Matthew L. Helm is the Executive Vice President and Chief Technology Officer for FamilyToolbox.net, Inc. He's the creator and maintainer of the award-winning Helm's Genealogy Toolbox, Helm/Helms Family Research Page, and a variety of other Web sites. Matthew speaks at national genealogical conventions, lectures to genealogical and historical societies, and is a director of the Federation of Genealogical Societies. Matthew holds an A.B. in History and an M.S. in Library and Information Science from the University of Illinois at Urbana-Champaign.

April Leigh Helm is the President of FamilyToolbox.net, Inc. April lectures on genealogy and other topics for various conferences and groups. She holds a B.S. in Journalism and an Ed.M. in Higher Education Administration from the University of Illinois at Urbana-Champaign.

Together, the Helms have coauthored several books in addition to the four editions of *Genealogy Online For Dummies*. They include *Family Tree Maker For Dummies, Your Official America Online Guide to Genealogy Online,* and *Get Your Degree Online*.

Although they collected notes on family members and old photographs for many years, it wasn't until 1990, while living and working in the Washington, D.C., area, that the Helms began seriously researching their family lines. Upon returning to central Illinois in 1994, the Helms found themselves with limited historical and genealogical resources for the areas in which their ancestors lived. It was then that they jumped into online genealogy.

Here's a little more information about a few of the genealogical Web sites maintained by the Helms:

Helm's Genealogy Toolbox (www.genealogytoolbox.com): An online clearinghouse of genealogical tools and links.

Sources2Go.com (www.sources2go.com): An online archive of digitized records and documents that enable genealogists to conduct primary research on the Internet.

GenealogyDirect.com (www.genealogydirect.com): Over 13,000 genealogical products are available for purchase through this site.

GenealogyPortal.com (www.genealogyportal.com): A site containing eight separate search engines that index sites of interest to genealogists. It was created as a joint project between Matthew and Stephen Wood, the creator and maintainer of the Genealogy Home Page.

Dedication

For Kyleakin and Cambrian

Authors' Acknowledgments

We wish to acknowledge the following people, without whom this book wouldn't exist:

Lisa Swayne, who sought us out to write our very first book, and Susan Barry, who currently keeps track of us.

Liz Kerstens, a fellow genealogist whom we greatly respect and trust to keep us honest.

Paul, Greg, Barry, Carmen, Megan, and Adrienne, who logged a lot of hours pulling together this book and its CD.

Our respective parents and ancestors, without whom our own genealogies wouldn't be possible.

Publisher's Acknowledgments

We're proud of this book; please send us your comments through our online registration form located at www.dummies.com/register/.

Some of the people who helped bring this book to market include the following:

Acquisitions, Editorial, and Media Development

Project Editor: Paul Levesque

Acquisitions Editor: Greg Croy

Copy Editor: Barry Childs-Helton

Technical Editors: Liz Kerstens

Editorial Manager: Kevin Kirschner

Permissions Editor: Carmen Krikorian

Media Development Manager: Laura Van Winkle

Media Development Supervisor: Richard Graves

Editorial Assistant: Amanda Foxworth

Cartoons: Rich Tennant (www.the5thwave.com)

Production

Project Coordinator: Adrienne Martinez

Layout and Graphics: Seth Conley, Andrea Dahl, Stephanie D. Jumper, Michael Kruzil, Lynsey Osborn, Heather Ryan, Jacque Schneider

Proofreaders: Andy Hollandbeck, Carl William Pierce, Dwight Ramsey, Charles Spencer, TECHBOOKS Production Services

Indexer: TECHBOOKS Production Services

Publishing and Editorial for Technology Dummies

Richard Swadley, Vice President and Executive Group Publisher

Andy Cummings, Vice President and Publisher

Mary C. Corder, Editorial Director

Publishing for Consumer Dummies

Diane Graves Steele, Vice President and Publisher

Joyce Pepple, Acquisitions Director

Composition Services

Gerry Fahey, Vice President of Production Services

Debbie Stailey, Director of Composition Services

Contents at a Glance

Table of Contents

Introduction

· ·

*T*ired of not knowing half of the people that your relatives are talking about at that annual family reunion? It can be quite embarrassing at times. Do you wish you could just pull out your laptop and show everyone that you're an expert on the history of your family? Then this might be just the book for you.

You may be interested in learning about your family history, or genealogy, for various reasons:

  ✔ Do you want to know what part your ancestors played in history?

  ✔ Do you need to conduct genealogical research for religious reasons or to join a lineage society?

  ✔ Do you simply enjoy solving puzzles?

No matter what the reason is for research, this is the best time in history to be looking into your genealogy.

In the past, genealogists had to load up the car with all of their notebooks and travel hundreds of miles to find clues about their ancestors. This meant that only a few had the time, energy, and money to do serious research. With the advent of the computer and genealogical resources on the Internet, the genealogy landscape has completely changed. You can now spend quality time sifting through the many resources available online, at any time of the day, without leaving the comfort of your home.

Of course, at this point we should give you a couple of warnings. First, genealogy is a very addictive pursuit. You just might find yourself staying up until all hours of the night chasing down that elusive ancestor. So, don't blame us if your boss begins to complain about you falling asleep at work due to your genealogical research routine. Also, on a more serious note, keep in mind that online research is merely one tool among many for finding information about your family. To thoroughly research your genealogy, you will have to employ a number of tools — many of which we talk about throughout this book.

Now that the disclaimers are out of the way, put the kids to bed, let your pets out, and boot up that computer. Your ancestors are just waiting to be found!

About This Book

Researching your family history online is like being a child in a candy store. There are so many neat things that catch your eye that it's difficult to decide which one to try. That's where this book comes in. We try to help you become a discriminating candy eater — well, a discriminating researcher anyway — by showing you not only the locations of useful genealogy sites but also how to effectively use them to meet your research goals.

Having said that, you're probably asking yourself how this book differs from the many other genealogy books on the shelf. Some books tell you only the traditional methods of genealogical research — which have you traveling hundreds of miles to visit courthouses and using the good old typewriter to summarize your results. Unfortunately, these books neglect the many opportunities that online research provides. Other books that do cover online genealogy tend to group resources by how users access them (all FTP sites are listed together, all World Wide Web sites are listed together, and so on), rather than telling you how you can integrate the many Internet resources to achieve your genealogical goal. As genealogists, we understand that researchers don't conduct searches by trying all the FTP sites, and then all the World Wide Web sites, and so on. We search by looking for surnames or places anywhere we can find them — through FTP sites, World Wide Web sites, e-mail, newsgroups, or whatever.

Also, some books become too computer-heavy — overkilling the ins and outs of each kind of Internet resource, and neglecting to help you with basic research techniques online *and offline* that you need to successfully meet your goal. We don't want you to have a bad experience online. So rather than focus on just one thing — genealogy *or* online resources — we try to balance the act. In this book, we show you how to integrate genealogical research with the use of online resources so you can learn to effectively and efficiently use your computer and the Internet in your family research.

What are the requirements for becoming an official genealogist? Well, do you have a mirror nearby? If so, go to the mirror and look at yourself. Now say out loud, "I declare myself an official genealogist." There you go. Of course, if you prefer, you're welcome to drag your family or pets into the room to witness this historic event. Whether you make your proclamation in a private ceremony for one or you have witnesses, it's official — you're a genealogist, and it's time to start pulling together the puzzle pieces of your family history.

Seriously, being a genealogist has no formal requirements. You simply need an interest in your ancestry and a willingness to devote the rest of your life to pursuing information and documents.

Foolish Assumptions

In writing and revising this book, we made a couple of assumptions. If you fit one of these assumptions, this book is for you:

- ✔ You've done at least a little genealogy groundwork, and now you're ready to use the Internet to pursue (and better prepare yourself for) your genealogy research both online and offline.

- ✔ You have at least a little computer experience, are now interested in pursuing your family tree, and want to know where and how to start.

- ✔ You have a little experience in genealogy and some experience with computers, but you want to learn how to put them together.

Of course, you can have a lot of computer experience and be a novice to genealogy or to online genealogy and still benefit from this book. In this case, you may still want to skim some of the basic sections on computers and the Internet in case you can find something else to use.

How to Use This Book

We know that you may not read this book from cover to cover, in order. (No, you're not hurting our feelings by skipping through the sections looking only for the information that you're interested in at that particular moment! We want this book to be useful. How you use it is up to you.) In fact, we've tried to write this book to accommodate you. Each section within each chapter can stand alone as a separate entity, so you can pick up the book and flip directly to a section that deals with what you want to know. If we think something relevant in another section can supplement your knowledge on the particular topic, we provide a note or reference telling you the other place(s) we think you should look. However, we've tried very hard to do this referencing in a manner that isn't obnoxious to those of you who choose to read the book from cover to cover. We hope we've succeeded in addressing both types of readers!

We use a couple of conventions in this book to make it easier for you to follow a set of specific instructions. Commands for menus appear with arrows between each selection. (For example, the command Format ➪ Tree Format tells you to choose Tree Format from the Format menu.)

If you need to type something, the explanation uses **bold type** to indicate what you need to type.

How This Book Is Organized

To help you get a better picture of what this book has to offer, we explain a little about how we organized it and what you can expect to find in each part.

Part 1: Getting Your Act Together

You need to have a good foundation before starting your online genealogical research. This part explores the fundamental family information that you need to collect first, how to form an online research plan, and how to start organizing your research and placing it into a genealogical database.

Part II: Focusing on Your Ancestor

Searching online for information about your particular ancestors can be a daunting task. Part II examines resources available for locating your ancestor by name and using government resources that can assist you in your ancestral hunt.

Part III: Adding Color to Your Research

Your family history is a lot more than just a list of names and birth dates. There are many details to be filled in so that your ancestors' lives are put in context. This part looks at geographical, ethnic, and religious resources that provide an insight into the everyday lives of your ancestors.

Part IV: Share and Share Alike

One of the most important aspects of genealogical research is using a coordinated effort to achieve success. This part takes a look at what goes into this effort, including using all available online resources, cooperating with other researchers, coordinating with groups and societies, and sharing the fruits of your research with the online community.

Part V: The Part of Tens

Ah, the infamous Part of Tens (infamous because every *For Dummies* book has one of these sections with profound advice or lists of things to do). Here you find a series of quick-reference chapters that give you useful genealogical hints and reminders. We include a list of online database sites we think you should know about, some tips for creating a genealogical Web page, hints to keep your online research sailing smoothly, and a list of sites that offer help to genealogists.

Appendixes

As you read this book (or skip from chapter to chapter, section to section, looking over only those parts that interest you), you may have additional questions in some areas. That's why we include the appendixes. One appendix helps you get some clarification or further information about going online. Another appendix provides definitions of many terms that you're likely to encounter in your genealogical research. And the last appendix gives you an overview of the software that we include on the CD-ROM that accompanies this book, as well as basic instructions for installing and using it.

The Genealogy Online For Dummies Internet Directory

This directory lists selected Internet sites that are of use and interest to genealogists. You can find sites for everything — from surnames to government records to comprehensive genealogical indexes to big search engines to commercial endeavors. For each site that we identify, we provide the name, URL (Uniform Resource Locator), and a brief overview of what the site has to offer.

We want you to be able to see immediately whether a site in the directory has a particular type of information or service of interest to you. For this reason, we created some mini-icons — or, if you prefer, *micons* (see The *Genealogy Online For Dummies* Internet Directory for details).

Icons Used in This Book

To help you get the most out of this book, we created some icons that tell you at a glance if a section or paragraph has important information of a particular kind.

Here we refer you to other books or materials if you'd like additional information.

This icon signals a Web site that has a search engine you can use to look for content within the site.

Here you can find concepts or terms that are unique to genealogy.

When you see this icon, you know we're offering advice or shortcuts to make your researching easier.

This icon points out software that's included on the CD-ROM.

We walk readers step by step through an example of something.

Look out! This is something tricky or unusual to watch for.

This icon marks important genealogical stuff, so don't forget it.

Where to Go from Here

Depending on where you're reading this introduction, your next step is one of two possibilities:

- ✔ You need to go to the front of the bookstore and pay for this book so that you can take it home and use it. (Many bookstores don't mind if you sit and read through parts of books — that's why they provide the comfortable chairs, right? But we're not sure they would look highly upon you whipping out your laptop computer, asking to borrow an Internet connection from them, and proceeding to go through this entire book right there in the store. Then again, we could be mistaken — so use your best judgment, based on your knowledge of the bookstore in which you're standing.)

- ✔ If you already bought the book and you're at home (or wherever), you can go ahead and start reading, following the steps for the online activities in the book as they come along.

Part I
Getting Your Act Together

The 5th Wave   By Rich Tennant

"They came here to help me with my genealogical research, but they stayed for the satellite T.V."

In this part . . .

So you wanna be an online genealogist? Well, you need to prepare yourself for that first online research trip by finding out about the basics of genealogy and how to form a research plan. Then you need to know how to organize and preserve what you find both online and offline. This part starts you off in the right direction.

Chapter 1

You Gotta Have Groundwork

*Y*ou're not going to believe it when we tell you this, but the first thing to do when researching your family history online doesn't involve a computer. That's right, you don't even need to flip that switch. Start by collecting some basic information about your family the "old-fashioned" way — interviewing relatives, digging through trunks in the attic, and visiting some better-known places for records. Then you can use some of this basic information to guide your research and help you make decisions about the quality of the information you find online.

Before we get too far down the path, we need to caution you that you can't complete your entire family history online. We say this not only to avoid the scorn of experienced genealogists, but we also want to make sure that your expectations of online research are appropriate. While you can find a lot of records online and the number of original records available online increases every day, several sets of crucial records are still not available through the Internet. The best way to think of online genealogy is as one of many tools that you use to put together the pieces of your family puzzle.

In this chapter, we give an overview of several resources that you can rely on for information before you begin your online genealogical research. We also provide some Web sites that can assist you in accessing these resources.

Starting Your Research with What You Already Know

You are really excited about getting started finding information on your great-great grandfather Benjamin Anderson. You fire up the computer, log on to your online service, and put good old Ben's name into one of the many genealogical search sites. The Results Web page comes up, showing entries for 450 Benjamin Andersons with the same name. Of course, the question is whether any of these people are the Benjamin you're looking for and, if so, which is the magic one? Well, if you know a little bit about Ben, then you can make some decisions as to which record or site is likely to contain information about him.

At this point, you might be asking yourself how you find information that can confirm whether the Benjamin on the screen is the one you're looking for. You're in luck because that's just what this section is all about. But before we go any further, we want to let you in on a little secret: Instead of starting your journey with Benjamin, it's better to begin by finding information about someone you already know a little bit better — yourself.

Making a few notes about yourself — the biographical sketch

You already know a great deal about yourself — probably more than anyone else knows about you. (That is, unless you're married. Then your spouse knows more about you, right?) You probably know your birth date, place of birth, parents' names, and where you've lived. (We recognize that not everyone knows all this information; adoptions or other extenuating circumstances may require you to do the best you can with what you know until you can discover additional information about yourself.) So, sit down at that computer, open your word processor, and create an autobiographical sketch. (Of course, if you prefer, you can take out a piece of paper and write down all those details instead.)

You can approach the sketch in several ways. Sometimes, the easiest method is to begin with current events and work back through your life. For instance, first note the basics: your current occupation, residence, and activities. Then move back to your last residence, occupation, and so on until you arrive at your birth date. Make sure that you include milestones like children's birth dates, marriage dates, military service dates, and other significant events in your life. If you prefer, you can cover your life by beginning with your birth and working forward to the present. Either way is fine, as long as all the important events are listed in the sketch.

Another method is to use index cards or a word processor to make notes on things that you recall over a certain period of time. Then you can arrange the cards or the paragraphs in the word-processing file to create a biographical sketch.

The biographical sketch that you create now may become an important research tool for one of your descendents who decides to conduct research about you in the future. So, when you have the time, we recommend that you turn that sketch into a full-blown autobiography and include it in your genealogy for the benefit of future generations. This way, your descendents not only know the facts about your life, they also will have some insight as to why you chose the paths you did throughout your life.

Finding primary sources

If you're like most of us, you probably think you know a lot about yourself. If we ask you what your birthday is, you can tell us without batting an eye. But how do you know the birth date? You were obviously there, but probably you were not in a condition to be a reliable witness — given that you were just born and most likely not fully aware of what was going on. This is where primary sources come in handy. Most likely there were people present who were witnesses and helped create a record of the event.

Primary sources are documents, oral accounts (if the account is made soon after the actual event and witnessed by the person who created the account), photographs, or any other items created at the time of a certain event's occurrence.

For example, a primary source for your birth date is your birth certificate. Typically, a birth certificate is prepared within a few days of the actual event and is signed by one or more actual witnesses to the birth. Because of the timeliness and involvement of direct witnesses, the information contained on the record (like the time, date, and parents' names) is usually a reliable first-hand account of the event. It's important to recognize that even if a record was prepared near the time of an event, such a unilateral account doesn't automatically mean that every fact provided on the record is correct. Cases arise where typographical errors occurred, or incorrect information was provided to the creator of the record. Often these errors are not caught when the certificate application is signed because new parents are preoccupied with things other than government paperwork during their stay at the hospital. So it's always a good idea to try to find other primary records that can corroborate the information found in any record.

Secondary sources are documents, oral accounts, and so on that are created some length of time after the event or for which information is supplied by someone who wasn't an eyewitness to the event. A secondary source can also be a person who was an eyewitness to the event but recalls it after a significant period of time passes.

Some records may be considered both primary and secondary sources. For example, a death certificate contains both primary and secondary source information. The primary source information is the death date and cause of death. These facts are primary because the certificate was prepared around the time of death, and the information is usually provided by a medical professional who pronounced the person dead. The secondary source information on the death certificate includes the birth date and place of birth of the deceased individual. These details are secondary because the certificate was issued at a time significantly later than the birth (assuming that the birth and death dates are at least a few years apart). Secondary sources don't have the degree of reliability or surety of primary sources. Often secondary source information, such as that found on death certificates, is provided by an individual's children or descendants who may or may not know the exact date or place of birth and who may be providing information during a stressful situation. Given the lesser reliability of secondary sources, backing up your secondary sources with reliable primary sources is always a good idea.

Although we've said that secondary sources are not as reliable as primary sources, that doesn't mean that secondary sources are always wrong or aren't useful. A good deal of the time, the information is correct, and such records provide valuable clues to locating primary source information. For example, in the case of a birth date and birthplace on a death certificate, the information provides a place and approximate time frame you can use as a starting point when you search for a birth record.

You can familiarize yourself with primary sources by collecting some information for your own biographical profile. Try to match up primary sources for each event in the sketch — for example, birth and marriage certificates, deeds, leases, military records, and tax records. For more information on finding these types of documents, see the appropriate sections later in this chapter. If you can't locate primary source documents for each event in your life, don't fret! Your biographical sketch can serve as a primary source document because you write it about yourself.

For additional information on primary sources, see The Historian's Sources page at the Library of Congress Web site at

`lcweb2.loc.gov/ammem/ndlpedu/lessons/psources/pshome.html`

For a comparison of primary, secondary, and *tertiary* sources (such as bibliographies, indexes, and encyclopedias), see the Randall Library Resource Guides site at

`library.uncwil.edu/is/infocycle.htm`

Chatting with Papa and Aunt Lola: Interviewing Your Family Members

There are some sources of genealogical gold out there, and you might not even recognize them. These sources hang around the food table at the family reunion, ask you embarrassing questions about your love life, and overstay their welcome in your home. Yes, they are your relatives.

Interviewing your relatives is an important step in the research process. They can provide family records and photographs, give you the dirt on other family members, and identify which other people would be beneficial to talk to about the family history. When talking with relatives, you want to collect the same type of information about their lives that you provided about your own when you wrote your biographical sketch.

Your parents, brothers, sisters, grandparents, aunts, uncles, and cousins are all good candidates for information sources about your family's most recent generations. Talking to relatives provides you with leads that you can use to find primary sources. (For more information on primary sources, see "Finding primary sources" in the preceding section.) You can complete family interviews in person or through a questionnaire — although we strongly recommend that you conduct them in person. For an example of a cover letter to send your family asking for an interview, go to the Family Tree Maker Web site at

`www.familytreemaker.com/00000059.html`

There's no easy way to say this, so please excuse us for being blunt — you may want to begin interviewing some of your older relatives as soon as possible, depending on their ages and health. If a family member passes on before you have the chance to interview him or her, you may miss the opportunity of a lifetime to learn more about his or her personal experiences and knowledge of previous generations.

TIP

Good interviewing questions

Before you conduct a family interview, pull together a set of questions to guide the discussion. A little planning on your part makes the difference between an interview in which the family member stays focused, or a question-and-answer session that invites bouncing from one unrelated topic to another. Here are examples of some questions that you may want to ask:

- What is your full name, and do you know why you were named that?

- Where were you born and when? Do you remember any stories that your parents told you about your birth?

- What do you remember about your childhood?

- Where did you go to school? Did you finish school? If not, why? (Remember to ask about all levels of schooling through college.)

- What were your brothers and sisters like?

- Where and when were your parents born? What did they look like? What were their occupations?

- Did your parents tell you how they met?

- Do you remember your grandparents? Do you recall any stories about them? What did they look like?

- Did you hear any stories about your great-grandparents? Did you ever meet your great-grandparents?

- When you were a child, who was the oldest person in your family?

- Did any relatives (other than your immediate family) live with you?

- Do you remember who your neighbors were when you were a child?

- Did your family have any traditions or celebrate any special holidays?

- Have any items (stories, traditions, or physical items) been handed down through several generations of the family?

- When did you leave home? Where did you live?

- Did you join the military? If so, what branch of service were you in? What units were you a part of? Did you serve overseas?

- What occupations have you had? Did you have any special training?

- How did you meet your spouse?

- When and where did you get married? Did you go on a honeymoon? Where?

- When were your children born? Do you have any stories about their births?

- Do you know who in the family originally immigrated to this country? Where did they come from? Why did they leave their native land?

You can probably think of more questions that are likely to draw responses from your family. If you want to see additional hints for conducting interviews, see the Capturing the Past Web site (www.byubroadcasting.org/capturingpast/).

Here are a few tips to remember as you plan a family interview:

✔ **Prepare a list of questions that you want to ask:** Knowing what you want to achieve during the discussion helps you get started and keeps your interview focused. (See the sidebar "Good interviewing questions" in this chapter for some ideas.) However, you also need to be flexible enough to allow the interviewee to take the conversation where he or she wants to go. Often some of the best information comes from memories that occur while the interviewee is talking — rather than being generated strictly in response to a set of questions.

✔ **Bring a tape recorder to the interview:** Make sure that you get permission from each participant before you start recording. If the interviewee is agreeable, you might consider videotaping the session. That way you can see the expressions on his or her face as he or she talks.

✔ **Use photographs and documents to help your family members recall events:** Often photographs can have a dramatic effect on the stories that the interviewee remembers. If there is a lull in the interview, pulling out a photo album is an excellent way to jump-start things.

✔ **Try to limit your interviews to two hours or less:** You don't want to be overwhelmed with information, and you don't want the interviewee to get worn out by your visit. Within two hours, you can collect a lot of information to guide your research. And remember, you can always do another interview if you want more information from the family member. (Actually, we strongly encourage you to do subsequent interviews — often the first interview stimulates memories for the individual that you can cover during a later interview.)

✔ **Be grateful and respectful:** Remember that these are people who have agreed to give you time and answers. Treat them with respect by listening attentively and speaking politely to them. And by all means, be sure to thank them when you've completed the interview.

Looking for Love Letters, Laundry Receipts, and Other Important Documents

Are you, or have you ever been, accused of being a pack rat? You know what we mean: someone who keeps every little scrap of paper that he or she touches. Ah, you know who you are. (And we know how to recognize you because — and here's a deep, dark confession — we're *both* pack rats of the serious variety!) If you are, then you're well suited for genealogy. In fact, if you're lucky, you descended from a whole family of pack rats who saved all those scraps from the past in their attics or basements. You may be able to share in their treasures — digging to find things that can further your genealogical research. For example, pay a visit to grandma's attic, and you may discover an old suitcase or cigar box full of documents like driver's licenses, wartime ration cards, and letters. These items may contain information that you can use to reconstruct your ancestor's past.

When you go through old family treasures, look for things that can serve as primary sources for facts that you want to verify. For more information on primary sources, see "Finding primary sources," earlier in this chapter. Here's a list (although not an exhaustive one) of some specific things to look for:

- ✔ Family Bibles
- ✔ Legal documents (such as mortgages, titles, and deeds)
- ✔ Insurance policies
- ✔ Wills
- ✔ Family letters
- ✔ Obituaries and newspaper articles
- ✔ Diaries
- ✔ Naturalization records
- ✔ Baptismal certificates and other church records
- ✔ Copies of vital records (such as birth, marriage, and death certificates, and divorce decrees)
- ✔ Report cards from school
- ✔ Occupational or personnel records
- ✔ Membership cards

For a list of other items to look for around the home, see the Treasures in the Attic page at

www.ancestry.com/library/view/ancmag/673.asp

as well as the Ancestors: Family Records page at

www.pbs.org/kbyu/ancestors/records/family/intro.html

Dusting Off the Old Photo Albums

A picture is worth a thousand words — so the saying goes. That's certainly true in genealogy. Photographs are among the most treasured documents for genealogists. Pictures show how your ancestors looked and what conditions they lived in. Sometimes the flip side of the photo is more important than the picture itself. On the back, you may find crucial information such as names, dates, and descriptions of places.

Photographs are also useful as memory-joggers for your family members. Pictures can help others recollect the past and bring up long-forgotten memories. Just be forewarned — sometimes the memories are good, and sometimes they're not so good! Although you may stimulate thoughts of some great moments long ago, you may also open a can of worms when you ask grandma about a particular person in a picture. On the plus side, in the end she may give you the lowdown on not only that person but every single individual in the family who has ever made her angry — this can provide lots of genealogical leads.

You may run into several different types of photographs in your research. Knowing when certain kinds of photographs were produced can help you associate a time frame with a picture. Here are some examples:

- **Daguerreotypes:** Daguerreotype photos were taken from 1839 to 1860. They required a long exposure time and were taken on silver-plated copper. The photographic image appears to change from a positive to a negative when tilted.

- **Ambrotypes:** Ambrotypes used a much shorter exposure time and were produced from 1858 to 1866. The image was made on thin glass and usually had a black backing.

- **Tintypes:** Tintypes were produced from 1858 to 1910. They were made on a metal sheet, and the image was often coated with a varnish. You can usually find them in a paper cover.

- **Cartes-de-visite:** Cartes-de-visite were small paper prints mounted on a card. They were often bound together into a photo album. They were produced between 1858 and 1891.

- **Cabinet cards:** Cabinet cards were larger versions of cartes-de-visite. They sometimes included dates on the borders of the cards. The pictures themselves were usually mounted on cardboard. They were manufactured primarily between 1865 and 1906.

- ✔ **Albumen prints:** These were produced on a thin piece of paper that was coated with albumen and silver nitrate. They were usually mounted on cardboard. These prints were used between 1858 and 1910 and were the types of photographs found in cartes-de-visite and cabinet cards.

- ✔ **Stereographic cards:** Stereographic cards were paired photographs that rendered a three-dimensional effect when used with a stereographic viewer. They were prevalent from 1850 to 1925.

- ✔ **Platinum prints:** Platinum prints have a matte surface that appears embedded in the paper. The images were often highlighted with artistic chalk. They were produced mainly between 1880 and 1930.

- ✔ **Glass-plate negatives:** Glass-plate negatives were used between 1848 and 1930. They were made from light-sensitive silver bromide immersed in gelatin.

When you deal with photographs, keep in mind that too much light or humidity can easily destroy them. For more information on preserving photographs, see Chapter 3. Also, some online resources can help you identify types of pictures. See the City Gallery Web site (www.city-gallery.com/learning/) for information about nineteenth-century photography, and visit the Everything You Ever Wanted to Know About Your Family Photographs page at

genealogy.about.com/library/authors/ucmishkin1a.htm

for descriptions of several types of photographs.

Sifting Through Birth, Death, Marriage, and Divorce Records

Vital records are among the first sets of primary sources typically used by genealogists (for more on primary sources, see "Finding primary sources," earlier in this chapter). Vital records include birth, marriage, divorce, and death records. For the most part, local governments keep the originals (although some governments have microfilmed them and stored them centrally). These records contain key and usually reliable information because they were produced near the time that the event occurred, and a witness to the actual event provided the information. (Outside the United States, vital records are often called *civil registrations*.)

Vital records are usually maintained in the county or parish, or in some cases the town, where the event occurred. Normally, you must contact the county, parish, or town clerk to receive a copy of a record. Some states centrally collect or microfilm their vital records, and they're available for public use at the state archives or library. You can find an online list of centralized vital record repositories in each of the United States at the Vital Records Information site (vitalrec.com). For information on where to find vital record (and civil registration) information online, see Chapter 5.

Each state has different laws regarding the release of vital records. It's a good idea to check the policy of the governing agency before making the trip or ordering a vital record. In some cases, the agency may only release a record for a good cause or to a close relative.

Birth records

Birth records are good primary sources for verifying — at a minimum — the date of birth, birthplace, and names of an individual's parents. Depending on the information requirements for a particular birth certificate, you may also learn the birthplace of the parents, their ages, occupations, addresses at the time of the birth, whether the mother had given birth previously, date of marriage of the parents, and the names and ages of any previous children. Sometimes, instead of a birth certificate, you may find another record in the family's possession that verifies the existence of the birth record. For example, instead of having a certified copy of a birth certificate, Matthew's grandmother had a Certificate of Record of Birth. This certificate attests to the fact that the county has a certificate of birth and notes its location. These certificates were used primarily before photocopiers became commonplace, and it became easier to get a certified copy of the original record.

Birth records were less formal in earlier times. Before modern record-keeping, a simple handwritten entry in a book sufficed as an official record of an individual's birth. So be very specific when citing a birth record in your genealogical notes. Include any numbers you find on the record and where the record is located (including not only the physical location of the building, but also the book number and page number of the information).

Marriage records

Marriage records come in several forms. Early marriage records may include the following:

- ✔ **Marriage bonds:** Financial guarantees that a marriage was going to take place

- ✔ **Marriage banns:** Proclamations of the intent to marry someone in front of a church congregation

- ✔ **Marriage licenses:** Documents granting permission to marry

- ✔ **Marriage records or certificates:** Documents certifying the union of two people

These records usually contain — at a minimum — the groom's name, the bride's name, and the location of the ceremony. They may also contain occupation information, birthplaces of the bride and groom, parents' names and birthplaces, names of witnesses, and information on previous marriages.

Here's one thing to be careful about when using marriage records: Don't confuse the date of the marriage with the date of the marriage bond, bann, or license — it's easy to do. The latter records were often filed anywhere from a couple of days to several weeks *before* the actual marriage date. Also, do not assume that because you found a bond, bann, or license that a marriage actually took place. Some people got *cold feet* then (as they do today) and backed out of the marriage at the last minute.

If you have trouble finding a marriage record in the area where your ancestors lived, try looking in surrounding counties or parishes or possibly even states. Other places to look are in the areas where the parents of the ancestors lived.

Divorce records

Genealogists often overlook divorce records. Later generations may not be aware that an early ancestor was divorced, and the records recounting the event can be difficult to find. However, divorce records can be quite valuable. They contain many important facts, including the age of the petitioners, birthplace, address, occupations, names and ages of children, property, and the grounds for the divorce.

Death records

Death records are excellent resources for verifying the date of death, but are less reliable for other data elements such as birth date and birthplace, because people who were not witnesses to the birth often supply that information. However, information on the death record can point you in the right direction for records to verify other events. More recent death records include the name of the individual, place of death, residence, parents' names, spouse's name, occupation, and cause of death. Early death records may only contain the date of death, cause, and residence.

Coming to Your Census

A lot of key dates in a person's life are recorded in vital records (see "Sifting Through Birth, Death, Marriage, and Divorce Records," earlier in this chapter for more details). However, unless your ancestors were consistently encountering life-events that resulted in numerous vital records, there will still be some gaps to fill in your research. Census records are one of the best record sets in the United States for filling in these gaps. *Census records* are periodic counts of a population by a government or organization. These counts can be regular (such as every ten years) or special one-time counts made for a specific reason. Some censuses contain just statistical information; others contain names and additional demographic information.

United States Census schedules

Federal census records in the United States have been around since 1790. Censuses were conducted every ten years to count the population for a couple of reasons — to divide up the number of seats in the U.S. House of Representatives, and to assess federal taxes. Although census collections are still done to this day, privacy restrictions prevent the release of any detailed census information on individuals for 72 years. Currently, you can find federal census data only for the census years 1790 to 1930. However, practically all of the 1890 Census was destroyed due to actions taken after a fire in the Commerce building in 1921 — for more on this, see "First in the Path of the Firemen," The Fate of the 1890 Population Census, at

`www.archives.gov/publications/prologue/spring_1996_1890_census_1.html`

Federal census records are valuable in that you can use them to take historical "snapshots" of your ancestors in ten-year increments. These snapshots enable you to track your ancestors as they moved from county to county or state to state, and to identify the names of parents and siblings of your ancestors that you may not have previously known.

Each census year contains a different amount of information, with more modern census returns (also called *schedules*) containing the most information. Schedules from 1790 to 1840 only list the head of household for each family, along with the number of people living in the household broken down by age classifications. Schedules from 1850 on have the names and ages of all members of the household.

The people who collected census details on individuals were called *enumerators*. Traveling door to door, these census-takers worked within an assigned district where they stopped at each residence to ask questions about the household. Being a census enumerator was not the most glamorous work. They were typically paid small amounts of money — usually barely enough to cover their expenses. Enumerators possessed differing levels of training and penmanship. These variations resulted in census returns that contained some readable information and some that had illegible entries and notes. Of course, on the plus side for genealogists, some enumerators went beyond the call of duty and made interesting notes on the families that they visited.

Using American Soundex to search United States census records

For the censuses conducted from 1880 to 1920, you can use microfilmed indices organized under the American Soundex system.

The *American Soundex* system is a method of indexing that groups names that are pronounced in a similar way but are spelled differently. This indexing procedure allows you to find ancestors who may have changed the spelling of their names over the years. For example, you find names like Helm, Helme, Holm, and Holme grouped together in the American Soundex.

The American Soundex code for a name consists of a letter and then three numbers. (Double letters count for only one number, and if your surname is short or has a lot of vowels in it, you use zeros on the end to bring the total numbers to three.) To convert your surname to American Soundex, use the first letter of your surname as the first letter of the American Soundex code, and then substitute numbers for the next three consonants according to the following table. (For example, the American Soundex code for the surname *Helm* is H450.)

1	B, P, F, V
2	C, S, K, G, J, Q, X, Z
3	D, T
4	L
5	M, N
6	R

We know that probably sounds confusing, so just follow these steps to convert your surname to a American Soundex code:

1. **Write down your surname on a piece of paper.**

   As an example, we convert the surname *Abell*.

2. **Keep the first letter of the surname and then cross out any remaining vowels (A, E, I, O, U) and the letters *W, Y,* and *H*.**

   If your surname begins with a vowel, keep the first vowel. If your surname does not begin with a vowel, cross out all the vowels in the surname. So, in the surname *Abell,* we keep the letters *A, B, L,* and *L.*

3. **If the surname has double letters, cross out the second letter.**

   For example, the surname Abell has a double *L,* so we cross out the second *L,* which leaves us with the letters *A, B,* and *L.*

4. **Convert your letters to the American Soundex code numbers according to the preceding chart.**

   We have the letters *A, B,* and *L* remaining. Because *A* is the first letter of the surname, it remains an *A*. The *B* converts to the number 1 and the *L* to the number 4. That leaves us with A14.

5. **Cross out the second occurrence of any repeated numbers that are side by side, including a number that repeats the value that the letter at the beginning would have.**

   The remaining numbers of the Abell (A14) surname do not have the same numerical code next to each other. But it could happen with a name like Schaefer. Ordinarily, the name Schaefer would have the American Soundex code of S216. However, because the *S* and the *C* would both have the code of 2 and are side by side, you would eliminate the second 2 and come up with a American Soundex code of S160.

6. **If you do not have three numbers remaining, fill in the rest with zeros.**

   Only two numbers remain in the Abell surname after we cross out the vowels and double letters. Because the American Soundex system requires a total of three numbers to complete the code, we must fill in the remaining numerical spot with a zero. Thus, our result for Abell is A140.

If you're like us, you want the most efficient way to do things. Although figuring out an American Soundex is not overly complicated, it can be a little time-consuming if you have several names to calculate. Fortunately, there are some free online sites that calculate American Soundex codes. Here are a few:

✔ **Yet Another Soundex Converter:**

   www.bradandkathy.com/genealogy/yasc.html

✔ **Surname to Soundex Code:**

   resources.rootsweb.com/cgi-bin/soundexconverter

✔ **Surname to Soundex Converter:**

   www.geocities.com/Heartland/Hills/3916/soundex.html

American Soundex indexes are subject to human error and in some cases are incomplete — for example, the 1880 Federal Census American Soundex primarily focuses on indexing those households with children age 10 years or younger. And those who carried out the actual indexing did not always handle American Soundex codes correctly or consistently. So the indexer may have made a coding error or failed to include some information. Therefore, if you're relatively certain that an ancestor *should* show up in a particular county in a census that uses American Soundex, but the American Soundex microfilm doesn't reflect that person, you may want to go through the census microfilm for that county anyway and look line-by-line for your ancestor.

We should also mention that population schedules were not the only product of the federal censuses. There were also special schedules including slave, mortality, agriculture, manufacturing, and veterans returns. Each type of special schedule contains information pertaining to a specific group or occupation. In the case of slave schedules (used in the 1850 and 1860 censuses), slaves were listed under the names of the slaveowner, and information was provided on the age, gender, and race of the slave. If the slave was over 100 years of age, his or her name was listed on the schedules (although names may have been included for other slaves if the enumerator felt inclined to list them).

Mortality schedules (used in 1850, 1860, 1870, and 1880) include information on people who died in the 12 months previous to the start of the census. Agricultural schedules were used between 1840 and 1910. However, only the schedules from 1840 to 1880 survive. They contained detailed demographic and financial information on farm owners. Manufacturing schedules (taken infrequently between 1810 and 1880) contain information on business owners and their business interests. Veteran schedules include the Revolutionary pensioner census, which was taken as part of the 1840 census, and the special census for Union veterans and their widows (taken in 1890).

Soundex improvements

Many of you have heard of the Soundex System — especially if you've already worked some with the United States census, or you live in a state that uses the Soundex as part of your driver's license number, or you're just a nut for indexing systems. However, you might not realize that there's more than one Soundex System. The American Soundex, which is the one used for the United States census and the one most widely recognized, is not alone. Nor was it the first system developed.

The ***Russell Soundex System.*** Robert C. Russell patented the first Soundex system in 1918. The Russell Soundex System categorizes the alphabet phonetically and assigns numbers to the categories. There are eight categories and four other rules to follow. The odd-looking terms that refer to parts of the mouth are technical descriptions of how to make the sounds; just try making the sounds of the letters shown with

each one, and you'll get the idea. Here's what they look (and sound) like:

Categories

1. Vowels or Oral Resonants: *a, e, i, o, u, y*

2. Labials and Labio-Dentals: *b, f, p, v*

3. Gutturals and Sibilants: *c, g, k, g, s, x, z*

4. Dental-Mutes: *d, t*

5. Palatal-Fricative: *l*

6. Labio-Nasal: *m*

7. Dento- or Lingua-Nasal: *n*

8. Dental Fricative: *r*

Other Rules

The code always begins with the first letter of the word.

If you have two letters in a row that are the same, they are represented in the code as one letter (for example, if you have "rr", it is represented as "r").

If the word ends in *gh, s,* or *z,* those letters are ignored.

Vowels are only considered the first time they appear.

The *American Soundex System:* The American Soundex System, the system with which most people are familiar, modified the Russell Soundex system. The changes include these:

The code disregards vowels altogether unless the first letter of the word is a vowel.

The letters *m* and *n* are categorized together and represented by the same number.

Words ending in *gh, s,* and *z* are treated the same as other words, and those letters are assigned values.

The American Soundex code begins with the first letter of the word and has three numbers following. Zeros are added to the code to ensure that it has three numbers. You can see the categories of letters and numbers assigned to them in the Using American Soundex to Search United States Census Records section of this chapter.

The *Daitch-Mokotoff Soundex System:* The Daitch-Mokotoff Soundex System builds upon the Russell and American Soundex Systems, and addresses difficulties in categorizing many Germanic and Slavic names that the other two systems encounter. The major points of this system are:

The code is made up of six numbers.

The first letter of the word is also represented by a number. If the first letter is a vowel, it has the code 0.

Some double-letter combinations that sound like single letters are coded as single.

If a letter or letter combination can have two sounds, it is coded twice.

If you want more detailed information about the various Soundex systems, take a gander at the Soundexing and Genealogy Web site at

```
www.avotaynu.com/soundex.html
```

And if you want to run some names through the American and Daitch-Mokotoff Soundex Systems at the same time, we recommend you visit the Generating American and Daitch-Mokotoff Soundex Codes in One Step converter at

```
stevemorse.org/census/soundex.
html
```

Other census records in the United States

You may also find census records at the state, territorial, and local level for certain areas of the United States. For example, the state of Illinois has federal census records for 1810 (one county), 1820, 1830, 1840, 1850, 1860, 1870, 1880, 1890 (small fragment), 1900, 1910, and 1920. In addition to these, Illinois has two territorial censuses taken in 1810 and 1818 — and eight state censuses taken in 1820, 1825, 1830, 1835, 1840, 1845, 1855, and 1865. Some city-census enumerations were taken in the 1930s, and a military census was taken in 1862. These non-federal census records can often help you piece together your ancestors' migration patterns or account for ancestors who may not have been enumerated in the federal censuses. Sometimes, these censuses can also provide more detail on your ancestors than the federal census schedules can.

Guides that offer information on census returns at the local and state level include *Ancestry's Red Book: American State, County and Town Sources,* edited by Alice Eicholz (Ancestry Publishing), *Your Guide to the Federal Census* by Kathleen Hinckley (Betterway Books), and *State Census Records* by Ann Smith Lainhart (Genealogical Publishing Company).

Searching census records from other countries

The United States isn't the only country that has collected information on its population. Census counts have taken place in several countries throughout history. Here are examples of a few countries with census records.

Australia

Although Australia has taken a census every ten years since 1901, the first Australia-wide census was conducted in 1911. Now for some bad news — every return has been destroyed, in accordance with law. There are other records that you can substitute for census returns in the form of convict returns and musters and post-office directories. These returns are available for some states for the years 1788, 1792, 1796, 1800, 1801, 1805, 1806, 1811, 1814, 1816, 1817, 1818, 1819, 1820, 1821, 1822, 1823, 1825, 1826, and 1837. Some of these records can be found at these locations:

- ✔ The State Library of New South Wales at

    www.sl.nsw.gov.au/find/databases/fhs.cfm

- ✔ The Archives Office of Tasmania at

    www.archives.tas.gov.au/genealres/census%20index.htm

- ✔ The Latrobe Library in Melbourne at

    www.statelibrary.vic.gov.au/slv/latrobe/ltguide.htm

- ✔ The Public Records Office of Victoria at

    www.prov.vic.gov.au

For more information on locating census returns, see the Censuses in Australian Colonies page at

www.users.on.net/proformat/census.html

Austria

Austrian censuses were taken in the years 1857, 1869, 1880, 1890, 1900, and 1910. The first census that listed individuals by name was the 1869 Census. These returns include surname, sex, year of birth, place of birth, district, religion, marital status, language, occupation, literacy, mental and physical defects, residence, and whether the household had farm animals.

Canada

Canadian census returns are available for the years 1851, 1861, 1871, 1881, 1891, and 1901. The returns from 1851 to 1891 contain the individual's name, age, sex, province or country of birth, religion, race, occupation, marital status, and education. The returns for 1901 also include birth date, year of immigration, and address. For more information on data elements in the 1901 Census, see the Description of Columns on the 1901 Census Schedule page at

freepages.genealogy.rootsweb.com/~wjmartin/census.htm

These returns are stored at the National Archives of Canada (www.archives.ca/).

If you're looking for online information on specific census records, see the Bob's Your Uncle, Eh! genealogy search engine at

indexes.tpl.toronto.on.ca/genealogy/index.asp

By selecting Census from the drop-down box marked *Topic,* you can see a variety of sites on census records including the 1753, 1921, 1935, and 1945 censuses of Newfoundland, French Canadian Heads of Households in the Province of Quebec in 1871, Index to the 1871 Census of Ontario, Index to the 1744 Quebec City Census, Nova Scotia Census Records, and the Toronto Census of 1837.

Denmark

The Danish Archives has census returns for the years 1787, 1801, 1834, and 1840 (as well as other years up to 1916) at

www.sa.dk/ra/engelsk/Roots.htm

The returns contain name, age, occupation, and relationship for each individual in the household. After 1845, census returns include information on the individual's place of birth. Census returns are available after 80 years.

Germany

The German central government held censuses in 1871, 1880, 1885, 1890, 1895, 1900, 1905, 1910, 1919, 1925, 1933, and 1939. Unfortunately, these census returns do not have much genealogical value because they were statistical in nature. For more information on the German census, see What About the German Census? at

www.genealogy.net/gene/faqs/sgg.html#census

Ireland

Countrywide census enumerations have been conducted every ten years since 1821. Unfortunately, the census returns from 1821 to 1851 were largely destroyed in a fire at the Public Record Office in 1922. Fragments of these census returns are available at the National Archives of Ireland (an online transcription of the census fragments is available at

home.iprimus.com.au/s_steffensen/1851IrelandCensus.htm

The government destroyed the returns from 1861 and 1871. Returns for 1901 and 1911 still survive and are available at the National Archives of Ireland at

www.nationalarchives.ie

Ireland suspended its law prohibiting the release of census returns for 100 years to make the 1901 and 1911 returns available to the public. For more information on censuses in Ireland, see the Census Records page at

scripts.ireland.com/ancestor/browse/records/census/index.htm

If you are interested in Northern Ireland, see the Public Record Office of Northern Ireland site:

proni.nics.gov.uk/research/family/family.htm

Italy

The Italian State Archives contains national censuses for the years 1861, 1871, 1881, 1891, and 1901. Its Web site is

www.archivi.beniculturali.it

Norway

The first census in Norway was conducted in 1769. A census by name was conducted for the first time in 1801, but was not repeated again until 1865. Each census after 1865 contained information such as name, sex, age, relationship to head of household, civil status, occupation, religion, and place of birth. For more information on Norwegian censuses, see the Documenting the Norwegian Census page at

`www.rhd.uit.no/census.html`

An online searchable index of the 1801, 1865, 1875, and 1900 censuses of Norway is available at

`digitalarkivet.uib.no/cgi-win/WebFront.exe?slag=vis&tekst=meldingar&spraak=e`

The 1865, 1875, and 1900 censuses of Norway are also available from the Norwegian Historical Data Centre. Here's the site:

`www.rhd.uit.no/folketellinger_engelsk_britisk.html`

United Kingdom

Since 1801, censuses have been taken in the United Kingdom every ten years (except 1941). Most of the returns from 1801 to 1831 were statistical and did not contain names, making them useless for genealogists. Beginning in 1841, the administration of the census became the responsibility of the Registrar General and the Superintendent Registrars, who were responsible for recording civil registrations (vital records). This changed the focus of the census from the size of the population to details on individuals and families. The Public Records Office releases information in the census only after 100 years, and can be found at

`www.pro.gov.uk`

You can find census returns for England and Wales at the Family Records Centre in London and for Scotland at the New Register House in Edinburgh:

`www.pro.gov.uk/research/familyhistory.htm`

If you are not in either of those places, you can find copies of area returns at district libraries or Family History Centers (for more on Family History Centers, see "Discovering Family History Centers" at the end of this chapter), as well as find some censuses online (flip over to Chapter 5 for more information). The 1881, 1891, and 1901censuses for Scotland are available at the ScotlandsPeople site maintained by the General Register Office for Scotland:

`www.scotlandspeople.gov.uk`

Location, Location, Location: Researching Land Records

In the past, ownership of land measured an individual's success. The more land your ancestors possessed, the more powerful and wealthy they were. This concept often encouraged people to migrate to new countries in the search for land.

Land records may tell you where your ancestor lived prior to purchasing the land, spouse's name, and the names of children, grandchildren, parents, or siblings. To use land records effectively, however, you need to have a good idea of where your ancestors lived and possess a little background information on the history of the areas in which they lived. Land records are especially useful for tracking the migration of families in the United States before the 1790 Census.

Most land records are maintained at the local level — in the town, county, or parish where the property was located. These records can come in multiple forms that reflect various types of land records and the locations in which they exist.

Finding land records in the United States

Your ancestors may have received land in the early United States in several different ways. Knowing more about the ways in which people acquired land historically can aid you in your research.

Your ancestor may have purchased land or received a grant of land in the public domain — often called *bounty lands* — in exchange for military service or some other service for the country. Either way, the process probably started when your ancestor petitioned (or submitted an application) for the land. Your ancestor may have also laid claim to the land, rather than petitioning for it.

If the application was approved, your ancestor was given a *warrant* — a certificate that allowed him or her to receive an amount of land. (Sometimes a warrant was called a *right.*) After your ancestor presented the warrant to a land office, an individual was appointed to make a *survey* — or detailed drawing and legal description of the boundaries — of the land. The land office then recorded your ancestor's name and information from the survey into a *tract book* (a book describing the lots within a township or other geographic area) and on a *plat map* (a map of lots within a tract).

After the land was recorded, your ancestors may have been required to meet certain conditions, such as living on the land for a certain period of time or making payments on the land. After they met the requirements, they were eligible for a *patent* — a document that conveyed title of the land to the new owner.

The Bureau of Land Management, Eastern States Land Office holds land records for public-domain land east of the Mississippi River. Here's its site:

`www.glorecords.blm.gov`

The National Archives (`www.archives.gov/research_room/federal_ records_guide/bureau_of_land_management_rg049.html`) holds the land records for the Western states. For secondary land transactions (those made after the original grant of land), you probably need to contact the recorder of deeds for the county in which the land was held.

Here are some Web sites with information on land records:

- **History and Use of Land Records:**
  `hometown.aol.com/CookCooke/historyanduse.html`
- **Legal Land Descriptions in the USA:**
  `www.outfitters.com/genealogy/land/land.html`
- **Georgia:** Georgia Department of Archives and History Land Records
  `www.sos.state.ga.us/archives/rs/land.htm`
- **Illinois:** Illinois Public Domain Land Tract Sales
  `www.sos.state.il.us/departments/archives/data_lan.html`
- **Indiana:** Land Office Records at the Indiana State Archives
  `www.in.gov/icpr/archives/databases/land/indiana_.html`
- **Maryland:** Land Records in Maryland
  `www.mdarchives.state.md.us/msa/refserv/genealogy/html/ land.html`
- **Ohio:** Introduction to Ohio Land History
  `users.rcn.com/deeds/ohio.htm`
- **Oklahoma:** Federal Tract Books of Oklahoma Territory
  `www.sirinet.net/~lgarris/swogs/tract.html`
- **Pennsylvania:** Pennsylvania Original Land Records Series
  `www.innernet.net/hively/PALand/About%20PA%20Land%20 Records.htm`

- ✔ **South Dakota:** Homesteading Records Information Page

  `members members.aol.com/gkrell/homestead/define.html`

- ✔ **Tennessee:** An Introduction to the History of Tennessee's Confusing Land Laws

  `web.utk.edu/~kizzer/genehist/research/landlaws.htm`

- ✔ **Texas:** Texas General Land Office Archives

  `www.glo.state.tx.us/central/arc/index.html`

- ✔ **Virginia:** Introduction to Virginia Land History

  `www.ultranet.com/~deeds/virg.htm`

Because the topic of land records is so expansive, many books have been devoted to the subject. When you're ready to tackle land records in more depth, you may want to look at William Thorndale's "Land and Tax Records" in *The Source: A Guidebook of American Genealogy,* edited by Loretto Dennis Szucs and Sandra Hargreaves Luebking, and published by Ancestry.

Finding land records in other countries

Depending on the country that you research, you may find a number of ways that land transactions occurred. These links can assist you in figuring out how to research land records in a particular country:

- ✔ **Canada:** Land Records — Genealogical Sources in Canada

  `www.archives.ca/02/020202/02020207_e.html`

- ✔ **England:** Land Conveyances: Enrolment of Deeds, and Registration of Title

  `catalogue.pro.gov.uk/ExternalRequest.asp?RequestReference=ri2225`

- ✔ **Ireland:** Land Records

  `scripts.ireland.com/ancestor/browse/records/land/index.htm`

Trial and Error at the Courthouse

Was your ancestor ever on the wrong side of the law? If so, you may find some colorful information at the courthouse in the civil and criminal court records. Even if you don't have an ancestor with a law-breaking past, you can find valuable genealogical records at your local courthouse. Typical records you can find there include land deeds, vital records, wills and probate records, tax records, and some military records (provided the ancestors who were veterans deposited their records locally). We discuss many of these types of records in more detail in Chapter 5.

It's a good idea to call ahead to the courthouse to find out whether the record you're looking for is actually at that facility. Sometimes records are kept off-site; it might be a waste of time to hit the road and go to the courthouse. Also, the more information you can provide to the clerk or customer service representative, the easier it will be for him or her to retrieve the record. Useful information includes full name of the ancestor, approximate date of the record, and any record identification number that you might find in an index to the record set.

Visiting Libraries, Archives, and Historical Societies

Collecting additional information on the area where your ancestor lived may inspire you to search for information in public (and some private) libraries. Although local history sections are not generally targeted toward genealogists, the information you can find there is quite valuable. For example, public libraries often have city directories and phone books, past issues of newspapers (good for obituary hunting), and old map collections. Libraries may also have extensive collections of local history books that can give you a flavor of what life was like for your ancestor in that area. For a list of libraries with online catalogs, see The Library Index site at www.libdex.com/.

Archives are another place to find good information. They exist at several different levels (national, state, and local) and have different owners (public or private). Each archive varies — some may have a large collection of certain types of documents, while others may just contain documents from a certain geographical area. To find archives, see the Repositories of Primary Sources page at

www.uidaho.edu/special-collections/Other.Repositories.html

A third place to find additional information is at a historical society. Generally, historical societies have nice collections of maps, documents, and local history books pertaining to the area in which the society is located. Also, they are repositories for collections of papers of people who lived in the community. Often, you can find references to your ancestors in these collections, especially if the person whose personal documents are in the collection wrote a letter or transacted some business with your ancestor. You can find links to historical societies on the Yahoo! site at

```
dir.yahoo.com/arts/humanities/history/organizations/
historical_societies/
```

Getting Involved with Genealogical Societies

There are times when dealing with all of the different record sets and methods of researching your family can be overwhelming. On such occasions it's nice to be able to sit down with some people who have similar experiences or more knowledge than you and discuss your research problems. One place that you can find such a group is your local genealogical society. Genealogical societies hold periodic meetings that focus on particular research methods. Some also have weekend seminars where they bring in genealogical lecturers to address topics of interest to their members.

If you have research needs in other areas of the country (or foreign countries for that matter), then you might consider joining a society in that area. Although you do not live there, you can still use the resources of the society to find answers to your questions, and you can contribute to the distant organization more than you realize by sharing your findings and experiences. Most societies have people who are well versed in the records that pertain to the area where the society is located. These individuals can be a great resource as you go through the research process.

To find a genealogical society in the United States, check out the Federation of Genealogical Societies Society Hall at

```
www.familyhistory.com/societyhall/main.asp
```

A general search engine (such as Google or AltaVista) can help you find societies in other countries.

Discovering Family History Centers

You may be surprised to discover that your own hometown has a resource for local genealogical research! Sponsored by the Church of Jesus Christ of Latter-day Saints (LDS), over 2,500 Family History Centers worldwide provide support for genealogical research. The FamilySearch collection of CD-ROMs is among the important resources found in Family History Centers. They contain databases with the following information:

- ✔ **Ancestral File:** A database with over 29 million names available in family group sheets and pedigree charts.

- ✔ **International Genealogical Index:** A list of over 284 million individuals who are reflected in records collected by the LDS.

- ✔ **United States Social Security Death Index:** An index of those persons for whom Social Security death claims have been filed.

- ✔ **Military Index:** A list of United States soldiers killed in the Korean and Vietnam Wars.

- ✔ **Family History Library Catalog:** A catalog of over 2 million rolls of microfilm, one-half million pieces of microfiche, and 400,000 books and CD-ROMs available at the Family History Library in Salt Lake City.

Many other resources are available from Family History Centers, including their collection of microfilmed records and indices.

You need not be a member of the LDS church to use a Family History Center; the resources contained within them are available to everyone. Keep in mind that the workers at a Family History Center cannot research your genealogy for you, although they're willing to point you in the right direction. To find a Family History Center, use the FamilySearch search interface, which you can find at

`www.familysearch.org/eng/Library/FHC/frameset_fhc.asp`

Otherwise you can consult your local telephone directory.

Chapter 2

Planning for Genealogical Success

All great projects start with a plan, right? Starting a genealogical project is no exception. A well thought out plan can save you hours of work and keep you focused on the goals that you have set for a particular research session. Now, we realize that not everyone enjoys coming up with a plan. It's finding your ancestors that is the fun part — not the planning. So, to help speed things along, we've come up with a basic process that we hope helps you make the most of your research time.

This chapter covers some of the basic things to keep in mind when you begin your research journey and offers some tips on what you can do when you hit *research bumps* along the way. Also, we provide some hints on how to select that first ancestor to kick off your genealogical pursuit.

Introducing the Helm Online Family Tree Research Cycle

No book on research would be complete without some sort of model to follow, so we created one just for you. Of course, wanting to take credit for our fabulous model, we like to call it the *Helm Online Family Tree Research Cycle*. Sounds impressive, doesn't it? Well, we have to admit that most of it is common sense. Figure 2-1 shows the five phases of the cycle: planning, collecting, researching, consolidating, and distilling.

Sticking with the *family tree* motif here, we liken the cycle to the steps you take to plant and sustain a tree:

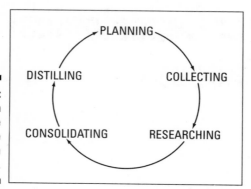

PLANNING

DISTILLING

COLLECTING

CONSOLIDATING

RESEARCHING

Figure 2-1:
The Helm
Online
Family Tree
Research
Cycle.

✔ **Planning:** The first step in planting a tree is figuring out what kind of tree you want and then finding a good place in your yard for the tree to grow. This step in the cycle is the *planning* phase. You want to select a family that you know enough about to begin a search and then think about the resources you want to use to find the information that you're looking for.

✔ **Collecting:** After you plan for the tree, you go to a nursery and pick out a suitable sapling and other necessary materials to ensure that the tree's roots take hold. The second phase of the cycle, *collecting,* is the same — you collect information on the family that you're researching by conducting interviews in person, on the phone, or through e-mail, and by finding documents in attics, basements, and other home-front repositories.

✔ **Researching:** The next step is to actually plant the tree. You dig a hole, place the tree in it, and then cover the roots. Similarly, you spend the *researching* phase of the cycle digging for clues, finding information that can support your family tree, and obtaining documentation. You can use traditional and technological tools to dig — tools like libraries, courthouses, your computer, and the World Wide Web.

✔ **Consolidating:** You planted the tree and covered its roots. However, to make sure that the tree grows, you put mulch around it and provide the nourishment the tree needs to survive. The *consolidating* phase of the cycle is similar in that you take the information you find and place it into your computer-based genealogical database or your filing system. These systems protect your findings by keeping them in a centralized location and provide an environment in which you can see the fruits of your labor.

> ✓ **Distilling:** After your tree has taken root and begins to grow, you need to prune the old growth, allowing new growth to appear. Similarly, the *distilling* phase is where you use your computer-based genealogical database to generate reports showing the current state of your research. You can use these reports to prune from your database those individuals you've proven don't fit into your family lines — and perhaps find room for new genealogical growth by finding clues to other lines you want to follow up.

We think that using our research model makes looking for genealogical information a lot easier and more fulfilling. However, this model is merely a guide. Feel free to use whatever methods work best for you — as long as those methods make it possible for someone else to verify your research (through sources you cite and so on).

Planning your research

You may have heard that the Internet puts the world at your fingertips. Discovering all the wonderful online resources that exist makes you feel like a kid in a candy store. You click around from site to site with wide eyes, amazed by what you see, tempted to record everything for your genealogy — whether it relates to one of your family lines or not.

Because of the immense wealth of information available to you, putting together a research plan before going online is very important — it can save you a lot of time and frustration by keeping you focused. Tens of thousands of genealogical sites are on the Internet. If you don't have a good idea of what exactly you're looking for to fill in the blanks in your genealogy, you can get lost online. And getting lost is even easier when you see a name that looks familiar and start following its links, only to discover hours later (when you finally get around to pulling out the genealogical notes you already had) that you've been tracking the wrong person and family line.

Now that we've convinced you that you need a research plan, you're probably wondering exactly what a research plan is. Basically, a *research plan* is a common-sense approach to looking for information about your ancestors online. A research plan entails knowing what you're looking for and what your priorities are for finding information.

If you're the kind of person who likes detailed organization (like lists and steps that you can follow to the tee), you can write your research plan on paper or keep it on your computer. If you're the kind of person who knows exactly what you want and need at all times, and you have an excellent memory of where you leave off when doing projects, your research plan can exist solely in your mind. In other words, your research plan can be as formal or informal as you like — as long as it helps you plot what you're looking for.

For example, say you're interested in finding some information on your great-grandmother. Here are some steps you can take to form a research plan:

1. **Write down what you already know about the person you want to research — in this case, your great-grandmother.**

   Include details like the dates and places of birth, marriage, and death; spouse's name; children's names; and any other details you think may help you distinguish your ancestor from other individuals. Of course, it's possible that all you know at this time is great-grandma's name.

2. **Conduct a search using a genealogically focused search engine to get an overview of what's available.**

   Visit sites like the GenealogyPortal.com (`www.genealogyportal.com`) to search for information by name and location. Using great-grandma's name and the names of some of the locations where she lived provides you with search results that give you an idea of what kind of resources are available. (Chapters 3 and 4 go into more detail about online trips and searching for this type of information.) You may want to make a list of the sites that you find on a sheet of paper or in your word processor.

3. **Prioritize the resources that you want to use.**

   Your search on a genealogically focused search engine may turn up several different types of resources, such as newsgroups, mailing lists, and Web sites. We recommend that you prioritize which resources you plan to use first. You may want to visit a Web site that specifically names great-grandma prior to signing up for a mailing list for all researchers interested in great-grandma's surname. (For more on using these resources, take a look at Appendix A.)

4. **Schedule time to use the various resources that you identify.**

   Genealogy is truly a lifelong pursuit — you can't download every bit of information and documentation that you need all at once. Because researching your genealogy requires time and effort on your part, we recommend that you schedule time to work on specific parts of your research. (Scheduling time is especially useful if you're paying by the hour for an Internet connection.)

Collecting useful information

After you generate a research plan (see the preceding section, "Planning your research," for more information), you may need to fill in a few details like dates and locations of births, marriages, and deaths. You can collect this information by interviewing family members and by looking through family documents and photographs. (See Chapter 1 for tips on interviewing and using family documents and photographs.) You may also need to look up a few things in an atlas or *gazetteer* (a geographical dictionary) if you aren't sure where certain locations are. (Chapter 4 provides more information on online gazetteers.)

For a list of things that may be useful to collect, see Chapter 1. In the meantime, here are a few online resources that identify items to collect for your genealogy:

- ✔ **Getting Started:**

  www.ngsgenealogy.org/edugetstart.htm

- ✔ **Introduction to Genealogy: First Steps:**

  genealogy.about.com/library/lessons/blintro2a.htm

- ✔ **Getting Started in Genealogy and Family History:**

  www.genuki.org.uk/gs/

Researching: Through the brick wall and beyond

Of course, researching your family history online is the topic of this entire book, so you can find the necessary resources to do a great deal of your online research in these pages.

A time will undoubtedly come when you run into what genealogists affectionately call the *Brick Wall Syndrome* — when you think you have exhausted every possible way of finding an ancestor. The most important thing you can do is to keep the faith — don't give up! Web sites are known to change frequently (especially as more people come online and begin sharing their information); although you may not find exactly what you need today, you may find it next week at a site you've visited several times before or at a new site altogether. Fortunately, a few people post some suggestions on how to get through that brick wall when you run into it. Check out these sites:

- ✔ **Breaking Down Walls, Brick by Brick: The Search for Henrietta:** genealogy.about.com/library/weekly/aa042602a.htm

- ✔ **Brick Wall Research:** genealogypro.com/articles/ brick-wall-research.html

Using a database to consolidate your information

After you get rolling on your research, you often find so much information that it feels like you don't have enough time to put it all into your computer-based genealogical database.

A *genealogical database* is a software program that allows you to enter, organize, store, and use all sorts of genealogical information on your computer.

When possible, try to set aside some time to update your database with information you recently gathered. This process of putting your information together in one central place, which we call *consolidating,* helps you gain a perspective on the work that you've completed and provides a place for you to store all those nuggets you'll need when you begin researching again. By storing your information in a database, you can always refer to it for a quick answer the next time you try to remember where you found a reference to a marriage certificate for your great-great-grandparents.

Distilling the information that you gather

The final step in the cycle is distilling the information that you gather into a report, chart, organized database, or detailed research log that you can use to find additional genealogical leads. Frequently, you can complete the distillation process by producing a report from your computer-based genealogical database. Most genealogical software programs allow you to generate reports in a variety of formats. For example, you can pull up a Pedigree chart (a chart showing a primary person with lines representing the relationships to his/her parents, then lines connecting them to their parents, and so on) or an outline of descendants from information that you entered in the database about each ancestor. You can use these reports to see what holes still exist in your research, and you can add these missing pieces to the planning phase for your next research effort — starting the whole cycle over again.

Another advantage to genealogical reports is having the information readily available so that you can *toggle* back to look at the report while researching online, which can help you stay focused. (*Toggling* is flipping back and forth between open programs on your computer. For example, in Windows you press Alt+Tab to toggle, or you can click the appropriate item on the taskbar at the bottom of the screen. On a Macintosh, you can use the Application Switcher in the upper-right corner of the screen.) Of course, if you prefer, printing copies of the reports and keeping them next to the computer while you're researching on the Internet serves the same purpose.

Selecting a Person to Begin Your Search

Selecting a person sounds easy, doesn't it? Just select your great-great-grandfather's name, and you're off to the races. But what if your great-great-grandfather's name was John Smith? You may encounter millions of sites with information on John Smith — unless you know some facts about the John Smith you're looking for, we can almost guarantee that you will have a frustrating time online.

Trying a unique name

The first time you research online, try to start with a person whose name is, for lack of a better term, semi-unique. By this we mean a person with a name that doesn't take up ten pages in your local phone book, but is still common enough that you can find some information on it the first time you conduct a search. If you're really brave, you can begin with someone with a very common surname such as Smith or Jones, but you have to do a lot more groundwork up-front so you can easily determine whether any of the multiple findings relate to your ancestor. (For more on groundwork, see Chapter 1.)

Also, consider any variations in spelling that your ancestor's name may have. Often, you can find more information on the mainstream spelling of his or her surname than on one of its rarer variants. For example, if you research someone with the surname Helme, you may have better luck finding information under the spellings *Helm* or *Helms*. If your family members immigrated to the United States in the last two centuries, they may have *Americanized* their surname. Americanizing a name was often done so that the name could be easily pronounced in English, or sometimes the surname was simply misspelled and adopted by the family.

To find various spellings of the surname, you may need to dig through some family records or look at a site like Table of Common Surname Variations & Surname Misspellings (www.ingeneas.com/alternate.html).

Narrowing your starting point

If you aren't sure how popular a name is, try visiting a site like Hamrick Software's surname distribution site (www.hamrick.com/names). At Hamrick's site, you can find the distribution of surnames in the United States based on the 1850 Census, 1880 Census, 1920 Census, and phone books from 1990 to the present. Here's what you do:

1. **Open your World Wide Web browser and go to Hamrick Software's surname distribution site (**www.hamrick.com/names**).**

   The Hamrick site appears with instructions and a form to use for searching.

Note: Need information on how to use a browser? Take a peek at Appendix A.

2. **Type the surname you're researching into the Surname field in the search form.**

   For help choosing a surname, see the preceding section.

3. **Use the drop-down menu to select the year(s) for which you want to see the surname distribution.**

   You can choose 1850, 1880, 1920, 1990, or all these years.

4. **Click the Display button.**

   A color map displaying the distribution of your surname appears.

Figure 2-2 shows a distribution map for the surname Abell in 1990. According to the map, only one out of every 1,000 individuals uses this surname in two states. In the remaining states, the name is even rarer. This gives you a good indication that the surname Abell is semi-unique. In contrast, during the same year, the surname Smith was held by at least one out of every 300 individuals in each state.

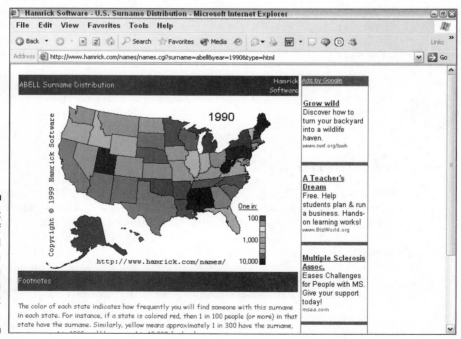

Figure 2-2:
A map of the Abell surname distribution in 1990 from Hamrick Software.

Note: Looking at Figure 2-2, you may find it difficult to determine which two states have one out of 1,000 individuals using the surname Abell because of the way the colors show up as black, white, or shades of gray. If you visit Hamrick's site, the maps come up in color and are easier to read. (And just in case you're curious, the two states were Maryland and Kentucky.)

A good reason to check out distribution maps is that you can use them to identify potential geographic areas where you can look for your family during the years covered by the site. This is especially true for maps generated from 1850 and 1880 Census data. For example, we generated another map on the Abell surname for the 1880 Census. We discovered that the name appeared more frequently in six states than in the rest of the country. If we hit a wall and can't find additional information online about a particular individual or the surname, we know we can start looking at records in these states to find more clues about families with the name and hopefully, by doing so, we'll find our branch.

Using a person who you know about

In addition to picking a person whom you're likely to have success researching, you want to use a person you already know something about. If you have a family line for which you know some basic information on your great-great-grandparents, use one of their names rather than a name for which you only know a few scattered details. The more details that you know about a person, the more successful your initial search is likely to be.

For example, Matthew used his great-grandfather William Abell because he knew more about that side of his family. His grandmother once mentioned that her father was born in Larue County, Kentucky, in 1876. This gives him a point of reference for judging whether a site has any relevant information on his family. A site is relevant if it contains any information on Abells who were located in or near Larue County, Kentucky, prior to or around the year 1876. Try to use the same technique with your ancestor. For more information on how to extract genealogical information from your family to use in your research, see Chapter 1.

Selecting a grandparent's name

Having trouble selecting a name? Why not try one of your grandparent's names? Using a grandparent's name can have several benefits. If you find some information on an individual but you aren't sure whether it's relevant to your family, you can check with relatives to see whether they know any additional information that can help you. This may also spur interest in genealogy in other family members who can then assist you with some of your research burden or produce some family documents that you never knew existed.

With a name in hand, you're ready to see how much information is currently available on the Internet about that individual. Because this is just one step in a long journey to discover your family history, keep in mind that you want to begin slowly. *Don't try to examine every resource right from the start.* You're more likely to become overloaded with information if you try to find too many resources too quickly. Your best approach is to begin searching a few sites until you get the hang of how to find information about your ancestors online. And keep in mind that you can always bookmark sites so you can easily return to them later, when you're ready for more in-depth researching. (A little rusty on how to set bookmarks on your Web browser? See Appendix A for a refresher.)

Too Many Ancestor Irons in the Research Fire

One last piece of advice: When you begin your research, take your time and don't get in a big hurry. Keep things simple and look for one piece of information at a time. If you try to do too much too fast, you risk getting confused, having no online success, and getting frustrated with the Internet. This result isn't very encouraging and certainly doesn't make you feel like jumping back into your research, which would be a shame because you can find a lot of valuable research help online.

Chapter 3

Fine-Tuning Your Organizational and Preservation Skills

*A*fter you collect all this great genealogical data, your findings don't do you much good if they're not easily accessed when you need them. You don't want to run all over your house trying to pull together all your precious scraps of paper — notes from your research at the library in your desk, letters from relatives in your mail-to-be-sorted basket, photocopies of some Pedigree charts mixed in with your magazines. You may forget where you placed a particular document and miss something important because your documents aren't organized and kept in a centralized location.

This chapter examines ways of organizing and preserving genealogical information and documents using traditional storage methods and preservation techniques. It also looks at how to use Family Tree Maker (a popular genealogical database) to store and organize information about your ancestors, as well as digitized documents and photographs. (Chapter 9 explores how to find and use other genealogical software.)

Getting a Firm Foundation in Traditional Methods of Genealogical Organization

No finer tradition exists in genealogy than collecting tons of paper and photographs. Until now, you've probably used any means possible to take notes while talking with relatives about your ancestors or looking up information in the local library — from notebook paper to receipts you have in your pocket or purse to stick-on notes. You may have used your camera to take pictures of headstones in the cemetery where some of your ancestors are buried, or of the old family homestead that's now abandoned and barely standing. And you've probably collected some original source documents — like the certified copy of your mother's birth certificate that grandma gave you, the family Bible from Aunt Lola, and the old photograph of your great-great-grandfather as a child that you found while digging through the attic. Now what are you supposed to do with all these things? Organize, organize, organize!

Even if you decide to use genealogical software to track your research progress, you're always going to have paper records and photographs you want to keep. The following sections offer some tips to help you become well organized (genealogically, anyway).

Establishing good organizational skills

You probably already discovered that taking notes on little scraps of paper works adequately at first, but the more notes you take, the harder the time you have sorting through them and making sense of the information on each. To avoid this situation, establish some good note-taking and organizational skills early by being consistent in how you take notes. Write the date, time, and place that you do your research, along with the names of the family members you interview, at the top of each page of your notes. This information can help you later on when you return to your notes to look for a particular fact or when you try to make sense of conflicting information.

You want to be as detailed as possible when taking notes on particular events, persons, books, and so forth — include the who, what, where, when, why, and how. And most importantly, always cite the source of your information, keeping the following guidelines in mind:

- **Person:** Include that person's full name, relationship to you (if any), the information, contact data (address, phone number, e-mail address), and the date and time that you and this person communicated.

- **Record:** Include the name or type of record, record number, book number (if applicable), the name and location of the record-keeping agency, and any other pertinent information.

- **Book or magazine:** Include all bibliographic information, including the name of the publication, volume number, date of issue, the publisher's name, and page number of the applicable article.

- **Microfilm or microfiche:** Include all bibliographic information and note the document media (microfilm roll, microfiche), document number, and repository name.

> ✔ **Web site or other Internet resource:** Include the name of the copyright holder for the site (or name of the site's creator and maintainer if no copyright notice appears on it), name of the site, address or Uniform Resource Locator (URL) of the site, the date the information was posted or copyrighted, and any notes with traditional contact information for the site's copyright holder or creator.

It's a good idea to print a copy of the Web page or other Internet resource that contains information about your research interest to keep in your paper files. Some Web sites have a tendency to disappear over time, so it's best to get documentation of the site while it exists.

If you need some help citing sources, check out *Evidence: Citation and Analysis for the Family Historian,* written by Elizabeth Shown Mills and published by Genealogical Publishing Company.

Understanding genealogical charts and forms

Many charts and forms can help you organize your research and make your findings easier to understand for those you share them with. Some examples include Pedigree charts that show the relationships between family members, Descendant charts that list every person who descends from a particular ancestor, and census forms in which you can record information enumerated about your ancestor during particular years. Some of these charts and forms are available online at sites like Genealogy Today at

www.genealogytoday.com/genealogy/enoch/forms.html

The sooner you become familiar with the most common types of charts and how to read them, the sooner you can interpret a lot of the information you receive from other genealogists. (Chapter 1 examines some of these charts and forms in greater detail; we discuss some forms you can generate using your computer in Chapter 9.)

Assigning unique numbers to family members

If you have ancestors who share the same name, or if you've collected a lot of information on several generations of ancestors, you may have trouble distinguishing one person from another. To avoid confusion and the problems that can arise from it, you may want to use a commonly accepted numbering system to keep everyone straight.

The ahnentafel (Sosa-Stradonitz) system

One well-known numbering system is called *ahnentafel,* which means "ancestor" (*ahnen*) and "table" (*tafel*) in German. You may also hear the ahnentafel system referred to as the *Sosa-Stradonitz* system of numbering because it was first used by a Spanish genealogist named Jerome de Sosa in 1676, and was popularized in 1896 by Stephan Kekule von Stradonitz.

The ahnentafel system is a method of numbering that shows a mathematical relationship between parents and children. Ahnentafel numbering follows this progression:

1. **The child is assigned a particular number: y**

   Of course, we recognize that y isn't really a number — it's a letter. In our mathematical (that is, algebraic) example, y represents a unique number for that particular person.

2. **The father of that child is assigned the number that is double the child's number: $2y$**

3. **The mother of that child is assigned a number that is double the child's number plus one: $2y + 1$**

4. **The father's father is assigned the number that is double the father's number: $2(2y)$**

   The father's mother is assigned the number that is double the father's number plus one: $2(2y) + 1$

5. **The mother's father is assigned a number that is double the mother's number: $2(2y + 1)$**

   The mother's mother is assigned a number that is double the mother's number plus one: $2(2y + 1) + 1$

6. **Continue this pattern through the line of ancestors.**

The mathematical relationship works the same way going forward through the generations — a child's number is one-half the father's number and one-half (minus any remainder) the mother's number.

In a list form, the ahnentafel for April's grandfather looks like the following list (see Figure 3-1 for the chart):

1 John Duff Sanders, b. 10 Mar 1914 in Benjamin, Knox Co., TX; d. 15 Mar 1996 in Seymour, Baylor Co., TX; ma. 24 Dec 1939 in Sherman, Grayson Co., TX.

2 John Sanders, b. 19 Oct 1872 in Cotton Plant, Tippah Co., MS; d. 2 Mar 1962 in Morton, Cochran Co., TX; ma. 28 Sep 1902 in Boxelder, Red River Co., TX.

3 Nannie Elizabeth Clifton, b. 1 Apr 1878 in Okolona, MS; d. 27 Apr 1936 in Morton, Cochran Co., TX.

4 Harris Sanders, b. 27 Mar 1824 in Montgomery Co., NC; d. 21 Feb 1917 in Tippah Co., MS; ma. 26 June 1853.

5 Emeline Crump, b. 20 Oct 1836; d. 21 Feb 1920 in Tippah Co., MS.

6 William Clifton, b. 5 Mar 1845 in SC; d. 9 Feb 1923 in Boxelder, Red River Co., TX; ma. 5 Nov 1872 in Birmingham, AL.

7 Martha Jane Looney, b. 8 Mar 1844; d. Boxelder, Red River Co., TX.

John Duff Sanders is number one because he's the base individual for the ahnentafel. His father (John Sanders) is number two (because 2 x 1 = 2), and his mother (Nannie Elizabeth Clifton) is number three (2 x 1 + 1 = 3). His father's father (Harris Sanders) is four (2 x 2 = 4), and his father's mother (Emeline Crump) is five (2 x 2 + 1 = 5). John Sanders' number (2) is one-half his father's number (4 ÷ 2 = 2), or one-half minus any remainder of his mother's number (5 ÷ 2 = 2.5; 2.5 minus remainder of .5 = 2) — well, you get the idea.

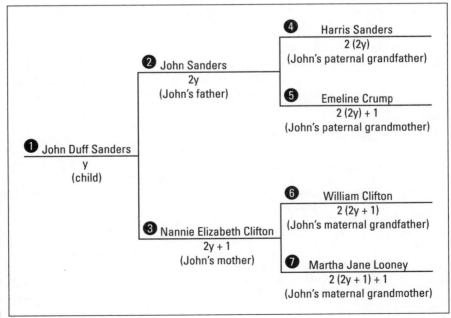

Figure 3-1: An ahnentafel for April's grandfather, John Duff Sanders.

As you can imagine, after a while you begin to tire from all these calculations — especially if you do them for ten or more generations of people. So, if your genealogy software supports it, we highly recommend that you run an ahnentafel report from it — saving you a lot of time and trouble. (We discuss software packages and some of their capabilities in The *Genealogy Online For Dummies* Internet Directory in this book.)

The tiny tafel system

Some people confuse ahnentafel with *tiny tafel,* which is a compact way to show the relationships within a family database. Tiny tafel provides only the Soundex code for a surname, and the dates and locations where that surname may be found according to the database. (For more on Soundex codes and how they work, check out Chapter 1.) Computer programs sometimes use tiny tafels to match the same individual in two different genealogy databases. The following example shows a tiny tafel:

C413	1845	1936	Clifton\South Carolina/Cochran Co. TX
C651	1836	1920	Crump/Mississippi
L500	1844		Looney/Red River Co. TX
S536	1824	1996	Sanders\Montgomery Co. NC/Baylor Co. TX

The Henry system

The *Henry* system is another well-known numbering system. This system assigns a particular number to the *progenitor,* or the ancestor farthest back (that you know about) in your family line. Then each of the progenitor's children is assigned a number in a sequence that starts with his number and adds the numbers one, two, three, and so forth through nine. (If the progenitor had more than nine children, the tenth child is assigned an X, the eleventh an A, the twelfth a B, and so on.) Then the children's children are assigned the parent's number plus a number in sequence (again one through nine, then X, A, B, and so on). For example, if progenitor number one (1) had 12 children, then his children would be 11, 12, 13, . . . 1X, and 1A. The eleventh child's children would be assigned the numbers 1A1, 1A2, 1A3, and so forth.

For example, suppose that one of your ancestors, John Jones, had 12 children. The names of these children were Joseph, Ann, Mary, Jacob, Arthur, Charles, James, Maria, Esther, Harriett, Thomas, and Sophia. Joseph had one child named Gertrude and Thomas had three children named Lawrence, Joshua, and David. Under the standard Henry system, the children's children are numbered like this:

1	John Jones
11	Joseph Jones
111	Gertrude Jones

12	Ann Jones	
13	Mary Jones	
14	Jacob Jones	
15	Arthur Jones	
16	Charles Jones	
17	James Jones	
18	Maria Jones	
19	Esther Jones	
1X	Harriett Jones	
1A	Thomas Jones	
	1A1	Lawrence Jones
	1A2	Joshua Jones
	1A3	David Jones
	1B	Sophia Jones

By no means are these systems the only genealogical numbering systems in existence. Ahnentafel and Henry are just two of the easier systems to learn. Several others have been designed to display genealogies in book form. If you're curious about some of these systems, take a look at the Numbering Systems in Genealogy page at www.saintclair.org/numbers/. There you can find descriptions of each major numbering system.

If you decide to use a numbering system, you can place the corresponding unique number for each individual on the file that you set up for that person in your paper record-keeping system, as well as in your genealogical software.

Making copies of source documents

You don't want to carry original records with you when you're out and about researching. The chances of misplacing or forgetting a document are too great. You have a few options:

- ✔ You can enter the information into a database and take a notebook computer with you.
- ✔ You can copy data from your desktop computer to a palmtop.
- ✔ You can print out your data.

- ✔ You can make photocopies of data that you must have with you for your research.
- ✔ You can scan the documents and store them on your laptop or notebook computer. (We talk more about using computers for your notes in Chapter 9.)

Then use your notes and copies out in the field. Place the original documents in the safest place you can think of that is available to you — a lockbox, fireproof file cabinet or safe, or a safety-deposit box.

Deciding on a storage method

How are you going to store all that information? A filing system is in order! You can set up a good filing system in many ways, and no one system is right or wrong. Just use one that's comfortable for you.

If you're at a loss as to how to start a system, here's one we like: We prefer to have both electronic and physical components to our filing system. To establish an electronic system, enter your ancestors' names into your database. Most genealogical programs enable you to enter numbers for each individual. Use the numbers that you create in the electronic system on file folders for paper documents that you collect on each individual. Although we like to scan all our paper documents, sometimes we get behind, so we set up temporary folders in which we can store the documents until we can scan them. After we scan the documents, we transfer them to permanent folders that we keep in a fireproof container. You may consider saving your scanned images to a notebook computer's hard drive, a Zip disk, or a writable CD-ROM so you can easily transport the images when you go on research trips.

Make backup copies of all your electronic documents as a safety precaution.

Preserving Your Treasured Family Documents

Time is going to take its toll on every document in your possession. The longer you want your records and pictures to last, the better care you need to take of them now. The following sections discuss some tips for preserving your family treasures so you can pass them down to future generations in the best possible shape.

Storing vital records under the right conditions

Place birth certificates, marriage licenses, and other records between sheets of acid-free paper in albums. Keep these albums in a dark, dry, and temperature-consistent place. Ideally, store these documents in a place that is 65 to 70 degrees Fahrenheit year-round, with a relative humidity of less than 50 percent. You may consider placing these albums in a steel file cabinet (but make sure it's rust-free). Also, try to avoid using ink, staples, paper clips, glue, and tape around your documents (unless you use archival products specifically designed for document repair).

For your precious documents (original birth certificates and family papers), rent a safety-deposit box or find another form of secure off-site storage. Of course, one of the best ways to ensure the success of your preservation effort is to make electronic copies of your documents using a scanner, then keep disk backups at a fire-safe, off-site location (again, a safety-deposit box is a good choice).

Protecting your photographs

Fight the urge to put all your photos of every ancestor on display, because light can damage them over time. Keep your most-prized pictures in a dark, dry, and temperature-consistent place. If you use a photo album for storage, make sure that it has acid-free paper or chemically-safe plastic pockets, and that you affix the pictures to the pages using a safe adhesive. Other storage options include acid-free storage boxes and steel file cabinets. Store the photographs in a place that stays around 65 to 70 degrees Fahrenheit year-round, with a relative humidity of less than 50 percent. Avoid prolonged exposure of photographs to direct sunlight and fluorescent lights. And, by all means, have negatives made of those rare family photos and store them in clearly marked, acid-free envelopes (the kind without gumming or glue!).

You can preserve photographs a couple of other ways. First, you can convert photographs from an earlier time to a newer and safer kind of film. A local photograph shop that specializes in preservation can do this for you. Because color photographs fade more quickly than their black-and-white counterparts, you may want to make black-and-white negatives of your color photographs. Also, as with documents, you can always preserve your photographs electronically by scanning them into your computer or by having a photo CD made by your photographic developer.

An electronic version isn't a real substitute for an original. Don't throw away the photos you scan (but you knew that).

Here are a few Web sites that provide more detailed tips on preserving your family treasures:

- ✔ **Just Black and White's Tips for Preserving Your Photographs and Documents** by David Mishkin: www.maine.com/photos/tip.htm

- ✔ **Guidelines For Preserving Your Photographic Heritage** by Ralph McKnight: www.geocities.com/Heartland/6662/photopre.htm

- ✔ **Document and Photo Preservation FAQ** by Linda Beyea: loricase.com/faq.html

And when you're looking for some of the chemically safe archival materials that we've described here (including albums, paper, boxes, adhesives, etc.), head on over to:

- ✔ Archival Methods at www.archivalmethods.com/

- ✔ Global Genealogy & History Shoppe: Archival Document & Artifact Preservation Supplies at globalgenealogy.com/archival/

Even though you want to preserve everything to the best of your ability, don't be afraid to pull out your albums to show visiting relatives and friends if you want to do so. On the other hand, don't be embarrassed to ask these guests to use caution when looking through your albums. Depending on the age and rarity of some of your documents, you may even want to ask guests to wear latex gloves when handling the albums so the oil from their hands doesn't get on your treasures. Upon realizing how important these treasures are to you, most guests won't mind using caution.

Entering Information into Family Tree Maker

To help you get a better idea of how software can help you organize your records and research, and to help you figure out what features to look for in particular software packages, this section examines how to use Family Tree Maker, one of the more popular genealogy software programs on the market today.

You can load a basic version of the Family Tree Maker software onto your computer from the CD-ROM accompanying this book. (For installation instructions, see Appendix C.)

When you open Family Tree Maker for the very first time and create a new family file, you get a form titled, "Start Your Family Tree." It is a small Pedigree chart where you can enter information about yourself, your parents, and your grandparents. Upon completing that page and clicking the Next button, you get a form where you can enter birth date and location information. Next is the page asking for death date and location. Lastly, Family Tree Maker informs you that you've now entered enough information to run a Family Finder search and asks whether you'd like to do so. After all of this, you see a blank Family Page with the cursor already set in the *Husband or Wife* field that holds your name. This page is the starting point for inserting detailed information about yourself and your family. Figure 3-2 shows a Family Page within Family Tree Maker.

Figure 3-2:
A Family
Page in
Family Tree
Maker for
William
Henry Abell
and
Elizabeth F.
Pickerrel.

Completing the Family Page

Usually, it's easiest to enter information about yourself, your spouse, and children, and then work backward through your parents, grandparents, great-grandparents, and so forth. After you complete your direct lines back as far as you can, come back and enter information on Family Pages for each of your siblings, nieces and nephews, cousins, and other relatives. Always enter as much information as you can in each of the fields on the Family Pages. Doing so may save you from returning to complete the page later or forgetting to do so. Follow these steps to fill in the Family Page:

1. **Enter your name.**

   Using the appropriate field *(Husband* or *Wife)* based on your gender or family role, enter your name in this order: first name, middle name, and last name (use your maiden name if you're female). Even if you're not married, use one of these two fields for your own information and just leave the spouse field blank.

   If you completed the initial "Start Your Family Tree" form when opening Family Tree Maker for the very first time, then your name already appears in either the Husband or Wife field. Verify that it is entered as we recommend here: first name, middle name, and last name (maiden if you're female).

   After you enter your name, Family Tree Maker automatically creates a Family Page for your parents. When you need to enter more detailed information about your parents, you can click the appropriate tab on the right side of the screen to access their Family Page.

2. **Enter your date of birth in the Date Born field, and enter your place of birth in the In field.**

   Press the Tab key to move among the fields on the page. Notice that some fields (Date Born, Died, and Location) are disabled when you first begin. As soon as you type your name, these fields become active.

   In the Date Born field, enter your birth date, including month, day, and full four-digit year. The software has a default format for dates, so you can spell out the date (January 15, 1965) or abbreviate it with numerals (01/15/1965). The system automatically converts the date to the spelled out format (January 15, 1965) unless you change the default format.

   Note: Uh-oh. Some people may say we just gave you incorrect instructions about the way to enter dates! Diehard genealogists and former military personnel often tell you that the order should be day, month, and *then* year instead (for example, 15 January 1965) — another perfectly acceptable method for dating, and one that is quite often international. Even though we're likely to get a lashing for saying this, we've seen both

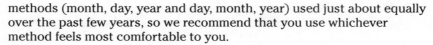
methods (month, day, year and day, month, year) used just about equally over the past few years, so we recommend that you use whichever method feels most comfortable to you.

If you inadvertently use only two numerals for the year, the software prompts you to use a four-digit year. For example, if you enter 01/15/65 into a Date Born field, a dialog box appears, asking you to choose a complete year for the date — 1965, 1865, 1765, and so forth. Additionally, if you aren't sure about the exact date of an event, Family Tree Maker enables you to use abbreviations for *circa* (or about). However, the software automatically defaults to Abt in the field when you enter one of the codes. For example, if you enter **cir. 01/15/1965**, the software converts it to Abt January 15, 1965. (Again, if you prefer Cir to Abt, you can change the default settings.)

Tab to the next field and enter your place of birth. Always include as much information as possible in every field, including the town, county or parish, state, and country of your birth.

3. **Click the appropriate fields and enter name and birth information about your spouse. If you don't have any spouse information to enter, go to Step 5.**

Enter your spouse's name in the appropriate Husband or Wife field. After the date and place of birth fields are active, tab down and enter your spouse's information in the Date Born and In fields just like you did for yourself.

After you enter your spouse's name, Family Tree Maker automatically creates a Family Page for the spouse's parents. When you need to enter more detailed information about your in-laws, you can click the appropriate tab on the right side of the screen to get to their Family Page.

4. **Enter your marriage information in the Marriage Date, Beginning Status, and Marriage Location fields.**

As with the birth and death fields, the Marriage Date and Marriage Location fields are disabled until you enter names in both the Husband and Wife fields. After the fields become active and you finish entering the basic information about you and your spouse, tab down to the Marriage Date field and enter the date of your wedding. In the Marriage Location field, enter the town, county/parish, state, and country where you were married.

The Beginning Status field reflects the relationship status between the persons whose information is contained in the Husband and Wife fields. The Beginning Status field starts out blank until both fields have information, and then it assumes Married. If the Beginning Status field reflects the wrong status for the relationship of the two people, use the drop-down menu to change the status. Your choices are Single, Married, Friends, Partners, Private, Unknown, and Other. Also, the Beginning Status field controls titles for some of the other fields on the Family Page. If you select

Friends or Partners for the relationship status of the two people, Family Tree Maker automatically changes Husband and Wife to Friend or Partner and Marriage Date and Marriage Location to Meeting Date and Meeting Location.

5. **Enter information about your children (if applicable) in the table at the bottom of the page. If you don't have any information to enter, skip this step.**

When you record information about your children, the software can be a little deceiving. At first glance, you may think that you can enter information about only one to four children, but this is not the case. To get to a fifth or subsequent child field, press Enter after recording the previous child's date of birth; the software brings up a fifth or subsequent line for you to use. (You can also use the scroll bar to get to additional lines — the scroll bar appears when you enter the fourth child's information.)

For each child, enter the child's full name, sex, and date of birth in the appropriate columns. As you begin entering the child's name, Family Tree Maker assumes that the child has the same last name as the father on this Family Page. If this is not the case, simply delete the last name that Family Tree Maker provides and type in the correct surname for the child.

After you enter a child's information, Family Tree Maker automatically creates a Family Page for that child. When you're ready to enter more detailed information about your children (such as their places of birth, marriage information, and so forth), click the appropriate child's tab on the right side of the screen to get to his or her Family Page. Or you can use the View drop-down menu to find the Index of Individuals, from which you can choose the child by name.

You probably noticed that we skipped over a few fields on your Family Page. These are the fields that hold death and burial information — so (for obvious reasons) if you're completing the Family Page on yourself, you do not yet need to enter information in them. You'll use these fields soon enough when entering information about your ancestors on their own Family Pages.

As you enter information about people, cite your data sources. Most genealogical software programs, including Family Tree Maker, allow you to enter source information. For specific instructions on how to enter info in your particular software, see the Help file or user's manual that comes with the software. In Family Tree Maker, you need to complete two processes in order to adequately cite your sources. First, create a master source by completing the window that you can access by selecting Edit ⇨ Edit Master Sources. After you've created a master source, select View ⇨ Source, and complete the fields in the Source Citation box that pops up. For example, if you were citing a source for information about your birth, you would first create a master source for your birth certificate, providing as much information as possible in the fields of the Master Source window and clicking OK. Then you would bring up the Source Citation box and complete its fields, including the field that references the Master Source. After you cite a source for a particular fact, notice that a little s appears next to the field(s) on the Family Page. In using our example here about entering a source citation for your birth certificate, a little s appears to the right of the Date Born and In fields.

Another feature of Family Tree Maker that you should know about — called Fastfields — tries to help you enter name and location information. (You may have already encountered this feature in your first Family Page.) Sometimes, this feature saves you time, but if the word that you're typing differs slightly from what you entered before, this feature can be a bit frustrating. As soon as the software recognizes that you're repeating characters in the same order as in a previous field, it populates that field with the same string so you can just press Enter to accept that name or location. For example, say you have several ancestors who were born in Larue County, Kentucky. After you type **Larue County, Kentucky** or **Larue Co., Kentucky** for one ancestor, then any time you begin typing it for additional ancestors, the software recognizes it and gives you the option to use the same phrase.

Another feature of Family Tree Maker — one we think is handy — is that all fields have instructional boxes that pop up after the mouse's pointer has been on the field for a couple of seconds. (See Figure 3-3.) The instructional boxes are very helpful if you aren't sure exactly what information to include in the field.

Figure 3-3:
The pop-up instructional box for a location field tells you what to include when entering information.

Working with the supplemental pages

On the Family Page, you find icons for some interesting features. You see three icons next to the Husband and Wife fields and two icons next to the Marriage Location field. These icons lead you to supplemental pages for information about these particular people or events.

The More icon takes you to a section where you can select pages with forms for recording particular types of information about yourself or your relatives, including Facts, Address, Medical, Lineage, and Notes. The following list explains how to use each page:

✔ **The Facts page:** Use this page to record facts about an ancestor. The page provides three fields for each fact — a Fact field (where you select a title for the event from a pull-down menu or type in your own fact title), a Date field (optional), and a Comment/Location field. There's also a Pref'd box where you can indicate which fact is preferred if you have multiple facts that are similar. Use this Facts page to record information such as the places and dates of an ancestor's christening, Bar Mitzvah, achievements, employments, or even where your ancestor lived during particular census years.

✔ **The Address page:** Use this page to enter the current or last-known address and phone number of the relative. You can use this information in another feature of the software to generate letters or address labels for those with whom you correspond by mail.

✔ **The Medical page:** Use this page to enter the individual's height, weight, cause of death, and other medical notes.

✔ **The Lineage page:** Use this page to record a number of items, such as any titles (Dr., Rev., Jr., Sr., Col., etc.) the person has, "also known as" information (such as nicknames, stage names, or aliases), and your filing system reference number. There's a box you can check if you want to exclude information about this person from any calendars you generate using Family Tree Maker. If the person whose Lineage page you're completing is female, there's a field for you to select the format in which her married name will appear in trees and reports — whether to provide her name as "First Maiden Married," "First Middle Married," or "First Middle Maiden." Also, you can record the nature of this person's relationship with the individuals who are identified as the person's father and mother, as well as select whether to include the relationship in any trees or kinship reports you generate using the software. For example, you can record whether the individual was the natural-born child, stepchild, foster child, and so on, of the ancestor identified as the individual's father. And if the individual was

> considered an illegitimate child of the ancestor or disowned for some reason, you can select to exclude them from any trees or reports by checking the Exclude This Relationship from Trees and Kinship box.
>
> ✔ **The Notes page:** Use this blank page to record any personal notes and stories about a particular ancestor.

Clicking the Scrapbook icon takes you to a section where you can link your software to photographs, sound files, and movies (called *objects*) about this particular ancestor that you've stored on your computer. To insert an object, choose Insert from the Picture/Object menu and follow the instructional boxes. (You can also get to the Scrapbook section at any time by clicking the Scrapbook button in the bar at the top of the page.)

If your ancestor was married more than once, click the Spouses icon to include information about the additional spouses. You can create "new" spouses and record other spousal information, as well as designate which spouse is the "preferred" one for your database. The preferred spouse automatically appears on the Family page and other reports with your ancestor.

Entering information for your other ancestors

After you enter all the information you have for your first person (most likely yourself), use the tabs that run down the right side of the screen to go to the Family Page for your parents and enter all the information you have about them. After you're done with them, use the tabs to get to the Family Pages for your grandparents and so on as you progress backward through your ancestors. Later, come back and add your siblings, aunts, uncles, and other relatives.

Part II
Focusing on Your Ancestor

The 5th Wave   By Rich Tennant

"Well, she now claims she's a descendant of the royal Egyptian line of cats, but I'm not buying that just yet."

In this part . . .

This part covers how to locate resources that provide information on your ancestors by name. You can also find search strategies for using a variety of government documents online to substantiate your ancestor's life.

Chapter 4

What's in a Name?

As a genealogist, you may experience sleepless nights trying to figure out all the important things in life — the maiden name of your great-great-grandmother, whether great-grandpa was really the scoundrel that other relatives say he was, and just how you're related to Daniel Boone. (Well, isn't everyone?) Okay, so you may not have sleepless nights, but you undoubtedly spend a significant amount of time thinking about and trying to find resources that can give you answers to these crucial questions.

In the past, finding information on individual ancestors online was compared with finding a needle in a haystack. You browsed through long lists of links in hopes of finding a site that contained a nugget of information to aid your search. Well, looking for your ancestors online has become easier than ever. Instead of merely browsing links, you can now use search engines and online databases to pinpoint information on your ancestors.

This chapter covers the basics of searching for an ancestor by name, presents some good surname resource sites, and shows you how to combine several different Internet resources to successfully find information on your family. If you need a refresher on how to use a Web browser, take a look at Appendix A before you read this chapter.

Finding the Site That's Best for You

Your dream as an online genealogist is to find a site that contains all the information that you ever wanted to know about your family. Unfortunately, these sites simply don't exist. However, during your search you may discover a variety of sites that vary greatly in the amount and quality of genealogical information. Before you get too deep into your research, it's a good idea to look at the type of sites that you are likely to encounter.

Personal genealogical sites

The vast majority of sites that you encounter on the Internet are personal genealogical sites. Individuals and families who have specific research interests establish these pages. You're likely to find information on the site maintainer's ancestry or on particular branches of several different families rather than on a surname as a whole. That doesn't mean valuable information isn't present on these sites — it's just that they have a more personal focus.

You can find a wide variety of information on personal genealogical sites. Some pages list only a few surnames that the maintainer is researching; others contain extensive online genealogical databases and narratives. A site's content depends on the amount of research, time, and computer skills the maintainer possesses. Some common items that you see on most sites include a list of surnames, an online genealogical database, Pedigree and Descendant charts (for information on these charts, see Chapter 9), family photographs, and the obligatory list of the maintainer's favorite genealogical Internet links.

Personal genealogical sites vary not only in content, but also in presentation. Some sites are neatly constructed and use soft backgrounds and aesthetically pleasing colors. Others sites, however, require you to bring out your sunglasses to tone down the fluorescent colors, or they use link colors that blend in with the background, making it very difficult to navigate through the site. You should also be aware that many personal sites use JavaScript, music players, and animated icons that can significantly increase your download times.

An example of a personal genealogical site is the Mastin Family Genealogy Site (www.curlywoods.com/mastin). The site includes transcribed family obituaries, American Civil War diaries, a description of the migration of the Mastin family from Pennsylvania to Iowa and Missouri, family photographs, cemetery records, family documents, and a Descendant chart. (See Figure 4-1.)

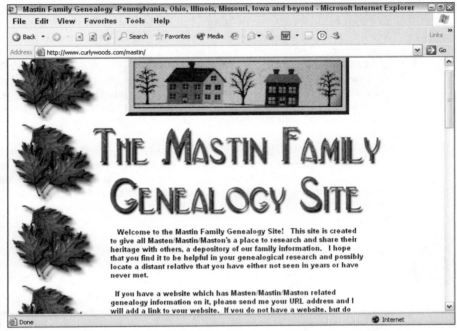

Figure 4-1:
The Mastin
Family
Genealogy
Site is an
example of
a personal
genealog-
ical site.

After you find a site that contains useful information, write down the maintainer's name and e-mail address and contact him or her as soon as possible if you have any questions or want to exchange information. Personal genealogical sites have a way of disappearing without a trace as individuals frequently switch Internet service providers or stop maintaining sites.

One-name study sites

If you're looking for a wide range of information on one particular surname, a one-name study site may be the place to look. These sites usually focus on one surname regardless of the geographic location where the surname appears. In other words, they welcome information about people with the surname worldwide. These sites are quite helpful because they contain all sorts of information about the surname, even if they don't have specific information about your branch of a family with that surname. Frequently they have information on the variations in spelling, origins, history, and heraldry of the surname. One-name studies have some of the same resources you find in personal genealogical sites, including online genealogy databases and narratives.

Although one-name study sites welcome all surname information regardless of geographic location, the information presented at one-name study sites is often organized around geographic lines. For example, a one-name study site may categorize all the information about people with the surname by continent or country — such as Helms in the United States, England, Canada, Europe, and Africa. Or the site may be even more specific and categorize information by state, province, county, or parish. So, you're better off if you have a general idea of where your family originated or migrated. But if you don't know, browsing through the site may lead to some useful information.

The Iseli Family World Wide Web site (www.iseli.org/) is a one-name study site with an international focus. From the home page (see Figure 4-2), you can choose to view the site in German, English, French or Afrikaans. The site's divided into several categories, including variations in surname spelling, family branches, notable Iselis, family heraldry, and links to Iseli researchers' Web sites.

The maintainers of one-name study sites welcome any information you have on the surname. These sites are often a good place to join research groups that can be instrumental in assisting your personal genealogical effort.

Figure 4-2:
The Iseli Family World Wide Web site is a one-name study with an international focus.

The *Genealogy Online For Dummies* Internet Directory in this book identifies some one-name study sites you may want to visit. It gives you just a sampling, though. To find one-name study sites pertaining to the surnames you're researching, you have to go elsewhere. Where, you say? One site that can help you determine whether any one-name study sites are devoted to surnames you're researching is the Guild of One-Name Studies (`www.one-name.org`).

The Guild of One-Name Studies

Gee, we bet you can't figure out what the Guild of One-Name Studies is! It's exactly as it sounds — an online organization of registered sites, each of which focuses on one particular surname. The Guild has information about more than 7,000 surnames. Follow these steps to find out whether any of the Guild's members focus on the surname of the person you're researching:

1. **Open your Web browser and go to** `www.one-name.org`.

2. **Scroll to** `The On-Line Searchable Register of One-Name Studies` **link.**

   You're taken to a page called Register of One-Name Studies. Near the bottom of the page is a field where you can type in the surname you're researching.

3. **Type a surname into the field and click Search.**

   The Results page contains entries from the database that match your search.

Family associations and organizations

Family association sites are similar to one-name study sites in terms of content, but they usually have an organizational structure (such as a formal association, society, or club) backing them. The association may focus on the surname as a whole or just one branch of a family. The goals for the family association site may differ from those for a one-name study. The maintainers may be creating a family history in book form or a database of all individuals descended from a particular person. Some sites may require you to join the association before you can fully participate in their activities, but this is usually at a minimal cost or free.

The Wingfield Family Society site (`www.wingfield.org`), shown in Figure 4-3, has several items that are common to family association sites. The site's contents include a family history, newsletter subscription details, a membership form, reunion news, queries, mailing list information, results of a DNA project, and a directory of the society's members who are online. Some of the resources at the Wingfield Family Society site require you to be a member of the society in order to access them.

Figure 4-3:
The
Wingfield
Family
Society site.

To find a family association Web site, your best bet is to use a search engine or a comprehensive genealogical index. For more on search engines see the sections "Focusing on genealogically focused search engines" and "Browsing Comprehensive Genealogical Indexes" later in this chapter.

Surnames connected to events or places

Another place where you may discover surnames is a site that has a collection of names connected with a particular event or geographic location. The level of information available on these sites varies greatly among sites and among surnames on the same site. Often, the maintainers of such sites include more information on their personal research interests than other surnames, simply because they have more information on their own lines.

Typically, you need to know events that your ancestors were involved in or geographic areas where they lived to use these sites effectively. Also, you benefit from the site simply because you have a general, historical interest in the particular event or location even if the Web site contains squat on your surname. Finding Web sites about events is easiest if you use a search engine, a comprehensive Web site, or a subscription database. Because we devote an entire chapter to researching geographic locations (Chapter 6), we won't delve into that here.

Taking the Plunge

After you've decided on a particular person to research (for more on selecting a good research candidate, see Chapter 2), it's time to research online. As we've mentioned frequently in this book, it's a good idea to arm yourself with some facts about the individual before venturing online.

Let's say that Matthew wants to research his paternal grandfather's line. His grandfather was Herschel Helm who lived in Macon County, Illinois. From memory and supported by a copy of a death certificate for Herschel, Matthew knows that his grandfather died in 1985 — information that can be used to distinguish him from another Herschel Helm found online.

Due to privacy laws, the amount of information online on people in the United States after 1930 is pretty limited. However, one source that does provide information on deceased individuals during this time period is the Social Security Death Index (SSDI), also called the Social Security Death Master file — a good place to get your feet wet.

As of late 2003, the SSDI contained more than 71 million records of deaths of individuals having a Social Security Number. The vast majority of these records deal with individuals who died after 1962 — although a few scattered records pre-date that year. Each entry includes the following:

- Name of deceased
- Birth date
- Death date
- Last residence
- Last benefit received
- Social Security Number
- State where person lived when Social Security card was issued

Several places exist online where the SSDI can be searched. Probably the most up-to-date version is found at

www.ancestry.com/search/rectype/vital/ssdi/main.htm

However, a subscription is required for access. For free access to the SSDI, try `ssdi.genealogy.rootsweb.com`.

To search the SSDI, try the following:

1. **Point your browser to** `ssdi.genealogy.rootsweb.com`.

   The Social Security Death Index Interactive Search page at Rootsweb.com appears with a search form near the bottom of the page.

2. **Type in the last name and first name of the individual and click the Submit button.**

   You can search for an exact match on the surname, or use a Soundex or metaphone (a phonetic code algorithm that is similar to Soundex) equivalent for the search. (For more information about Soundex, flip back to Chapter 1.) These sound-based equivalents can be used to find names that are not spelled exactly as you expect them to be. In our case, we typed "helm" in the last name and "herschel" in the first name fields.

3. **Browse the results page for the appropriate individual.**

   The results are presented in a table with nine columns. Our search yielded four results, and only one of those has the last residence of Macon County and a death date of 1985.

Whenever you use this database and find someone for whom you're searching, you have the opportunity to generate a letter to order the original Social Security application (Form SS-5) from the Social Security Administration.

Family Trees Ripe for the Pruning (Finding Compiled Genealogical Resources)

Using online databases to pick pieces of genealogical fruit is wonderful. But you want more, right? Not satisfied with just having Social Security information on his grandfather, Matthew is eager to know more — in particular, he'd like to know who Herschel's grandfather was. There are a couple of research routes to take at this point. Perhaps the first is to see if someone has already completed some research on Herschel and his ancestors.

When someone publishes his or her genealogical findings (whether online or in print), the resulting work is called a *compiled genealogy*.

Compiled genealogies can give you a lot of information about your ancestors in a nice, neat format. When you find one with information relevant to your family, you get this overwhelming feeling of instantaneous gratification. But don't get too excited yet! When you use compiled genealogies, it's important to remember that you need to verify any information in them that you're adding to your own findings. Even when sources are cited, it's wise to get your own copies of the actual sources to ensure that the author's interpretation of the sources was correct and that no other errors occurred in the publication of the compiled genealogy.

Compiled genealogies take two shapes online. One is the traditional narrative format — the kind of thing that you typically see in a book at the library. The second is in the form of information exported from an individual's genealogical database and posted online in a lineage-linked format (lineage-linked means that the database is organized by the relationships between people).

Narrative compiled genealogies

Narrative compiled genealogies usually have more substance than their exported database counterparts. Authors sometimes add color to the narratives by including local history and other text and facts that can help researchers get an idea of the time in which the ancestor lived. An example of a narrative genealogy is found at the Glen Family Genealogy page at

`www.bedfordhouse.net/sites/genus/compiled/GlennCompiled.htm`

To locate narrative genealogies, try using a search engine or comprehensive genealogical index. (For more information on using these resources, see the sections later in this chapter.) Often, compiled genealogies are part of a larger, personal or family association Web site.

In addition to using a search engine or comprehensive site to find compiled narratives, check out the HeritageQuest Genealogy and Local History Online collection at `www.heritagequestonline.com`. The HeritageQuest collection is available to libraries and institutions. However, you can access it as an individual through the Family and Local Histories collection at Genealogy.com (`www.genealogy.com`).

Compiled genealogical databases

Although many people don't think of lineage-linked, online genealogical databases as compiled genealogies, these databases serve the same role as narrative compiled genealogies — they show the results of someone's research in a neatly organized, printed format. Even so, finding information in these databases can sometimes be tough. There isn't a grand database that indexes all the individual databases available online. While general Internet search engines have indexed quite a few, some very large collections are still only accessible through a database search — something that general Internet search engines don't normally do. Let's look at some of the larger collections.

In the previous section, we conducted a search on Matthew's grandfather, Herschel Helm. Now we want to find out more about his ancestry. We can jump start our research by using a lineage-linked database in hopes of finding some information compiled from other researchers that can help us learn who his ancestors were (perhaps even several generations worth). From documents such as his birth and death certificates, we learn that Herschel's father was named Emanuel Helm. And from interviews with family members, we also learn that Emanuel was born in Fayette County, Illinois, in the early 1860s. Armed with this information, we can search a compiled genealogical database.

FamilySearch

The FamilySearch Internet Genealogy Service (www.familysearch.org) is the official research site for the Church of Jesus Christ of Latter-day Saints (LDS). This free Web site allows you to search several LDS databases including the Ancestral File, International Genealogical Index, Family History Catalog, Research Guidance, census records, and a collection of abstracted Web sites — all of which are currently free. The two resources that function much like lineage-linked databases are the Ancestral File and the Pedigree Resource File. Fortunately, you don't have to search each of these resources separately. A master search is available that allows you to search all seven resources on the site at once.

To search the FamilySearch site, do the following:

1. **Open your Web browser and go to** www.familysearch.org.

   The home page for FamilySearch contains three columns under the Features label: Search for Ancestors, Share Information, and Family History Library System.

2. **Click the Search for Ancestors link in the first column.**

   This takes you to a page showing several fields that you can fill in to conduct a search on the site. (The fields form a small Pedigree chart.)

3. **Type the first and last name of the ancestor you're researching into the fields marked** First Name **and** Last Name.

   If you decide to include information on the spouse or mother or father and you don't receive adequate results, try doing the search on only the name of the ancestor. You can also fill in optional fields such as Event, Year, Year Range, Country, State, or Use Exact Spelling. (Keep in mind that filling in any of these fields may reduce the overall number of results you receive.) We typed in "Emanuel" in the first name box and "Helm" in the last name box. Notice that we did not select the exact-spelling option. We did this because Emanuel Helm is not that common a name. However, if you are searching a common name and expect a lot of results, you might want to check that option.

4. **After you select the search options, click the Search button.**

   The Results page contains links (with descriptions) to the resources that met your search criteria. For example, our search for Emanuel Helm yielded 45 results. These results come from six different resources on the site. The far-right column, Sources Searched, provides a breakdown of the number of results you received from each FamilySearch resource, as shown in Figure 4-4.

5. **Click the link of any result to see more information.**

   A few results jump out at us. The first is the Emanuel Helm born about 1863 in Fayette, Illinois. Looking for other records from Illinois, we find Manuel Helm in the 1880 U.S. Census and an Emanuel Helm born about 1863 in Fayette, Illinois, in the International Genealogical Index. As it turns out, all of these are the same person — in the 1880 Census his name was misspelled as *Manuel,* something we would not have found out if we'd turned on the exact-spelling option.

If we select the Ancestral File entry for Emanuel Helm, we are taken to the Individual record page. This page shows the sex of the individual, the event prompting the record, the parent names (if known), and information on the submitter of the record. From this record, we see that someone submitted a record showing Emanuel's parents as Uriah Helm and Rebecca Norris. The source information for this is not here, so it would be worthwhile to contact the submitter to locate the source. The other links on the page allow us to generate a Pedigree chart of Emanuel's ancestors or a Family Group Sheet of his immediate family. Looking at the Family Group Sheet, the submission shows that Uriah and Rebecca had six children and that Uriah's parents' names were William Helm and Elizabeth Guffey. Clicking the Pedigree link generates a chart that shows ancestors of Emanuel going back five generations to George Helm (born in 1723 in Virginia). Matthew can use this information to look for primary records to document these generations.

Although the LDS Church is well known for its large genealogical collection, don't expect to find the complete collection online — the vast majority of LDS resources reside in their library and Family History Centers. Also, you need to verify — with the help of the *original* records — any information that you do find online. Much of the information currently on the site was contributed by other family-history researchers, who may or may not have been careful in researching and documenting their family history.

Figure 4-4:
The results
of a search
for Jacob
Helm at
Family
Search.org.

We should also mention that there is another search site for the Pedigree Resource File component of the LDS site at www.findyourfamilytree.com. This site allows you to directly order the CD-ROM that contains the results of your search.

There are other lineage-linked collections that may contain useful information. The following list gives you details on some of the better-known collections:

✔ **GENDEX:** Before a lot of the genealogical software programs offered users the possibility of posting the data online, there were utilities that could convert GEDCOM files (the standard file format that genealogical databases can create) into HTML to be placed on the World Wide Web. One of the oldest of these is the GED2HTML program. (For more on posting genealogical databases to the Web and GED2HTML, see Chapter 12. And for even more about the GED2HTML program, see the section on genealogical software utilities in The *Genealogy Online For Dummies* Internet Directory in this book.) Once people began posting their information using this program, the GENDEX World Wide Web Genealogical Index (www.gendex.com/gendex/) was created so a person could search all GED2HTML databases in one location. As of late 2003, the database contained an index of over 70 million individuals in 27,569 databases.

✔ **Ancestry World Tree:** Part of the Ancestry.com site, the Ancestry World Tree (www.ancestry.com/trees) is a free area where researchers can contribute GEDCOM files from their individual databases, as well as search through the files of other researchers. Currently, the database contains over 250 million names.

✔ **WorldConnect:** The WorldConnect Project (worldconnect.rootsweb.com) is part of the RootsWeb.com site. The Project has over 300 million names in its database.

✔ **MyTrees.com:** MyTrees.com (www.mytrees.com) is a site maintained by Kindred Konnections. The site has a lineage-linked database numbering 90 million records. Most of the rest of the site is available only by subscription.

✔ **OneGreatFamily.com:** OneGreatFamily.com (www.onegreatfamily.com) hosts a subscription-based lineage-linked database. The database contains 55 million names contributed by over 300,000 users.

✔ **GenCircles:** GenCircles (www.gencircles.com) is a free, lineage-linked database site with a twist: Its SmartMatching feature compares individuals from different files and attempts to match them together. Thus a researcher who contributes to GenCircles can get in contact with another who may be working on the same family lines. The database currently has over 60 million names.

Letting Your Computer Do the Walking: Using Search Engines

Imagine spending several hours clicking from link to link and not finding anything that related to your research. Wouldn't it be nice to be able to just type in your ancestor's name and see if there are any sites that contain that name? Well, that's exactly what search engines allow you to do.

Search engines are programs that search huge indexes of information generated by robots. *Robots* are programs that travel throughout the Internet and collect information on the sites and resources that they run across. You can access the information contained in search engines through an interface, usually through a form on a Web page.

The real strength of search engines is that they allow you to search the full text of Web pages instead of just the title or a brief abstract of the site. For example, say that we're looking for information on one of Matthew's ancestors whom we found by using a lineage-linked database: George Helm, who lived around the turn of the nineteenth century in Frederick County, Virginia.

We could start by consulting a comprehensive genealogical index site (for more on comprehensive genealogical indexes, see "Browsing Comprehensive Genealogical Indexes," later in this chapter). There we could look for a Web site with *George Helm* in the title, or find an abstract of the site. Even if the comprehensive index contains tens of thousands of links, the chances of a Web site having *George Helm* in its title or its abstract is relatively small. Even so, by conducting a search through a search engine that indexes the full text of Web sites, we can find George Helm listed in a tax list from Grayson County, Virginia, in 1800 (along with 611 other individuals at `www.ls.net/~newriver/va/gray1800.htm`). Not only do we find information on George Helm on a Web site — we find him in a county we did not expect.

Different kinds of search engines are available to aid your search. These include genealogically focused search engines, general Internet search engines, and general Internet meta-search engines. For a list of some to use, check out The *Genealogy Online For Dummies* Internet Directory in this book.

Focusing on genealogically focused search engines

Your first stop on a search for a particular ancestor should be a search engine that's already set up for that purpose.

Genealogically focused search engines are sites that send out robots that index the full text of only those sites that contain information of interest to genealogists. By indexing just such sites, you receive fewer extraneous results when you type in your ancestor's name as a search term. An example of a genealogy-focused search engine is GenealogyPortal.com.

Technically, GenealogyPortal.com (`www.genealogyportal.com`) contains eight separate genealogically focused search engines. It includes search engines dedicated to the following categories: Archives and Libraries, Guides to Research, Historical Sites, Location-Specific Sites, Names and Personal sites, Primary Records, Research Supplies, and Software and Utilities. The Genealogy Portal.com search interface allows free-form text (your entry doesn't have to be a name) and Boolean searching. (*Boolean* searches involve using the terms *and, or,* or *not* to narrow your results.) You may have to use more than one of the GenealogyPortal.com's search engines to get complete coverage.

1. **Using your browser, go to** `www.genealogyportal.com`.

   The home page for GenealogyPortal.com contains a Search for Names and Personal Sites search box. If you want to switch to one of the other seven search engines, click one of the links located at the bottom of the search box.

2. **Type your search term in the field located in the gray box and click the Search button.**

   For example, we typed **George Helm** and clicked Search. The Results page appeared with 222 results. (See Figure 4-5.)

3. **Click a link that interests you.**

   The Results page shows the title of the page and an abstract of the site.

Using general Internet search engines

General search engines send out robots to catalog the Internet as a whole, regardless of the content of the site. Therefore, on any given search you're likely to receive a lot of hits, perhaps only a few of which hold any genealogical value — that is, unless you refine your search terms to give you a better chance at receiving relevant results.

Figure 4-5: Some of the results from a Genealogy Portal.com search on the names George and Helm.

You can conduct several different types of searches with most search engines. Looking at the Help link for any search engine to see the most effective way to search is always a good idea. Also, search engines often have two search interfaces — a simple search and an advanced search. With the *simple search,* you normally just type your query and click the Submit button. With a typical *advanced search,* you can use a variety of options to refine your search. The best way to become familiar with using a search engine is to experiment on a couple of searches and see what kinds of results you get.

One search engine that has proven successful for us when we search for genealogical data is Google (www.google.com). To conduct a search on Google, do the following:

1. **Point your Web browser to** www.google.com.

    The Google home page is simple. It consists of a field where you can enter search terms and two buttons marked *Google Search* and *I'm Feeling Lucky.*

2. **Type your ancestor's name into the search field and click Google Search. (We typed** george helm**.)**

    The Results page appears with a list of URLs and an abstract of the site, showing the search term bolded. (See Figure 4-6.) In our case, the search resulted in 105 pages.

3. **Click a search result that looks like it relates to your ancestor.**

If you're looking for additional leads, Google allows you to view other pages that are similar to results that you receive from your original search. You can also refine your search by using quotation marks in order to search for a complete phrase — for example, you can search for George Helm using **"George Helm"** as your search term, which filters out results dealing with the countless other Georges in this world. For more search hints, you can click the Search Tips link available at the top of the Results page.

Looking at general Internet meta-search engines

Wouldn't it be nice if we never had to visit multiple sites to search the Internet? This burning question led directly to the creation of *meta-search engines,* which use a single interface (or form) to execute searches using several different search engines. They then return the results of all the individual search engines back to a single page that you can use to view the results. The number of results from meta-search engines can be overwhelming, so it's important for you to have a good search term and to know something substantial about the person you're researching. That way, you can quickly determine whether a result is relevant to your search. You also need to have patience because you may have to trudge through several sets of results before you find something useful. Some general Internet meta-search engines include the following:

- ✔ **Vivisimo:** `vivisimo.com`
- ✔ **Ixquick:** `ixquick.com`
- ✔ **Dogpile:** `www.dogpile.com`
- ✔ **MetaCrawler:** `www.metacrawler.com`
- ✔ **Search.com:** `www.search.com`

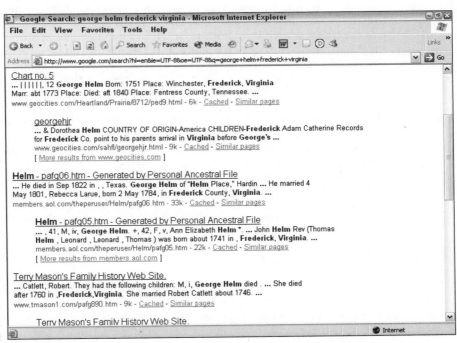

Figure 4-6: Search results from Google.

Online Subscription Databases: Gold Mines of Genealogy?

Some of your ancestors may have been prospectors. You know the type — they roamed from place to place in search of the mother lode. Often, they may have found a small nugget here or there, but they never seemed to locate that one mine that provided a lifetime supply of gold. Searching on the Internet can be very similar to this situation. You may be able to sympathize with the prospectors as you check out results from search engines only to find small nuggets of information here and there. However, don't lose hope. There may be some goldmines waiting for you if you can only stumble upon the right site — and the right site may be in the form of an online subscription database.

Online subscription databases are repositories of information that you can retrieve by paying a monthly, quarterly, or yearly fee. Most online subscription databases are searchable and allow you to type in your ancestor's name and execute a search to determine whether any information stored in the database relates to that particular name. Databases can be large or small; they can focus on a small geographic area or have a broad scope that encompasses many different areas. Each database may also have its own unique search method and present information in its own format.

You can find online subscription databases in many ways. You can find references to them through search engines (see the section "Letting Your Computer Do the Walking: Using Search Engines" earlier in this chapter), comprehensive genealogical indexes (see "Browsing Comprehensive Genealogical Indexes" later in this chapter), and links that appear on personal and geographic-specific Web sites. To give you a flavor of the type of goldmines that are available, we take a look at some of the larger online subscription databases.

Ancestry.com

Ancestry.com (www.ancestry.com) is a commercial site that contains information on over 2 billion names and adds new databases daily. The site also has a lot of free content, including weekly columns and a few databases. To access the text of the databases, you must be a member (although Ancestry.com does put the majority of its new databases online for free for ten days, and usually has a free period for all of its databases in December or January of each year). The major collections at the Ancestry.com site include

- ✔ U.S. Records Collection
- ✔ U.S. Census Images and Indexes
- ✔ U.K. and Ireland Records Collection
- ✔ Historical Newspapers
- ✔ U.S. Immigration Collection

Genealogy.com

Genealogy.com (`www.genealogy.com`) is a subscription site that was, until recently, the chief competitor to Ancestry.com. Now, however, its owned by the same parent company as Ancestry.com, although it's still maintained as a separate site. It also places new databases online daily. The contents of the site are periodically made available for free for a limited time, which gives you a good chance to decide whether the contents are beneficial to your research. Collections on Genealogy.com include

- ✔ Genealogy Library
- ✔ International and Passenger Records
- ✔ U.S. Census Collection
- ✔ Family and Local Histories
- ✔ World Family Tree Collection

Browsing Comprehensive Genealogical Indexes

If you're unable to find information on your ancestor through a search engine or online database (or you want to find additional information) another resource to try is a comprehensive genealogical index. A comprehensive genealogical index is a site that contains a categorized listing of links to online resources for family history research. Comprehensive genealogical indexes can be organized in a variety of ways, including by subject, alphabetically, or by resource type. No matter how the links are organized, they usually appear hierarchically — you click your way down from category to subcategory until you find the link you're looking for.

Some examples of comprehensive genealogical indexes include the following:

- ✔ **Cyndi's List of Genealogy Sites on the Internet:** www.cyndislist.com
- ✔ **Genealogy Home Page:** www.genealogyhomepage.com
- ✔ **Genealogy Resources on the Internet:** www-personal.umich.edu/ ~cgaunt/gen_int1.html
- ✔ **Helm's Genealogy Toolbox:** www.genealogytoolbox.com

To give you an idea of how comprehensive genealogical indexes work, try the following example:

1. **Fire up your browser and go to Cyndi's List (www.cyndislist.com).**

   This launches the home page for Cyndi's List.

2. **Scroll down to the portion of the main page labeled Cyndi's List Main Category Index.**

   Note: You have to scroll down almost one-third of the page to get to the Category Index.

3. **Select a category, such as Surnames, Family Associations & Family Newsletters.**

   For example, we're looking for a page that may contain information on our ancestors. Two categories on the list may have this info: Personal Home Pages and Surnames, Family Associations & Family Newsletters. We decide to try the Surnames category.

4. **Select a subcategory.**

   We can actually access the subcategories within the Surnames category in two ways. We can click the link for Surnames, Family Associations & Family Newsletters and then click another link for the letter of the alphabet that corresponds to the name we're looking for. Or we can simply click the letter of the alphabet contained in the table beneath the Surnames, Family Associations & Family Newsletters link.

   Say we're interested in finding some information on the Helm family. We select the H link and we're taken to the appropriate subcategory page. We then scroll down to the section titled Surname-Specific Sites and Resources and look for Helm resources. (See Figure 4-7.) We find one possible resource; however, it's on the Helms — not Helm — family.

5. **Click a promising link.**

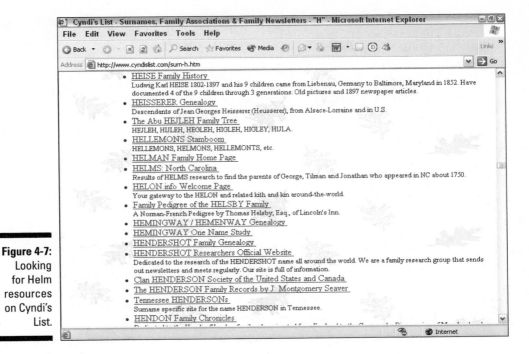

- HEISE Family History
  Ludwig Karl HEISE 1802-1897 and his 9 children came from Liebenau, Germany to Baltimore, Maryland in 1852. Have documented 4 of the 9 children through 3 generations. Old pictures and 1897 newspaper articles.
- HEISSERER Genealogy
  Descendants of Jean Georges Heisserer (Heusserer), from Alsace-Lorraine and in U.S.
- The Abu HEJLEH Family Tree
  HEJLEH, HIJLEH, HEGLEH, HIGLEH, HIGLEY, HIJLA.
- HELLEMONS Stamboom
  HELLEMONS, HELMONS, HELLEMONTS, etc.
- HELMAN Family Home Page
- HELMS: North Carolina
  Results of HELMS research to find the parents of George, Tilman and Jonathan who appeared in NC about 1750.
- HELON info Welcome Page
  Your gateway to the HELON and related kith and kin around-the-world.
- Family Pedigree of the HELSBY Family
  A Norman-French Pedigree by Thomas Helsby, Esq., of Lincoln's Inn.
- HEMINGWAY / HEMENWAY Genealogy
- HEMINGWAY One Name Study
- HENDERSHOT Family Genealogy
- HENDERSHOT Researchers Official Website
  Dedicated to the research of the HENDERSHOT name all around the world. We are a family research group that sends out newsletters and meets regularly. Our site is full of information.
- Clan HENDERSON Society of the United States and Canada
- The HENDERSON Family Records by J. Montgomery Seaver
- Tennessee HENDERSONs
  Surname specific site for the name HENDERSON in Tennessee.
- HENDON Family Chronicles

Figure 4-7:
Looking for Helm resources on Cyndi's List.

Of course, one drawback to comprehensive genealogical indexes is that they can be time-consuming to browse. It sometimes takes several clicks to get down to the area where you believe links that interest you may be located. And, after several clicks, you may find that no relevant links are in that area. This may be because the maintainer of the site has not yet indexed a relevant site, or the site may be listed somewhere else in the index.

Integrated Genealogical Search Sites

Clearly, search engines and comprehensive genealogical indexes can help you find information online about your ancestors. Wouldn't it be nice, though, if you could use both resources at the same time? We're proud to say that one Web site does integrate both full-text searching of genealogical Web sites with a comprehensive genealogical index. The site is, drum roll please, Helm's Genealogy Toolbox (www.genealogytoolbox.com).

Helm's Genealogy Toolbox is one of the oldest genealogical Web sites — growing out of a list of links first placed on the Web in September 1994. The site currently contains links to sites of interest to genealogists, a set of eight search engines that index the full-text of online genealogical sites, and digitized images of microfilmed original records. All these resources are integrated together into a single site that's divided into the following categories:

- Computers
- How-to and Help
- Media
- People
- Places
- Supplies and Services
- Original Records

You can search Helm's Genealogy Toolbox a couple of different ways. You can search all the resources of the site at the same time through the Global Search or you can browse through the categories much like a comprehensive genealogical index. Here's an example search using the Global Search option:

1. **Launch your Web browser and type in the address for Helm's Genealogy Toolbox** (www.genealogytoolbox.com).

   The home page for the site appears. At the bottom of the page, there's a section with a blue background and a number three (3) that contains the field and instructions for the Global Search.

   On other windows within Helm's Genealogy Toolbox site, the Global Search interface appears in the left column of the page. The section's blue background makes it easy to find.

2. **Type your ancestor's name into the field and click the Search button.**

   The Results page returns a list of links that met your search criteria. These links include resources from the categorized list of links, the full-text search engines, queries from other researchers, and names from digitized records.

3. **Click a link that may relate to your ancestor.**

To browse links on Helm's Genealogy Toolbox site, complete the following steps:

1. **Launch your Web browser and type in the address for Helm's Genealogy Toolbox** (www.genealogytoolbox.com).

   The Site Categories are accessible through the column on the left or through a section in the middle of the page that has a number two (2) and has links to the seven site categories and descriptions of each.

2. **Click the** `People` **link.**

The resulting page contains links to surname subcategories arranged by letter of the alphabet. (The letter of the alphabet corresponds to the first letter of the surname that's the subject of the Web site.)

3. **Choose a link to a surname subcategory or select a link that looks interesting.**

On some pages, you may encounter further subcategories that break down the letters of the alphabet into smaller sections. Other pages merely contain links to other Web sites.

Query for One: Seeking Answers to Your Surname Questions

Even if you can't find any surname-specific sites on your particular family, you still have hope! This hope comes in the form of queries. *Queries* are research questions that you post to a particular Web site, mailing list, or newsgroup so other researchers can help you solve your research problems. Other researchers may have information that they haven't yet made available about a family, or they may have seen some information on your family, even though it isn't a branch that they're actively researching.

Web queries

One of the quickest ways of reaching a wide audience with your query is through a query site on the Web. (Appendix A has some information about the Web if you need help.) For an example of a query site, try GenForum:

1. **Open your Web browser and go to** `www.genforum.com`.

2. **In the field under Forum Finder, type the surname you're looking for and click the Find button.**

In our case, we enter **Helm**. But feel free to enter a surname that interests you. If you feel like browsing the forums, you can also select a letter beneath the word *Surnames*.

Don't worry if your surname doesn't have a forum. The GenForum section is constantly growing and adding surnames, so you should check back every so often to see if one's been added or you may consider requesting that a new forum be added for your surname. (Look for the little link called Add Forum near the bottom of the GenForum pages.)

You may also want to search other forums to see if the name is included in a variant spelling or if someone else mentioned the name in a passing reference in another forum. (See the next section for details.)

3. **After you find a forum, read a message by clicking its link.**

   As soon as your browser loads the message board page, you should see a list of bulleted messages to choose from. You can also navigate to other pages of the message board if the messages don't all fit on a single page. If you don't want to read all messages, you have the option to see only the latest messages, only today's messages, or any messages posted in the last seven days. These options are available at the top of the page.

4. **To post a new query, click the Post New Message button near the top of the message board page.**

   If you're not already a registered user of GenForum, you get a page with instructions on registering.

   If you're already a registered user or after you become one, a page containing the fields that generate your message pops up. This page includes the Name, E-Mail, Subject, and Message fields, as shown in Figure 4-8.

5. **Fill out the appropriate fields and then click the Preview Message button.**

   Make sure that your message contains enough information for other researchers to determine if they can assist you. Include full names, birth and death dates and places (if known), and geographic locations where your ancestors lived (if known).

   Clicking the Preview Message button is an important step because you can see how the message will look when it's posted. This option can prevent you from posting an embarrassing message — you know, one filled with those embarrassing typos.

6. **If you're satisfied with the way the message looks, click the Post Message button.**

Mailing-list queries

When you think of mailing lists, you may have nightmares of the endless stream of *junk* mail that you receive every day as a result of some company selling your name to a mailing list. Well, fear no more. The type of mailing list we refer to delivers mail that you request. Such lists also provide a way you can post queries and messages about your surnames and genealogical research in general.

Post New Message - Microsoft Internet Explorer

File   Edit   View   Favorites   Tools   Help

Back ▾   ⦿   ▾   ☒   ☒   ⦿   🔍 Search   ⭐ Favorites   🎬 Media   ⦿   ▾   🖾 ▾   □ ⓞ 3   Links »

Address   http://genforum.genealogy.com/cgi-genforum/forums/helm.cgi?   ⤷ Go

Home: Post New Message

Helm Family Genealogy Forum
If you want to post to this forum, type your subject and message below and then click "Post Message".

If you are not **Matthew Helm** click here to log in.

Posting To: Helm Family Genealogy Forum
Your Name: Matthew Helm   (this name appears with your posted message)
Your E-Mail: (click here to change your email address)
Subject:

Internet

Figure 4-8:
The Helm
Family
Genealogy
Forum
at Gen
Forum.com.

Mailing lists are formed by groups of people who share common interests, whether those interests are in surnames, specific geographic areas, particular topics, or ethnic groups. A list consists of the e-mail addresses of every person who joins (subscribes to) the group. When you want to send a message to the entire group, you send it to a single e-mail address that in turn forwards the message to everyone on the list. To join a mailing list, you send an e-mail to a designated address with a subscription message. You should then receive a confirmation e-mail that lets you know you're subscribed to the list and tells you where to send an e-mail if you want to send a message to everyone on the list.

Okay, even when you're hip to what a mailing list is, how do you find one of interest to you? One way is to consult the comprehensive list of mailing lists found on the Genealogy Resources on the Internet site (www.rootsweb.com/ ~jfuller/gen_mail.html). The site breaks down the mailing lists into various categories: Countries other than USA, USA, Surnames, Adoption, African-Ancestored, Cemeteries/Monuments/ Obituaries, Computing/Internet Resources, General Information/Discussion, Genealogical Material/Services, Jewish, Native American, Religions/ Churches (other than Jewish), Software, Wars/Military, Uncategorized.

Here's how you can find and join a mailing list for your surname:

1. **Point your Web browser to** `www.rootsweb.com/~jfuller/gen_mail.html` **and select the first letter of a surname you're interested in under the surnames section.**

   The letters appear near the bottom of the page. We select Hei-Hen because we're looking for a mailing list on the surname Helm. A list of surnames with mailing lists pops up.

2. **Scroll through the list and click one of the surname links on the page.**

   By scrolling through the list, you can see if your surname is represented. We scrolled through until we found our surname (see Figure 4-9) and clicked that link. It took us to a page that had information on a mailing list pertaining to Helm.

3. **Follow the subscription instructions for your mailing list.**

   The instructions for the Helm mailing list tell us to send an e-mail message with the word *subscribe* as the only text in the message body to one of two addresses.

   Typically, you can receive mailing lists in one of two ways. The first way, *mail mode,* simply forwards e-mail messages to you every time someone posts to the mailing list. Although this practice is fine for small mailing lists, you probably don't want hundreds of messages coming in individually — unless you like to have lots of e-mail sitting in your inbox. To avoid this, try the second way of receiving the mailing list — *digest mode.* This mode groups several messages together and then sends them out as one large message. Instead of receiving 30 messages a day, you may receive only two messages, with the text of 15 messages in each.

4. **Start your e-mail program and subscribe to the mailing list.**

   We decide to subscribe to the digest mode of the Helm mailing list. To do this, we start our e-mail program, create a new message with only the word *subscribe* in the body, and send the message to the digest address — `helm-d-request@rootsweb.com`. (See Figure 4-10.) Within a couple of minutes, we receive a confirmation message welcoming us to the mailing list.

5. **Read the messages without responding or posting your own messages for a while. Begin posting your own queries and responses to others' messages when you feel comfortable.**

   Reading messages but not posting your own messages is called *lurking.* You may want to lurk on the mailing list to see what other messages look like and to become familiar with the general culture of the list. After you get a feel for the structure and attitude of the messages, jump in and begin sending your own queries and messages!

Figure 4-9:
Identifying
mailing lists
at the
Genealogy
Resources
on the
Internet site.

Figure 4-10:
An e-mail
message to
subscribe
to a mailing
list.

Using E-Mail to Get Help

In the section "Query for One: Seeking Answers to Your Surname Questions" earlier in this chapter, we discuss a couple of ways to research surnames through e-mail by using queries. You can also use e-mail to directly contact other researchers of your surname. You just need to know where to find them.

Identifying potential e-mail pals by using online directories to find everyone with the surname you're researching, getting their e-mail addresses, and then mass e-mailing all of them about your research and questions is a bad idea. Although mass e-mailing everyone you can find with a particular surname generates return e-mail for you, we can almost guarantee that the responses will be hateful, not helpful. Sticking with genealogical sites (such as those we identify in a moment) when you're looking for other researchers interested in the same surnames is a better way to go about it.

The Roots Surname List

One of the oldest of the Internet genealogy resources is the Roots Surname List at rsl.rootsweb.com/. The Roots Surname List (RSL) is simply a list of surnames (and their associated dates and locations) accompanied by contact information for the person who placed the surname on the list. So if you want to contact other submitters about particular surnames, all you have to do is look at the contact information and send them e-mail messages or letters in the mail detailing your interest in the surnames.

The format for the list looks like this:

```
Helm 1723 now FrederickCo,VA>FentressCo, TN>FayetteCo,IL,USA
mhelm
```

The line contains the surname, earliest date for which you have information on the surname, most recent date that you have for the surname, locations through which your family passed showing migration patterns (using a list of standard abbreviations), and a name tag for the submitter.

Every surname entry has a companion entry, called the *name tag*. This entry shows how to contact the submitter. The name tag contains the submitter's name, e-mail address, and an optional mailing address. The following is a name tag that could be the companion to the preceding surname example:

```
mhelm Matthew Helm, mhelm@tbox.com, P.O. Box 111, Anytown,
Anystate, 11111
```

You can submit surnames to the RSL through e-mail or with a form on the Web. Before you submit something for the first time, take a few minutes to read the RSL instructions (helpdesk.rootsweb.com/help/rsl6.html).

You can search the information on the RSL by pointing your browser to rsl.rootsweb.com/cgi-bin/rslsql.cgi#search and filling in the surname and an optional location.

Surname-related e-mail resources

A number of resources are available that use e-mail as their primary communication tool. You can find a list of these at the Genealogy Resources on the Internet site (www.rootsweb.com/~jfuller/gen_mail.html). Among these resources are e-mail addresses of specific family associations, archives, and newsletters.

Verifying Your Information: Don't Believe Everything You Read!

We have one last piece of advice for you when you're researching — surnames or otherwise. *Don't believe everything you read.* Well, actually a pure genealogist would say, "Don't believe anything that you read." Either way, the point is the same — always verify any information that you find online with primary records. (For more on primary records, see Chapter 1.) If you can't prove it through a census record, vital record, or some other authoritative record, then the information simply may not be worth anything. However, just because you can't immediately prove it doesn't mean that you shouldn't hold on to the information. At some time in the future, you may run across a record that does indeed prove the accuracy of the information.

Chapter 5

Government Records

As we all know, governments love paper. Sometimes it seems government workers can't do anything without a form. Luckily for genealogists, governments have been this way for a number of years — otherwise it might be next to impossible to conduct family history research. In fact, the number of useful government records available online has exploded in the past few years. Not only have government entities been placing records and indexes online — private companies have also put great effort into digitizing and indexing government records for online use.

In this chapter, we show you what kinds of records are currently available and some of the major projects that you can use as keys for unlocking government treasure chests of genealogical information.

Counting on the Census

Census records are one of the most valuable tools to a genealogist, at least in the United States. Many countries periodically count and gather information about their populations, although most didn't conduct nationwide censuses regularly until the nineteenth century.

Census records are valuable for tying a person to a place and for discovering relationships between individuals. For example, suppose you have a great-great-great-grandfather by the name of Nimrod Sanders. You're not sure who his father was, but you do know that he was born in North Carolina. By using a census index, you may be able to find a Nimrod Sanders listed in a North Carolina census index as a child of someone else. If Nimrod's age, location, and siblings' names fit, then you may have found one more generation to add to your genealogy.

Often a census includes information such as a person's age, sex, occupation, birthplace, and relationship to the head of the household. Sometimes the *enumerators* (the people who conduct the census) added comments to the census record (such as a comment on the physical condition of an individual) that may give you further insight into the person's life. For additional information about the value and format of censuses, see Chapter 1.

Getting the lowdown on censuses

Several Web sites provide background information about census records in particular countries. They explain what years the census records cover, how the censuses were conducted, and what information is valuable to genealogists. Also, they give you the details on where you can find and obtain copies of these census records. Here's a list of general census information sites from various countries:

- **Australia:** Australian C19th Censuses

    www.users.on.net/proformat/census.html
- **Canada:** National Archives of Canada

    www.archives.ca/02/02020205_e.html
- **England, Scotland, and Wales:** Genuki Census Information

    www.genuki.org.uk/big/eng/Census.html
- **Ireland:** Irish Ancestors Census Records

    www.genealogy.ie/categories/cenna/
- **Norway:** Norwegian Censuses

    www.rhd.uit.no/indexeng.html
- **United States:** Availability of Census Records About Individuals

    www.census.gov/prod/2000pubs/cff-2.pdf

To find information on census records for some other countries, see the appropriate Research Helps at the FamilySearch Web site:

www.familysearch.org/Eng/Search/RG/frameset_rhelps.asp

For a summary of the contents of each United States census return and advice on how to use the censuses, see *The Census Book* by William Dollarhide (published by Heritage Quest). If you run into abbreviations that you don't understand, take a look at the Abbreviations Found in Genealogy page at

`www.rootsweb.com/~rigenweb/abbrev.html`

Finding your ancestors in census records

Imagine that you're ready to look for your ancestors in census records. You hop in the car and drive to the nearest library, archives, or Family History Center. On arrival, you find the microfilm roll for the area where you believe your ancestors lived. You then go into a dimly lit room, insert the microfilm into the reader, and begin your search. After a couple hours of rolling the microfilm, the back pain begins to set in, cramping in your hands becomes more severe, and the handwritten census documents become blurry as your eyes strain from reading each entry line by line. You come to the end of the roll and still haven't found your elusive ancestor. At this point, you begin to wonder if a better way exists.

Fortunately, a better way *does* exist for a lot of census records: census indexes. A *census index* contains a listing of the people who are included in particular census records, along with references indicating where you can find the actual census record. Traditionally, these indexes come in book form, but you can now find these indexes online or on CD-ROM.

Although no single World Wide Web site contains indexes of all available census records for all countries (at least not yet), some sites contain substantial collections of census indexes.

So how do you find these online indexes? Well, you can check a comprehensive index site or use a search engine (both of which we discuss in Chapter 3) to find an index that interests you.

For example, say you want to find an Alan McSwain who lived in Ontario sometime around 1870. Your first step is to determine whether a census was taken in or around 1870. To do so, follow these steps:

1. **Fire up your Web browser and go to Cyndi's List of Genealogy Sites on the Internet (`www.cyndislist.com`).**

   Note: For more information about using a Web browser, take a look at Appendix A.

2. **Click the** Ontario **link (under the Canada Index category).**

   This page contains many subcategories.

3. **Under the "Category Index for this page," click the** Records: Census, Cemeteries, Land, Obituaries, Personal, Taxes and Vital **link.**

   Doing so takes you down this list of links to the Records section. You see links to several records projects online.

4. **Scroll down near the bottom of the list of Records links and click the** Ontario 1871 Census **link.**

   The link takes you to a searchable index of the 1871 Census. (See Figure 5-1.)

5. **In the box next to Family Name, type** mcswain **(or another name that interests you) and click Submit.**

   A search on the McSwain name yields two results: Alan McSwain and Mary McSwain.

Figure 5-1:
The 1871
Census of
Canada —
Ontario
online
search form.

This same search strategy works for a census index for any country. If you can't find an index for the census you're looking for in a comprehensive site, try using one of the large Internet search engines, such as Google (www.google.com), Lycos (www.lycos.com), or AltaVista (www.altavista.com), or one of the genealogical search engines, such as GenealogyPortal.com (www.genealogy portal.com), or the Internet FamilyFinder (www.genealogy.com/ifftop. html). For more information about using search engines, check out Appendix A.

If you find one of your ancestors in a census index, be sure to write down the county, township, house number, and page on which you find the ancestor. Then you can make a specific request for a copy of the census record, reducing the amount of time it takes to have it sent to you (and reducing the frustration levels of those pulling records for you). Or, of course, you can always try to find the record and make a copy of it for yourself through a site containing digitized census records or at your local library, archives, or Family History Center.

Remember that the objective of a census index is only to let you know who was included in the census return and where the record is located. Keep in mind, too, that transcribed indexes may have omissions and typographical errors and may include only the names of heads of households. If you're in doubt, you can always check a copy of the actual record.

Finding individuals in the United States Census

Census indexes are a very important resource for finding individuals in the United States Census. Currently, the largest United States Census index collections are found on the subscription-based Ancestry.com, GenealogyLibrary. com (owned by the same company as Ancestry.com), and HeritageQuest Online (available to libraries and other institutions) sites. Ancestry.com (www.ancestry.com) and GenealogyLibrary.com (www.genealogylibrary. com) both have census indexes for the years 1790 through 1870, generated from print indexes. Ancestry.com also has re-indexed 1790–1850; partially indexed 1860; indexed 1870; uses the 1880 index produced by the Church of Jesus Christ of Latter-day Saints; indexed 1890; partially indexed 1920; and indexed 1930. Genealogy.com has indexes for 1790–1820; 1860–1870; 1890–1910; and a partial index of 1920. HeritageQuest Online has re-indexed census entries for the years 1790–1930.

We should mention that you need to be careful about using these indexes. First of all, not all indexes include every person in the census. Some are merely head-of-household indexes. So, it's a good idea to read the description that comes with the index to see how complete it is. Also, the same quality control may not be there for every census year even within the same index-producing company. If you do not find your ancestor in one of these indexes, don't automatically assume that he or she is not in the census. Another point to remember is that a lot of these indexes were created outside of the United States by people who are not native English speakers and who were under time constraints. It is quite possible that the indexer was incorrect in indexing a particular entry — possibly the person you are searching for.

If you don't want to pay a fee to access census indexes online, you can find some Census indexes under the USGenWeb Archives Census Project at

www.rootsweb.com/~usgenweb/census/

The Census Project is a volunteer effort to index the United States censuses and provide them online for free. If you can't find an index there, try a site dedicated to providing links to online census resources, such as Census Online (www.census-online.com) or CensusLinks (www.censuslinks.com), or a geographic-specific site, such as the county-level pages in the USGenWeb Project (www.usgenweb.org). Also, a number of independent sites have census indexes; typically you can find them by using a search engine such as Google (www.google.com).

Say you want to find Samuel Abell, who lived in St. Mary's County, Maryland, in 1790. Your first step is to see if an index is available for that county during the 1790 Census. To do this, try the following:

1. **Fire up your Web browser and go to Census Online (**www. census-online.com**).**

   For more information about using a Web browser, take a look at Appendix A.

2. **Click the** Links to Online Census Records **link.**

   This page contains a number of links represented by a state or province (depending on whether it's a state in the United States or province in Canada).

3. **Click the** Maryland **link.**

   A page appears, showing a column (on the left) with state-wide links to censuses and the names of counties for the state, and a second column containing a map of the state.

4. **Select a county from the left column or from the map.**

   In this case, St. Mary's County has five links.

5. **Click** 1790 Federal Census **link.**

This takes you to a file listing on the USGenWeb Census project. Clicking the `index.txt` file opens an index of individuals for the county. The sixteenth person on the list is Samuel Abell.

Researchers can use one additional resource to find individuals in United States records: the Family Archive CD Index.

The Family Archive CD Index (`www.familytreemaker.com/cdhome.html`) is produced by Genealogy.com. The Index contains names from census records, marriage records, Social Security records, death records, and family trees on CD-ROMs. You can use the Index to conduct a preliminary online search for individuals in census records from 1790 to 1870 and the 1890 Veterans Schedules. The Index provides the name of an individual, estimated date, location, and the name of the CD-ROM where the name appears. Here's an example:

1. **Point your Web browser to the Family Archive CD Index (**`www.familytreemaker.com/cdhome.html`**).**

   You see a page with a search form in the right column that enables you to search by first, middle, and last names.

   Note: Check out Appendix A for more information about using a browser.

2. **Type a name that interests you in the text boxes and click the Go button.**

   We're interested in finding census indexes that contain one of Matthew's ancestors, Uriah Helm, so we type **Uriah** in the First Name text box, type **Helm** in the Last Name text box.

3. **Select Census Indexes from the drop-down menu titled "Or By Record Type" and click the Go button.**

   This generates a Search Results page.

4. **Review the Results page that appears for the estimated date and location of the selected individual.**

   In our case, we see four entries for Uriah Helm. One entry indicates that a Uriah Helm was present in 1860 in Illinois. (See Figure 5-2.)

After you know whether the Family Archive CD Index identifies entries that pertain to your ancestor, you can decide what route to take to get the documentation. You have a few options: You can see whether Genealogy.com or some other company has digitized that particular census. If so, you can get a copy of the CD-ROM or online census record in which Uriah Helm's name shows up, or you can go through the traditional means to obtain a copy of the actual census record (from microfilm) at an archives or Family History Center.

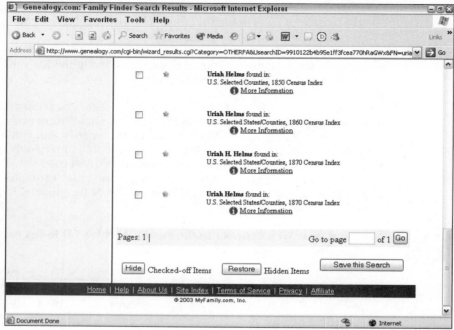

Figure 5-2:
The results
of a Family
Archive
CD Index
search on
Uriah Helm.

Using a transcribed online census

As an online genealogist, what you want is to be able to search all the census records for information on Aunt Bettie with just the click of a mouse. Unfortunately, the genealogy world isn't quite up to speed yet. Efforts are currently underway to transcribe census records for use online. Some of these transcriptions cover only a portion of the entire census, while others feature the complete census returns for a certain area.

As with any transcribed record, you should always verify your findings with either a digitized or microfilm copy of the original record. Often, census records are difficult to read because of their age, the quality of the handwriting, and so on — so mistakes do occur in the transcription process. But these transcribed records are better than nothing at all.

Finding transcribed records on the Internet is very similar to finding census indexes. You can try one of the comprehensive genealogical sites under a geographical category or a genealogically focused search engine. For a list of comprehensive sites, see The *Genealogy Online For Dummies* Internet Directory. To see a step-by-step walk-through of a search using a comprehensive site or genealogically focused search engine, see Chapter 4.

Census records in the United States are a mainstay of genealogists, so most transcribed censuses that you see on the Internet come from the United States (although that doesn't mean that censuses from other countries aren't online — as we explain later in this section). Until recently, these censuses weren't transcribed in any systematic fashion. Fortunately, a couple of projects undertaken by USGenWeb volunteers are trying to change this situation. You can find the USGenWeb Archives Census Project at `www.rootsweb.com/~usgenweb/census/` and the USGenWeb Census Project On-Line Inventory of Transcribed Censuses at `www.us-census.org/inventory/inventory.htm`. A similar project is underway for the United Kingdom census at the UK Census Online site (`freecen.rootsweb.com`). Individuals simply transcribed those censuses in which they were interested, or those associated with a geographical area they were researching. This fact doesn't diminish the importance of these efforts; it only explains why you may see a census record for one county but not for the county right next to it.

Here's a sample search on the USGenWeb Archives Census Project site:

1. **Go to the USGenWeb Archives Census Project site (`www.rootsweb.com/~census/states.htm`).**

   You see a page with a map and list of states and territories for which census transcriptions are available.

   Note: If you want more information about using a browser, flip to Appendix A.

2. **Select a state for your search by clicking the state on the map or its link in the list.**

   For our example, we're looking for census information on an Isaac Metcalf who lived in Baylor County, Texas, around 1880, so we select Texas. A list of available census schedules for the state appears at the top of the screen.

3. **Click a year or type of schedule that interests you.**

   We select 1880. The resulting page contains a table listing the location, roll number, status of the project, and transcriber's name.

4. **Click the status button for an available census.**

   We choose the transcription for Baylor County by clicking the status button marked Images, which takes us to a page of transcribed census entries where we can scroll down to an individual named Isaac Metcalf. You can also use your browser's Find in Page option to find the name you're looking for.

The transcriptions you can use at this site are the works of volunteers; it's possible that you may find errors here and there. Typographical errors may crop up, some censuses may not be indexed, or the status of the project for a particular county may be incorrect.

The most plentiful type of transcribed census records you're likely to encounter is what we refer to as the *plain-text census,* which is a Web page or text file that's simply a transcription of the actual census record without any kind of search function. You either have to skim the page or use your Web browser's Find in Page option to find the person you're looking for. The 1870 Census for Penn Township, Stark County, Illinois, at

```
members.aol.com/ZCyberCat/private/castleton.html
```

is an example of this type of census return. (See Figure 5-3.) For each individual, the record includes the house number of the household, last name, first name, age, sex, race, occupation, real-estate value, personal-property value, and birthplace. This site is also typical of smaller census sites in its focus on the records on one county (actually, one township in one county).

Some sites contain collections of several census returns for a specific geographic area (over an extended period of time). A good example of this type of site is the Transcribed Census Records for Vernon County, Missouri, at

```
freepages.genealogy.rootsweb.com/~jrbakerjr/census/census1.htm
```

which has several transcribed census returns for the county from 1860–1930.

Figure 5-3: An online transcription of the 1870 Census for Penn Township, Stark County, Illinois.

Another site with a simple search engine that displays census records is the Census of Norway (digitalarkivet.uib.no/index-eng.htm), which used a nationwide approach for the 1801 Census. At this site, you can search for individuals who lived in each parish in Norway as of February 1, 1801. You can search by farm name, first name, or surname. Also, you can follow a link from this site to the Digital Archive, which includes the 1865, 1875, and 1900 Censuses.

Looking for more elaborate search capabilities? Point your browser to the Danish Demographic Database at ddd.sa.dk/kiplink_en.htm. The database is a joint project of the Danish Data Archives, the Danish Emigration Archives, and the Centre of Microfilming at the Danish State Archives. It contains partial census records from 1787 to 1916 — not all the paper records have been computerized. You can search for particular individuals online (by using searches by parish, district, county, birthplace, name, occupation, position in household, and year of census).

The future of census information: Digitized images

Many genealogists are no longer satisfied with using transcribed information. After all, even if you find useful information, you must take a second step to confirm the information through a copy of the primary record. In response to this demand, a few companies are now developing electronic versions of census records that you can use on your personal computer. Many of these resources are available online, as well as on CD-ROM. The following sections describe some of these currently available resources.

HeritageQuest Online

HeritageQuest Online (www.heritagequestonline.com), a fee-based site produced by ProQuest Information and Learning Company, houses digitized images of United States census population schedules from 1790 to 1930. The collection numbers more than 10 million images taken from 12,555 rolls of microfilm. These images are bitonal (black and white) and require a TIFF viewer plug-in for your Web browser. Indexes for the images are included for 1790–1820, 1860–1870, 1890–1930. In the case of the 1870 index, only selected individuals are indexed. If you're looking for individuals in other censuses, you must browse the images much as you would when using microfilm. A unique feature of the site is a sticky-note feature that enables you to annotate the census images. For example, if you have a correction or more information on a census entry, you can post a sticky note mentioning that fact. You can also use the feature to tell others that you're researching that family so they can share information with you. The images available on HeritageQuest Online.com are also available on CD-ROMs through Heritage Quest.

GenealogyLibrary.com and U.S. Census Collection

GenealogyLibrary.com (`www.genealogylibrary.com`) is another subscription site — this one maintained by Genealogy.com. In addition to its collection of transcribed family histories and historical texts, the site also contains 283,000 bitonal digitized images from the 1850 census (including the states of Alabama, Arkansas, California, Connecticut, Illinois, Indiana, Kentucky, Louisiana, Massachusetts, Maine, Mississippi, New Hampshire, North Carolina, New Mexico, Oregon, Pennsylvania, Rhode Island, Tennessee, Texas, Utah, Vermont, and Virginia). These images are also available on CD-ROM. In a separate sub-scription area (`www.genealogy.com`), users can access bitonal images of federal census population schedules from 1790–1930. Out of these, nine years are indexed, and one is partially indexed.

Sources2Go.com

Sources2Go.com contains digitized images in 256-color grayscale (shades of black, white, and gray) of Illinois state and territorial census records for the years 1810, 1818, 1835, and 1840 — as well as some federal census population schedules from 1790. (Figure 5-4 shows an image of a handwritten record.)

U.S. Census Images and Indexes

Ancestry.com offers a subscription-based service that it calls U.S. Census Images and Indexes at

`www.ancestry.com/search/rectype/census/usfedcen/main.htm?o_iid=3717`

This resource contains the 1790–1930 census population schedules. The images are 256-color grayscale, which typically makes them clearer than bitonal images. The site offers a plug-in viewer that displays the images in your Web browser.

Some noncommercial efforts also provide digitized census images. The pri-mary source for these is the USGenWeb. Its census images are available at

`www.rootsweb.com/~usgenweb/cen_img.htm`

The images are of various qualities and, in some cases, are difficult to read. You can't zoom in on these images (as you can with some commercial offer-ings), but they're available to researchers free of charge.

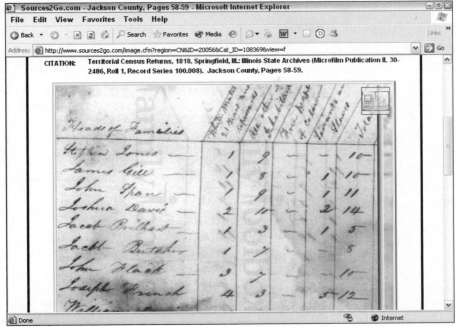

Figure 5-4:
A Sources 2Go.com digitized image of a handwritten 1818 Census record for Jackson County, Illinois.

Censuses around the world

Of course, this section would not be complete without mentioning projects for censuses outside the United States.

Canada

As with United States census records, you can find Canadian census returns online in many different forms. The National Archives of Canada has placed online images of the 1901 Census at www.archives.ca/02/020122_e.html and the 1906 Census of the Northwest Provinces. However, the returns are not indexed by name. So, you have to know the residence of your ancestor and then browse line-by-line through the images. The National Archives of Canada has also placed online a name index of the 1871 Ontario Census heads of household (created by the Ontario Genealogical Society), which you can find at www.archives.ca/02/02010803_e.html. The index entries contain name, sex, birthplace, religion, origin, district, subdistrict, division, page, microfilm reel, and reference. An index of the 1881 Canadian census is available on the FamilySearch site at www.familysearch.org. (Select the Search link at the top of the site, then choose the Census link on the left side to search census records at this site.)

There are also a number of indexes to individual portions of census records. A few examples of these are

- ✔ 1901 Census: Alberta District at

  www.agsedm.edmonton.ab.ca/1901_census_202_online.html

- ✔ 1881 Canada Census, Yale District, British Columbia; 1891 Canada Census, Yale District, British Columbia; 1877 Indian Reserve Commission Census, southern interior of British Columbia; 1877 Okanagan (Native) Census taken by the Oblates of Mary Immaculate at

  royal.okanagan.bc.ca/census/index.html

- ✔ Queens County, New Brunswick Census records for 1871 and 1891 at

  www.rootsweb.com/~nbqueens/cen-intro.htm

- ✔ Newfoundland 1836 Census at

  ngb.chebucto.org/C1836/index.shtml

England and Wales

Government-based World Wide Web sites featuring census information have also appeared for England and Wales. The 1901 Census for England and Wales is available at www.census.pro.gov.uk. You can search the site at no cost. However, if you want to view a digitized image of the census, you must enter a credit card number or purchase a voucher. The 1881 Census index for the British Isles is available on the FamilySearch site www.familysearch.org. (Select the Search link at the top of the site, then choose the Census link on the left side to search census records at this site.)

The 1891 Census index and images is available for the Channel Islands, England, Isle of Man, and Wales on the subscription-based Ancestry.com site.

Individual sites also contain indexes to portions of the censuses including:

- ✔ 1851 and 1881 Hampshire, England Census Index:

  www.rootsweb.com/~wellsfam/country/hampshir/hamcen.html

- ✔ 1861 census for Lincoln South West:

  www.wparkinson.com/1861.htm

- ✔ 1871 census for Glapthorn:

  www.lds.co.uk/glapthorn/1871.htm

Scotland

The first place to search for Scottish census records is the Scotland's People site at www.scotlandspeople.gov.uk. The site, maintained by the General Register Office for Scotland, contains a variety of records including census, births, marriage, and death. In particular, the site contains indexes and images for the 1891 and 1901 censuses and index only for the 1881 census. By the end of spring 2004, the site expects to have information from the 1841, 1851, 1861, 1871, and images for the 1881 censuses. Keep in mind that the site does charge a fee for use.

These Records Are Vital

It seems that some kind of government record accompanies every major event in our lives. One is generated when we are born, another when we get married (as well as get divorced), another when we have a child, and still another when we pass on. Vital records (also called *civil registrations*) is the collective name for records of these events. Traditionally, these records were kept at the local level. States and countries have only recently made an effort to collect and centralize their holdings of vital records. In a similar manner, the record holders have just recently begun to expand the number of vital record indexes available online. You're likely to encounter three types of vital record sites: *general information sites, vital record indexes,* and *transcribed vital records.*

Vital record information sites

If you're looking for information on how to order vital records within the United States, you can choose among a few sites. Vital Records Information — United States (vitalrec.com/index.html) is probably the most comprehensive site. A page for each state lists the type of record, its cost, the address to which you should send requests, and additional remarks, such as the time period during which records were kept and to whom to make the check payable. (See Figure 5-5.) You also can find information on obtaining vital records for foreign or high-sea births and deaths of United States citizens.

Although the Vital Records Information site doesn't contain any online indexes or records, using it is a good way to become familiar with where each state stores its vital records. Later on, as you locate records on more ancestors, you can use this site as a quick reference for getting mailing addresses for your many records requests.

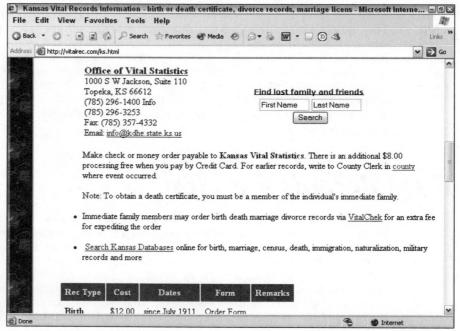

Figure 5-5:
The Vital
Records
Information
page for
Kansas.

Outside the United States and Canada, vital records are called *civil registrations*. For those of you looking for these records, the following list describes some helpful sites:

✔ **Australia:** For Australian records, you can find an article on purchasing certificates from the General Registrar's offices at

www.cohsoft.com.au/afhc/certs.html

✔ **Canada:** For a list of addresses to request copies of civil registrations in Canada, see the National Archives of Canada page on Records of Births, Marriages, and Deaths at

www.archives.ca/02/02020202_e.html

✔ **Denmark:** For background on and the contents of vital records in Denmark and Greenland, see the Civil Registration System in Denmark site at

www.cpr.dk/Index/dokumenter.asp?o=7&n=0&d=141&s=5

✔ **England and Wales:** You can find links to information on civil registrations in the Births, Marriages, and Deaths page at

www.familyrecords.gov.uk/topics/bmd.htm

The English Origins site (www.englishorigins.com) contains Boyd's Marriage Index — containing 6.4 million names from English marriages between 1538 and 1840 — and a marriage-license allegations index.

✔ **France:** For a helpful article on civil registers in France, check out the Genealogy in France page on About.com at

genealogy.about.com/library/weekly/aa070700b.htm

✔ **Ireland:** You can find Irish civil records — birth, marriage and death registrations — at

www.groireland.ie/fees.htm

✔ **New Zealand:** You can find information on birth, marriage, death, and name change records at the New Zealand Births, Deaths, and Marriages Office site at

www.bdm.govt.nz/diawebsite.nsf/wpg_URL/Services-Births-Deaths-and-Marriages-Index?OpenDocument

✔ **Northern Ireland:** The General Register Office (Northern Ireland) has information on birth, death, and marriage registers on its Historical Records page available from

www.groni.gov.uk/index.htm

✔ **Philippines:** A Frequently Asked Questions page on civil registrations is available from the National Statistics Office

www.census.gov.ph/data/civilreg/

✔ **Poland:** You can find a sample letter for requesting civil registration records from the Polish Civil Registration Office at

www.polishroots.org/genpoland/certif.htm

✔ **Scotland:** If your interests lie in Scottish records, look at the Frequently Asked Questions page at

www.gro-scotland.gov.uk/grosweb/grosweb.nsf/pages/bdm

The General Register Office for Scotland maintains this site. You can also find birth, marriage, and death records at the General Register Office's pay-per-view site, ScotlandPeople, at

www.scotlandspeople.gov.uk

✔ **Slovakia:** The State Archives keeps information on births, marriages, and deaths up to the year 1900. You can find contact information for the State Archives on the Embassy of the Slovak Republic page at

www.iarelative.com/embassy.htm

✔ **Other countries:** The Research Guidance page at the FamilySearch Web site includes information on civil registrations for various other countries at

www.familysearch.org/Eng/Search/RG/frameset_rg.asp

If the country you're researching isn't in the preceding list, try looking at one of the comprehensive genealogy sites (you can find a list of these in The *Genealogy Online For Dummies* Internet Directory in this book) or conduct a search on one of the genealogically focused search engines (www.genealogyportal.com) or general Internet search engines such as Google (at www.google.com) or AltaVista (at www.altavista.com) to see whether a similar site exists with vital records for the country you're interested in.

Don't overlook these information sites just because they don't contain primary resources. You still need to use more traditional ways of collecting records because very few transcribed or digitized records exist online. And even if you find a transcribed record online, you may want to order a copy of the original record to place in your filing system — in which case you need addresses from these sites.

Vital record indexes

Vital record indexes serve much the same purpose as census indexes: They point to the locations of original records. You can use indexes to confirm that an ancestor's vital records are available prior to submitting a request for the record. And knowing the exact location of the record can often make retrieval of the record a lot easier.

The easiest way to find vital record (and civil registration) indexes on the Internet is to search along geographical lines. Suppose you're looking for registrations in British Columbia — you want to use a search engine with narrow search criteria.

1. **Go to Google (www.google.com).**

   The home page for Google contains a search box.

   Note: See Appendix A for how-to information about using a browser.

2. **Type your search terms into the box and click the Google Search button.**

   In our case, we typed **british columbia vital record indexes**.

3. **Check the results page for something relevant to your search.**

   The first link in our search was for Vital Event Indexes kept at the British Columbia Archives.

4. **Click a link to go to a site featuring civil registrations (vital records).**

   If you click the `Vital Events Indexes` link on the Google page, it takes you to a site that the British Columbia Archives maintains, containing indexes to birth, marriage, and death registrations. Depending on the site you selected in Step 3, you may need to go through additional steps to find the information you're looking for.

The site that we mention in the preceding steps includes a query page for the marriage index that enables you to search by surname, given name, place, and date. (See Figure 5-6.) The results of the search provide you with the bride's name and groom's name, event date, event place, registration number, British Columbia Archives microfilm number, and Genealogical Society of Utah (GSU) microfilm number (the number used for retrieving the microfilm at Family History Centers). It also indicates whether a digital image of the registration is available for purchase directly from the site.

Figure 5-6: Searching the marriage index at the British Columbia Archives Vital Events site.

Another approach to finding vital statistics (civil registrations) is to go to the USGenWeb (www.usgenweb.org) or WorldGenWeb (www.worldgenweb.org) site for the appropriate state or country. For example, we want to find a death certificate for Matthew's great-grandfather, William Henry Abell of Larue County, Kentucky. To do so, we go through the following steps:

1. **Go to the USGenWeb site (**www.usgenweb.org**).**

   You see a page with two columns on it.

   Note: See Appendix A for more details about using browsers.

2. **Click the link titled** The Projects State Pages **and then click the** Text Only State List.

   This link takes us to a page with a list of states and the URLs associated with each state page.

3. **Click a state that interests you.**

   In our case, we select Kentucky because we're looking for someone who died in the state of Kentucky.

   As a shortcut, you can always access any USGenWeb state page by typing www.usgenweb.org and the two letter postal code for the state. For example, for Kentucky, you can type www.usgenweb.org/ky.

4. **At the USGenWeb state page for the state that you choose, look for a link to vital records information or research links.**

   We choose the Vital Statistics link in the table under the Welcome to Kentucky heading on the Kentucky USGenWeb page. This takes you to a page with search interfaces for the Kentucky Death Index, Birth Index, and Marriage Index.

5. **Scroll down to the appropriate section and type the name that you want to search in the text box and then click Submit Query.**

   Sticking with the example, we go to the Kentucky Death Index for 1911–2000 section, type **Abell** and **William H.**, and click **Search**. We then wait for the results to return.

6. **Scan the results of your query.**

   In our case, the results page contains two individuals named William H. Abell. One died in Larue County and the other in Jefferson County. The location seems right for the William from Larue County. We check the death date, September 7, 1955, and the age, 82, both of which are consistent with what we've heard from interviews with family members. The database also supplies us with the record volume number and certificate number, which we can use to obtain a copy of the certificate.

A few other projects are currently transcribing civil registrations. The FreeBMD project (freebmd.rootsweb.com) currently contains indexes of registrations in England and Wales from 1837 to 1983 online (although its coverage for these years is not complete). Currently, over 68 million records exist in the database. You can search the database on type of record, surname, first name, spouse surname, spouse first name, death age, date range, volume, page, districts, and counties. Results of the search include type of record, surname, first name, age, district, volume, page, and contributor name. A companion to the FreeBMD site is the FreeREG site (`freereg.rootsweb.com`). This site focuses on baptism, marriage, and burial records transcribed from parish and nonconformist church registers. The International Internet Genealogical Society Births, Deaths and Marriages Exchange (`www.iigs.org/global_village/bdm/`) is also creating indexes of civil registrations for nine countries and hosts "exchanges" for 36 countries.

Transcribed vital records

If you aren't lucky enough to have a copy of your great-grandfather's marriage certificate, you need a way to discover the information that the document contains. The best way to find this information is to order a copy of the certificate from the appropriate government source. (For more information on this strategy, see "Vital record information sites," earlier in this chapter.) But before you spend the money to get a copy, you want to find out whether the record is really of interest to you — this is where transcribed vital records come in handy.

Transcribed records can come in several forms. A researcher may have transcribed a series of records of a particular county, a state may have established a database of records, or a commercial company may have created or bought a transcription. Either way, these sites can be helpful in determining whether the record you're looking for is useful.

To find a transcribed record, you could use a *meta-search engine* (a site that groups together the results from several search engines). When using meta-search engines, you tend to find links to commercial databases as well as to free databases — so be sure to check several results before subscribing to a commercial site just to get access to its database. For example, we can use Dogpile (`www.dogpile.com`) to search for a transcribed marriage record for Jacob Gardner, who was married sometime around 1850.

1. **Go to Dogpile (`www.dogpile.com`).**

   The page loads with the Web Search tab open and a search box displayed.

2. **Enter your search terms into the search box and click Go Fetch!**

   In our example, we typed **indiana marriage index**. We used the word index, rather than transcribed record, because the transcribed records are more likely to be accessed as part of a larger index — especially when held by a governmental institution. Also, with older records there are so few items to index that often the contents of the whole record are indexed.

3. **Click a link that looks promising.**

   We received multiple results. Scrolling through the list, we look for a promising link — finding one in the Indiana State Library marriage index, which offers free access.

4. **Once on the new site, follow the instructions to view the transcribed record.**

   We chose a link to the marriage database with last name E-F-G. This led us to a search form, where we typed **Jacob Gardner** and clicked Start Search. The result page we got lists a marriage between Jacob Gardner and Harriet Simmons in Jefferson County on November 2, 1848.

We could have taken a similar path to locate the same information with a commercial site, such as Ancestry.com (www.ancestry.com), which also had a database titled Indiana Marriages to 1850 (as well as a database titled Indiana Marriages, 1845–1920 — although that database did not have an entry for Jacob).

Investigating Immigration and Naturalization Records

You may have heard the old stories about your great-great-grandparents who left their homeland in search of a new life. Some of these stories may include details about where they were born and how they arrived at their new home. Although these are great stories, as a genealogist you want to verify this information with documentation.

Often the document you're looking for is an immigration or naturalization record. *Immigration records* are documents that show when a person moved to a particular country to reside; *naturalization records* are documents showing that a person became a citizen of a particular country without being born in that country. Sometimes these documents can prove difficult to find, especially if you don't know where to begin looking. Unless you have some evidence in your attic or have a reliable family account of the immigration, you may need a record or something else to point you in the right direction. Census records are one useful set of records. (For more information about census records, see "Counting on the Census," earlier in this chapter.) Depending on the year your ancestors immigrated, census records may contain the location of birth and tell you the year of immigration and the year of naturalization of your immigrant ancestor.

Emigration records — documents that reflect when a person moved out of a particular country to take up residence elsewhere — are also useful to researchers. You find these records in the country your ancestor left; they can often help when you can't find immigration or naturalization records in the new country.

Locating immigration, emigration, and naturalization records online can be challenging. The common types of records that genealogists use to locate immigrants — passenger lists, immigration papers, emigration records — are just now becoming available on the Internet. A good starting point for determining an ancestor's homeland is to look at census records. (For more information about census records, see "Counting on the Census," earlier in this chapter.) Because a great deal of early immigration and naturalization processing occurred at the local level, census records may give you an indication of where to look for immigration records.

Some examples of online records include the following:

- ✓ **Immigration/Naturalization Records:** McLean County, Illinois, Immigration Records (www.mclean.gov/cc/imgrecs/imgrecs.html)
- ✓ **Passenger Lists:** *Mayflower* Passenger List (members.aol.com/calebj/passengers2.html)
- ✓ **Immigration Indexes:** Canadian Immigration Records for 1925–1935 (www.archives.ca/02/020118_e.html)

If you don't have a lot of details on when your ancestor may have immigrated but have a general idea of the time or place of immigration, you may want to consider looking for information on a comprehensive genealogical index. (See The *Genealogy Online For Dummies* Internet Directory for a list of comprehensive genealogy indexes.) As you look at comprehensive genealogy sites, you're likely to find these types of records categorized under immigration, naturalization, passenger lists or by geographical area. If you know more details, try using a genealogy-focused search engine or a general Internet search engine.

As an example, suppose that you have a family legend that Martin Saunders immigrated to America on a ship called *Planter* sometime in the first part of the seventeenth century. The following steps show you how to search for a passenger list to confirm the legend:

1. **Go to the Yahoo! search engine (www.yahoo.com).**

   On the home page, the search box is located at the top of the page.

2. **Type your search terms into the Search the Web field and click the Yahoo! Search button.**

   For this example, you type **martin saunders planter**.

3. Click a promising link from the list of results.

The results page shows the first 20 links of over 1,300 links found for these search terms. One of the top links goes to a transcription of the passengers on the *Planter*, which sailed on April 6, 1635 — the first on the list being "Martin Saunders, aged 40 years." Another link on the Results page reads `Passengers of the Planter, sailed April, 1635`. In the abstract that you access by clicking the link, you see that a Martin Saunders, age 40, sailed on the *Planter*.

Another source for passenger lists is the Immigrant Ships Transcribers Guild passenger-list transcription project (`www.immigrantships.net`). Currently, the transcriptions made by the Guild are divided into six volumes, including information on more than 5,000 ships and over 500,000 passenger arrivals. The passenger lists are organized by date, ship's name, port of departure, port of arrival, passenger's surname, and captain's name. You can also search the site to find the person or ship that interests you. Other pages containing links to passenger lists include these:

- ✔ Olive Tree Genealogy at

  `olivetreegenealogy.com/ships/index.shtml`
- ✔ Passenger Lists on the Internet at

  `members.aol.com/rprost/passenger.html`
- ✔ Ships Indexes and Records Online at

  `www.standard.net.au/~jwilliams/ships.htm`

There are also some significant commercial database collections of immigration records. Ancestry.com's U.S. Immigration Collection contains information on over 10 million names and immigration records from more than 100 countries. Highlights of the collection include

- ✔ New York passenger lists
- ✔ Passenger and immigration list indexes (1500s to 1900s)
- ✔ Passenger lists from Boston, Philadelphia, Baltimore, and New Orleans
- ✔ Naturalization records (1700s to 1900s)

Genealogy.com's International and Passenger Records collection also contains several databases, including

- ✔ Immigrants to the New World (1600s to 1800s)
- ✔ German and Swiss settlers in America
- ✔ Scottish immigrants to North America

✔ Philadelphia naturalization records (1789–1880)

✔ Passenger and immigration lists for Baltimore, Boston, New Orleans, New York and Philadelphia

Looking for some background information on immigration and naturalization within the United States? Take a look at the Naturalization Records page of the National Archives and Records Administration site at

```
www.archives.gov/research_room/genealogy/research_topics/
naturalization_records.html
```

or the Immigration and Ships Passenger Lists Research Guide page at

```
home.att.net/~arnielang/shipgide.html
```

You can also check out Chapter 13, "Immigration: Finding Important Immigrant Origins," written by Kory L. Meyerink and Loretto Dennis Szucs, in *The Source: A Guidebook of American Genealogy,* edited by Szucs and Sandra Hargreaves Luebking (published by Ancestry, Inc.). Other sources to refer to include *They Became Americans,* written by Loretto Dennis Szucs (Ancestry Publishing), and *They Came in Ships,* Third Edition, written by John Philip Colletta (Ancestry Publishing). Both provide more information about immigration and naturalization within the United States.

For general information on Canadian immigration records, see the National Archives of Canada pages on immigration records at

```
www.archives.ca/02/02020204_e.html
```

For information on citizenship, see the naturalization pages at

```
www.archives.ca/02/020202/02020219_e.html
```

To search Canadian passenger lists, see the InGeneas site at `www.ingeneas.com`.

Land Lovers

Land records are among the most plentiful sources of information on your ancestors. Although a census would have occurred only once every ten years, land transactions may have taken place two or three times a year, depending on how much land your ancestor possessed. These records don't always contain a great deal of demographic information, but they do place your ancestor in a time and location, and sometimes in a historical context as well. For example, you may discover that your ancestors were granted military bounty lands. This discovery may tell you where and when your ancestors acquired the land, as well as what war they fought in. You may also find out how litigious your ancestors were by the number of lawsuits they filed or had filed against them as a result of land claims.

Getting a foundation in the history of land records prior to conducting a lot of research is probably a good idea. Here are some sites with general information on land records:

- **Canada:** Land Records in Ontario:

  www.archives.ca/02/020202/02020207_e.html

- **Denmark:** Denmark Research Outline:

  www.familysearch.org/Eng/Search/RG/frameset_rg.asp?Dest=
  G1&Aid=&Gid=&Lid=&Sid=&Did=&Juris1=&Event=&Year=&Gloss=
  &Sub=&Tab=&Entry=&Guide=Denmark.ASP

  Click the Land and Property link in the list on the resulting page to get to the land information.

- **England:** GENUKI Land and Property:

  www.genuki.org.uk/big/eng/#Land

- **Germany:** Germany Research Outline:

  www.familysearch.org/Eng/Search/RG/frameset_rg.asp?Dest=
  G1&Aid=&Gid=&Lid=&Sid=&Did=&Juris1=&Event=&Year=&Gloss=
  &Sub=&Tab=&Entry=&Guide=Germany.ASP

  Click the Land and Property link in the list on the resulting page to get to the land information.

- **Ireland:** Irish Ancestors — Land Records:

  scripts.ireland.com/ancestor/browse/records/land/
  intro.html

- **Latin America:** Latin America Research Outline:

  www.familysearch.org/Eng/Search/RG/frameset_rg.asp?Dest=
  G1&Aid=&Gid=&Lid=&Sid=&Did=&Juris1=&Event=&Year=&Gloss=
  &Sub=&Tab=&Entry=&Guide=Latin_America.ASP

  Click the Land and Property link in the list on the resulting page to get to the land information.

- **Norway:** Norway Research Outline:

  www.familysearch.org/Eng/Search/RG/frameset_rg.asp?Dest=
  G1&Aid=&Gid=&Lid=&Sid=&Did=&Juris1=&Event=&Year=&Gloss=
  &Sub=&Tab=&Entry=&Guide=Norway.ASP

Click the Land and Property link in the list on the resulting page to get to the land information.

- **Philippines:** Philippine Research Outline:

  `www.familysearch.org/Eng/Search/RG/frameset_rg.asp?Dest=`
  `G1&Aid=&Gid=&Lid=&Sid=&Did=&Juris1=&Event=&Year=&Gloss=`
  `&Sub=&Tab=&Entry=&Guide=Philippines.ASP`

  Click the Land and Property link in the list on the resulting page to get to the land information.

- **Scotland:** GENUKI Land and Property:

  `www.genuki.org.uk/big/sct/#Land`

- **United States:** Land Records Reference at

  `www.ultranet.com/~deeds/landref.htm`

  and Chapter 8, "Research in Land and Tax Records," by Sandra Hargreaves Luebking, in *The Source: A Guidebook of American Genealogy*, edited by Loretto Dennis Szucs and Luebking (published by Ancestry, Inc.).

Of course, these are only a few examples of some sites offering background information about land transactions in those particular countries. To see if a similar site exists for a country you're interested in (or if you're looking for any kind of land record), visit a comprehensive genealogical site and look under that location, as well as under a directory heading or category for land records (if you see one).

One exciting site relating to land records in the United States is the Bureau of Land Management, Eastern States, General Land Office Official Land Patents Records Site (`www.glorecords.blm.gov`). This site enables you to search the more than 2 million federal land title records for the Eastern States office issued between 1820 and 1908. Recently the database was expanded to include serial patent records issued after 1908, but this is still an ongoing project.

Follow these steps to search the records on this site:

1. **Go to the Land Patents Records Site (`www.glorecords.blm.gov`).**

   Note: For more information about using a browser, see Appendix A.

2. **In the left green bar at the top of the page, click the Search Land Patents button link and, on the following page, enter your Zip code in the appropriate space and click the Continue button.**

   This brings you to a page displaying a form that you can fill out to search the patents. Matthew's interest, for example, is in finding land that one of his ancestors, Jacob Helm, owned in Illinois.

3. **Select the state that you're interested in from the State drop-down list.**

   We select Illinois.

4. Type a first name and last name in the text boxes in the section where you enter the name of the patentee or warrantee, and then click the Search button.

We type **Helm** in the Last Name text box and **Jacob** in the First Name text box and then click the Search button. This brings us to a page listing one result for Jacob Helm. The table tells us the name of the patentee, state, county, issue date, land office, document number, and accession number, and provides a button link that we can click for details on the entry or a button to view the image (looks like a piece of paper).

5. Click the Patentee Name or Warrantee Name link.

The Land Patent Details page loads with the Patent Description showing. From this information, we can obtain the document number of the purchase, how many acres, how and when the land was purchased, and which land office recorded the transaction. Most databases stop here, but this site offers more as you can see from the four tabs — Patent Description (what you're currently viewing), Legal Land Description, Document Image, and Certified Copy.

6. Click the Document Image tab to view a digitized copy of the patent.

We can choose one of four ways to view the document: a small GIF image, a large GIF image, a TIFF image, or a PDF document. We can then save the copy of the document on our computer.

Some other government entities have also placed land records online. Here are a few examples:

- Illinois public-domain land-tract sales:

  www.sos.state.il.us/departments/archives/data_lan.html

- Fort Wayne land office entries, 1823–1852:

  www.in.gov/icpr/archives/databases/land/fwintro.html

- Oregon Historical Records Index:

  genealogy.state.or.us/start.lasso?location=search

- Virginia land office grants:

  ajax.lva.lib.va.us/F/?func=file&file_name=find-b-clas30&local_base=CLAS30

In addition to the methods we mention so far in this section, you may want to check out geography-related resources, such as the USGenWeb project (www.usgenweb.org) or the WorldGenWeb project (www.worldgenweb.org). These sites organize their resources by location (country, state, and/or county, depending on which you use). For more information about USGenWeb, see Chapter 4 or The *Genealogy Online For Dummies* Internet Directory that we include with this book; for more information about WorldGenWeb, see the directory as well. Of course, if your attempts to find land records and information through comprehensive sites and geographical-related sites don't prove as fruitful as you'd like, you can always turn to a search engine such as AltaVista (www.altavista.com) or Google (www.google.com). (See Appendix A for more information about using search engines.)

Marching to a Different Drummer: Searching for Military Records

Although your ancestors may not have marched to a different drummer, at least one of them probably kept pace with a military beat at some point in life. Military records contain a variety of information; the two major types of records that you're likely to find are service and pension records. Draft or conscription records may also surface in your exploration.

Service records

Service records chronicle the military career of an individual. They often contain details about where your ancestors lived, when they enlisted or were *drafted* (or *conscripted*, enrolled for compulsory service), their ages, their discharge dates, and, in some instances, their birthplaces and occupations. You may also find pay records (including muster records that state when your ancestors had to report to military units) and notes on any injuries that they sustained while serving in the military. Although most of the information contained in service records seems to be of little genealogical value, you can use these records to determine the unit in which your ancestor served. This information can lead you to pension records that do have genealogical importance because of the level of detail required to prove service in order to receive a pension. Also, service records can give you an appreciation of your ancestor's place within history — especially the dates and places where your ancestor fought or served as a member of the armed forces.

Pension records

Pensions were often granted to veterans who were disabled or who demonstrated financial need after service in a particular war or campaign; widows or orphans of veterans also may have received benefits. These records are valuable because, in order to receive pensions, your ancestors had to prove that they served in the military. Proof entailed a discharge certificate or the sworn testimony of the veteran and witnesses. Pieces of information that you can find in pension records include your ancestor's rank, period of service, unit, residence at the time of the pension application, age, marriage date, spouse's name, names of children, and the nature of the veteran's financial need or disability. If a widow submitted a pension application, you may also find records verifying her marriage to the veteran and death records (depending on when the veteran ancestor died).

Locating military records

Some military records (such as a discharge certificate or copy of orders) may turn up in your own home or in the home of a relative. For other military records, you may need to visit a national archive or contact the appropriate military department. These Web sites contain general information on military records:

- **Australia:** If you're interested in researching Australian military records, see the Society of Australian Genealogists Basics on Australian Military, Naval, Etc. Records page at

  www.sag.org.au/ozsources/military.htm

  The Society maintains an index of soldiers and marines from 1787–1830 at

  svc007.bne009i.server-web.com/catalogue/onlinebook/gatewaysearchmarine.ehtml

  Also, for unit histories, see the Australian Army Regiments — Index of Web Sites at

  regiments.org/milhist/australia/austral.htm

- **Austria:** You can find a list of the collections maintained in the Austrian State Archives War Archive:

  www.genealogienetz.de/reg/AUT/krainf-e.htm

- **Bangladesh:** For unit histories, see the India, Pakistan, and Bangladesh Army Regiments — Index of Web Sites at

  regiments.org/milhist/southasia/bangla.htm

- **Canada:** For a description of the military records that you can find in the Archives of Canada, see

  www.archives.ca/02/020203_e.html

  To see regimental histories, see the Canadian Army Regiments — Index of Web Sites at

  regiments.org/milhist/na-canada/canada.htm

✔ **Germany:** Addresses for finding German military records can be found at

www.faqs.org/faqs/genealogy/german-faq/part3/
section-1.html

Information on military records is also located at

www.familysearch.org/Eng/Search/Rg/guide/Germany24.
asp#military_records

✔ **India:** For unit histories, see the India Army Regiments — Index of Web Sites at

regiments.org/milhist/southasia/india.htm

✔ **Malawi:** For unit histories, see the Malawi Regiments — Index of Web Sites at

regiments.org/milhist/africacentral/malawi.htm

✔ **New Zealand:** For unit histories, see the New Zealand Army Regiments — Index of Web Sites at

regiments.org/milhist/newzealand/nzealand.htm

✔ **Pakistan:** For unit histories, see the Pakistan Army Regiments — Index of Web Sites at

regiments.org/milhist/southasia/pakistan.htm

✔ **South Africa:** For unit histories, see the South African Army Regiments — Index of Web Sites at

regiments.org/milhist/southafrica/safrica.htm

✔ **United Kingdom:** In general, you can find military records at the Public Record Office, now part of the newly formed (British) National Archives; its Web site has a series of Family Fact Sheets on British military records:

www.pro.gov.uk/leaflets/riindex.asp

For regimental histories, see the British Army Regiments — Index of Web Sites at

regiments.org/milhist/uk/uk.htm

✔ **United States:** The National Archives and Records Administration (www.archives.gov/index.html) houses several types of military records, including service and pension records. For guides on the types of military records kept by the National Archives, see

www.archives.gov/research_room/genealogy/research_topics/
military.html

You can also request information from the National Personnel Records Center (www.archives.gov/facilities/mo/st_louis.html) for more recent military records.

- **Zambia:** For unit histories, see Zambia Regiments — Index of Web Sites at

    `regiments.org/milhist/africacentral/zambia.htm`

- **Zimbabwe:** For unit histories, see Zimbabwe Regiments — Index of Web Sites at

    `regiments.org/milhist/africacentral/zimbabwe.htm`

As we mention at the beginning of this section, military records come in various forms. Here are examples of the online version of these types:

- **Casualty Lists:** Canadian Books of Remembrance:

    `collections.ic.gc.ca/books/remember.htm`

- **Cemetery Records:** Confederate Graves at Brice's Crossroads:

    `sunset.backbone.olemiss.edu/~cmprice/cavalry/brice_cem.html`

- **Draft Registrations:** Civilian Draft Registration Database:

    `userdb.rootsweb.com/ww1/draft/search.cgi`

- **Military Census:** Cumberland, Providence County, Rhode Island, 1777 Military Census:

    `ftp://ftp.rootsweb.com/pub/usgenweb/ri/providen/military/militry1.txt`

- **Muster/Recruitment Records:** National Archives of Canada, Canadian Expeditionary Force Database:

    `www.archives.ca/02/020106_e.html`

- **Pension Records:** 1835 Federal Pension List for Virginia:

    `www.rootsweb.com/~usgenweb/va/vapensio.htm`

- **Regimental Histories:** Confederate Regimental History Links:

    `www.tarleton.edu/~kjones/confeds.html`

- **Service Records:** Civil War Soldiers and Sailors System:

    `www.itd.nps.gov/cwss`

- **Unit Rosters:** Ohio Historical Society Military Rosters Searchable Database:

    `www.ohiohistory.org/resource/database/rosters.html`

If you're researching United States military units, you may want to consult the United States Internet Genealogical Society Military Links Collection site at

`www.usigs.org/library/military/links/`

This site has links to other sites all across the United States that contain some form of military records. The sites are categorized by major war.

For military records for countries outside the United States, consult one of the comprehensive genealogy sites or conduct a search using a general Internet search engine. (You can find sites for both of these types in The *Genealogy Online For Dummies* Internet Directory.)

A useful guide to military records is "Military Service Records in the National Archives," General Information Leaflet 7, available from the National Archives and Records Administration, Room G-7, 700 Pennsylvania Avenue, NW, Washington, DC 20408.

Taxation with Notation

Some of the oldest records available for research are tax records — including property, inheritance, and church taxation records. Most early tax records you encounter were most likely collected locally (that is, at the county or parish level). However, many local tax records have since been turned over to state or county archives — some of which now make tax records available on microfilm, as do Family History Centers. (If you have a Family History Center in your area, you may be able to save yourself a trip, call, or letter to the state archives — check with the Family History Center to see whether it keeps copies of tax records for the area in which you're interested.) And a few maintainers of tax records — including archives and Family History Centers — are starting to make information about their holdings available online. Generally, either indexes or transcriptions of these microfilm records are what you find online.

Here are just a few examples of the types of online resources that you can find pertaining to tax records:

✔ **General Information:** Chapter 8, "Research in Land and Tax Records," by Sandra Hargreaves Luebking, in *The Source: A Guidebook of American Genealogy,* edited by Luebking and Loretto Dennis Szucs (published by Ancestry, Inc.).

✔ **Tax List:** 1790–1800 County Tax Lists of Virginia at

`homepages.rootsweb.com/~ysbinns/vataxlists/`

✔ **Transcribed Hearth Tax:** 1662 Hearth Tax Assessments — Caldwell (`freepages.genealogy.rootsweb.com/~brett/census/ cald1662_ht.htm`)

To identify sites that contain tax records for countries other than the United States, visit a comprehensive genealogical site or the appropriate WorldGenWeb site (www.worldgenweb.org). For more information about WorldGenWeb, see The *Genealogy Online For Dummies* Internet Directory.

If you're locating records in the United States, try a USGenWeb site for the state or county. Here's what to do:

1. **Go to the USGenWeb site (www.usgenweb.org).**

   You see a page with two columns on it.

   Note: See Appendix A for more details about using Web browsers.

2. **Click** The Project's State Pages **link and click the** Text Only State List **link.**

   This link takes you to a page with a list of states and the URLs associated with each state page.

3. **Click a state that interests you.**

   In our case, we select the Pennsylvania link because we're looking for tax records in Lancaster County.

   As a shortcut, you can always get to any USGenWeb state page by typing www.usgenweb.org and the two letter postal code for the state. For example, for Pennsylvania, we can type **www.usgenweb.org/pa**.

4. **From the USGenWeb state page (for the state that you choose), find a link to the county in which you're interested.**

   On the Pennsylvania Counties page, we click the Lancaster link to get to the Lancaster County GenWeb site.

5. **Click the link for Courthouse Records.**

   We click the Courthouse Records link because tax records were often kept in county courthouses. This leads us to another link called Tax Lists.

6. **Click the link for Tax Lists.**

   Clicking this link takes us to another page that offers tax lists for the county.

The state and county Web sites in the USGenWeb Project vary immensely. Some have more information available than the Pennsylvania and Lancaster County pages, while others have less. The amount of information that's available at a particular USGenWeb site affects the number of links you have to click through to find what you're looking for. Don't be afraid to take a little time to explore and become familiar with the sites for states and counties in which your ancestors lived.

Was Your Ancestor a Criminal?
Using Court Records

There's good news — your ancestor may not have to have been a criminal for court records to be useful in your genealogical research. Court records may also contain information about your model-citizen ancestors — those fine, upstanding citizens who made good witnesses.

Court cases and trials aren't just a phenomenon of today's world. Your ancestor may have participated in the judicial system as a plaintiff, defendant, or witness. Some court records can provide a glimpse into the character of your ancestors — whether they were frequently on trial for misbehavior or called as character witnesses. You can also find a lot of information on your ancestors if they were involved in land disputes — a common problem in some areas where land transferred hands often. Again, your ancestor may not have been directly involved in a dispute but may have been called as a witness. Another type of court record that may involve your ancestor is a probate case. Often, members of families contested wills or were called upon as executors or witnesses, and the resulting file of testimonies and rulings can be found in a probate record. Court records may also reflect appointments of ancestors to positions of public trust such as sheriff, inspector of tobacco, and justice of the peace.

Finding court records online can be tricky. They can be found using genealogy-focused search engines such as GenealogyPortal.com (`www.genealogyportal.com`), a general search engine such as Lycos (`www.lycos.com`), or a subscription database service. Note, however, that good data can also be tucked away inside free databases that are not indexed by search engines. In this case, you will have to search on a general term such as "Berks County wills" or "Berks County court records." Here is an example:

1. **Go to the Lycos search engine site** (`www.lycos.com`).

   Near the top of the page is the search box (in the yellow area).

2. **Type your search terms into the search box and click the Search button.**

   The results page is displayed. In our case, we typed **Berks County wills** and received 22,817 results.

3. **Click a link that looks relevant to your search.**

   We selected the link to the Berks County Register of Wills at

   `www.berksregofwills.com`

   At this site, there is a database where you can search over 1 million records covering a variety of areas including birth, death, marriage, and estate.

Part III
Adding Color to Your Research

The 5th Wave   By Rich Tennant

"Hold your horses. It takes time to locate the ancestors for someone of your background."

In this part . . .

These chapters help you add some pizzazz to your research by examining how to find geographically related and ethnic-based resources. These types of resources often offer perspectives into your ancestors' lives. We also explore some interesting genealogical byways, such as adoption records, molecular genealogy, and records associated with religious groups and fraternal orders.

Chapter 6

Locating Your Ancestors (Geographically Speaking)

In This Chapter

▶ Finding out where your ancestors lived

▶ Locating places on maps and in history

▶ Using maps in your research

▶ Getting information from local sources

▶ Preparing for genealogical research trips

*W*hile researching census records, you find that your great-great-great grandfather lived in Winchester, Virginia. But where is Winchester? What was the town like? Where exactly did he live in the town? What was life like when he lived there? To answer these questions, you need to dig a little deeper than just retrieving documents — you need to look at the geographical surroundings of your ancestor.

Geography played a major role in the lives of our ancestors. It often determined where they lived, worked, and migrated (as early settlers often migrated to lands that were similar to their home state or country). It can also play a major role in how you research your ancestor. Concentrating on where your ancestor lived can often point you to area-specific record sets or provide clues about where to research next. In this chapter, we look at several ways to use geographical resources to provide a boost to your family history research.

Are We There Yet? (Researching Where "There" Was to Your Ancestors)

What did "there" mean for your ancestors? You have to answer this question to know where to look for genealogical information. These days, a family that lives in the same general area for more than two or three generations is rare. If you're a member of such a family, you may be in luck when it comes to genealogical research. However, if you come from a family that moved around at least every couple of generations (or not all members of the family remained in the same location), you may be in for a challenge.

So how do you find out where your ancestors lived? In this section, we look at several resources you can use to establish their location, including using known records, interviewing relatives, consulting gazetteers, looking at maps, using GPS devices, and charting locations using geographical software. As we go through these resources, we use a "real-life" example to show how the resources can be used together to solve a research problem — finding the location of the final resting place of Matthew's great-great grandfather.

Using documentation you already have in your possession

When you attempt to geographically locate your ancestors, start by using any copies of records or online data that you or someone else has already collected. Sifting through all of those photocopies and original documents from the attic and printouts from online sites provides a good starting point for locating your ancestors geographically. Pay particular attention to any material that provides a definite location during a specific time period. You can use these details as a springboard for your geographical search.

For example, Matthew's great-great grandfather, Uriah Helm, is listed in the Ancestral File on the FamilySearch Web site (for more on the FamilySearch site — www.familysearch.org — see Chapter 4). In the record, the submitter states that Uriah was buried in the German Reformed Cemetery in Fayette, Illinois, sometime after 20 February 1911 (the date of Uriah's death). The mention of Fayette, Illinois, gives us a place to begin our search.

If you have information about places where your ancestors lived, but not necessarily the time frame, you can still be reasonably successful in tracking your ancestors based on the limited information you do have. Aids are available to help you approximate time frames, such as the Period Approximation Chart (www.myroots.net/extras/tidbits3.htm). For example, say you know the birth dates of your great-great-grandmother's children, but you don't know when great-great-grandma and great-great-grandpa were married. You can use the Period Approximation Chart to calculate a date range in which you can look for the marriage record. The Period Approximation Chart uses average ages for events in history and typical lifespans during certain periods of time to make the calculations.

For additional information about using documents you already have, take a look at "Starting Your Research with What You Already Know" in Chapter 1.

Grilling your relatives about what they know

Your notes from interviews with family members, or from other resources you've found on your ancestors, most likely contain some information about locations where the family lived and hopefully the approximate time frames.

Chances are you have at least some notes with statements, such as "Aunt Lola recalled stories about the old homestead in Fayette County, Kentucky." Of course, whether Aunt Lola recalled stories firsthand (those that she lived through or participated in) or her recollections were stories she heard from those before her has an effect on the time frames within which you look for records in Fayette County. Either way, these stories give you a starting point.

For details on interviewing your family members, see the section "Chatting with Papa and Aunt Lola: Interviewing Your Family Members," found in Chapter 1.

Where is Llandrindod, anyway?

At some point during your research, you're bound to run across something that says an ancestor lived in a particular town or county, or was associated with a specific place, but contains no details of where that place was — no state or province or other identifiers. How do you find out where that place was located?

A *gazetteer,* or geographical dictionary, provides information about places. By looking up the name of the town, county, or some other kind of place, you can narrow your search for your ancestor. The gazetteer identifies every place by a particular name and provides varying information (depending on the gazetteer itself) about each. Typically, gazetteers provide at least the names of the principal region where the place is located. Many contemporary gazetteers also provide the latitude and longitude of the place.

By adding the information you get from the online gazetteer to the other pieces of your puzzle, you can reduce the list of common place names to just those you think are plausible for your ancestors. By pinpointing where a place is, you can look for more records to prove whether your ancestors really lived there.

For research in the United States, one of your first stops should be the U.S. Geological Survey's Geographic Names Information System (GNIS) Web site. The GNIS site contains information on more than 2 million places within the United States and its territories (including those in Antarctica).

To find the precise location of the cemetery were Uriah Helm is buried, we can use the Geographic Names Information System (GNIS) site.

1. **Start your Web browser and head to the U.S. Geological Survey's Geographic Names Information System (GNIS) at** geonames.usgs.gov.

   Note: For information on using a browser, see Appendix A.

2. **Select the link called Query GNIS: <u>U.S. and Territories</u> link.**

   When you click the <u>U.S. and Territories</u> link, you go to the query form. (See Figure 6-1.)

3. **Enter any information that you have, tabbing or clicking between fields; click the Send Query button when you're finished.**

   If you're not sure what a particular field asks for but you think you may want to enter something in it, click the <u>GNIS Query Help Page</u> link at the bottom of the page.

   We entered **German Reformed Cemetery** in the Feature Name field and selected **Illinois** from the state drop-down box.

Figure 6-2 shows the result of the search. The only result was the German Reformed Cemetery in Fayette County, located at 38 degrees, 55 minutes, 58 seconds North latitude and 88 degrees, 54 minutes, 18 seconds West longitude. With this information, we can now plot the location on a map. (See the following section, "Mapping your ancestor's way," for more details on using maps.)

In addition to the GNIS database, which limits itself to the United States and its territories, some online gazetteers identify places in other countries as well as places in the United States. Here are some for you to check out:

   ✔ **Alexandria Digital Library Gazetteer Server** (which has a worldwide focus):

   fat-albert.alexandria.ucsb.edu:8827/gazetteer

- ✔ **Geoscience Australia Place Name Search:**

  www.ga.gov.au/map/names

- ✔ **Canada's Geographical Names:**

  geonames.nrcan.gc.ca

- ✔ **Gazetteer for Scotland:**

  www.geo.ed.ac.uk/scotgaz/

- ✔ **Gazetteer of British Place Names:**

  www.abcounties.co.uk/newgaz/section0.htm

- ✔ **GEOnet Names Server (GNS):**

  gnswww.nima.mil/geonames/GNS/index.jsp

- ✔ **Swedish Gazetteer:**

  www.sna.se/gazetteer.html

- ✔ **National Gazetteer of Wales:**

  www.gazetteer-wales.co.uk

Figure 6-1:
Use the
query form
on the U.S.
Geological
Survey's
Geographic
Name
Information
System
(GNIS) site
to search
the system
for places in
the United
States.

Figure 6-2:
The results
of a GNIS
search for
"German
Reformed
Cemetery"
in Illinois.

Most online gazetteers are organized on a national level and provide information about all the places (towns, cities, counties, landmarks, and so on) within that country. However, there are exceptions. Some unique gazetteers list information about places within one state or province. One such example is the Kentucky Atlas and Gazetteer (www.uky.edu/KentuckyAtlas), which has information only about places within — you guessed it — Kentucky. For each place, it provides the name of the place, the type of place (civil division, school, cemetery, airport, and so on), source of information, topoquad (topographic-map quadrangle that contains the feature), latitude, longitude, area (if applicable), population (if applicable), date of establishment, elevation, and a link to a map showing you where the place is.

In addition to online gazetteers, there are also a number of software gazetteers. One such gazetteer geared toward genealogists is the World Place Finder by Progeny Software (www.progenysoftware.com).

If you can't find a place in current gazetteers, you may need to consult a historical gazetteer. Some examples of these include the On-Line Historical Gazetteer (British) based on the 1911 Census parish table — available at www.geog.qmul.ac.uk/gbhgis/gaz/start.html — and the Early American Gazetteer by GenRef, Inc, available on CD-ROM.

Mapping your ancestor's way

Once you find out where the place is located, it's time to dig out the maps. Maps can be an invaluable resource in your genealogical research. Not only do maps help you track your ancestors, but they also enhance your published genealogy by illustrating some of your findings.

Different types of online sites have maps that may be useful in your genealogical research:

- ✔ **Historical maps:** Several Web sites contain scanned or digitized images of historic maps. In a lot of cases, you can download or print copies of these maps. Such sites include these:

  - **David Rumsey Map Collection:**

    www.davidrumsey.com

  - **Perry-Castañeda Library Map Collection, University of Texas at Austin:**

    www.lib.utexas.edu/Libs/PCL/Map_collection/Map_collection.html

  - **American Memory Map Collections of the Library of Congress:**

    memory.loc.gov/ammem/gmdhtml/gmdhome.html

  You can also find local collections of maps at several university and historical-society sites.

- ✔ **Digitized historical atlases:** In addition to map sites, individuals have scanned portions or the entire contents of atlases, particularly those from the nineteenth century. Examples include

  - **Countrywide atlases.** An example is the 1895 U.S. Atlas:

    www.livgenmi.com/1895.htm

  - **County atlases.** An example is the 1904 Maps from the New Century Atlas of Cayuga County, New York:

    www.rootsweb.com/~nycayuga/maps/1904/

  - **Specialty atlases.** An occupational example is the 1948 U.S. Railroad Atlas:

    nyow.railfan.net/pfmsig/atlas48.html

✔ **Interactive map sites:** A few sites have interactive maps that you can use to find and zoom in on areas. After you have the view you want of the location, you can print a copy of the map to keep with your, genealogical records. Two such sites are

- **MapQuest** (www.mapquest.com) has interactive maps for many countries (including the United States, Canada, Germany, Italy, New Zealand, and the United Kingdom), although some of these look down from too high a level to get much detail.

- **The U.K. Street Map Page** (www.streetmap.co.uk) identifies streets in London or places in the United Kingdom. Interactive maps are especially helpful when you're trying to pinpoint the location of a cemetery or town you plan to visit for your genealogical research, but they're limited in their historical helpfulness because they typically offer only current information about places.

✔ **Specialized maps:** You can view specialized maps on Web sites such as these:

- **Topozone** has interactive topographic maps for the entire United States:

  www.topozone.com

- **Microsoft TerraServer USA** offers satellite maps of the United States:

  terraserver-usa.com

- **OffRoute.com** lets you order custom-made waterproof topographical maps, perfect for those cemetery trips:

  www.offroute.com

Zeroing in

In the cemetery example used in the previous sections, we know two pieces of information about where that cemetery is located. The FamilySearch information states that the cemetery is in Fayette, Illinois; the GNIS tells us that the cemetery is in Fayette County, Illinois, at a specific latitude and longitude. As Matthew wants to see the gravestone for himself, we can consult an interactive atlas site to give us an idea of how to get to the cemetery.

Using the MapQuest atlas, we typed in **Fayette** in the city field and **IL** in the state field and clicked on the Get Map button. The resulting map provides us with a bit of a problem. Fayette, Illinois, is not located in Fayette County — it is actually located in Greene County (some 72 miles from the coordinates given by the GNIS). So, the submitter's information was probably referring only to the county name and not the city of Fayette (although the information should have been specific enough to say Fayette County, to avoid confusion). So, we decide to use the GNIS coordinates to plot the general location of the cemetery on a map (we'll then print out the map to use for driving directions).

Here is how to generate a MapQuest map by latitude and longitude:

1. **Using your Web browser, go to MapQuest at** `www.mapquest.com`.

   Note: See Appendix A for more details on using a browser.

   MapQuest's main page comes up.

2. **Click the Maps icon and then the link titled <u>Lat/Long</u>.**

   The link appears near the top of the page, just under the MapQuest banner.

3. **Enter the latitude and longitude and click the button marked Get Map.**

   If you are entering West longitude, use the negative sign in the Degrees field. For example, we entered 38 degrees, 55 minutes, 58 seconds in the Latitude fields and -88 degrees, 54 minutes, 18 seconds in the Longitude fields.

Figure 6-3 shows the map generated from the GNIS coordinates. The cemetery is located on Highway 185 outside of a town called Confidence.

Figure 6-3:
A map generated on Map-Quest using latitude and longitude.

While MapQuest maps are good for getting a general idea of where a place is, more specific maps are necessary for feature types such as cemeteries. Topographic maps are especially good set to use for these purposes; they contain not only place names, but also information on features of the terrain (such as watercourses, elevation, vegetation density, and, yes, cemeteries). At the TopoZone site (www.topozone.com), you can view interactive topographic maps produced by the United States Geological Survey.

To generate a topographic map from GNIS coordinates do the following (or, you can click on the TopoZone.com link directly from the GNIS results page that we generated in the earlier section titled, "Where is Llandrindod, anyway?").

1. **Direct your browser to** www.topozone.com.

2. **Click on the link marked <u>View Maps</u>, which takes you to a form.**

3. **Click the <u>Deg/min/sec</u> link in the left column, and you pop down to that section of the form.**

4. **Type the latitude and longitude and click on the Map button.**

   You will need to use the negative sign in the degrees field to denote west longitude.

The topographic map produced by TopoZone appears in Figure 6-4. A small red cross marks the location of the coordinates. On the topographic map, the letters *CEM* indicate the location of a cemetery. You can also get an idea of the area surrounding the cemetery — which appears to be quite rural.

Crossing the line

Just as maps help you track your ancestors' movements and where they lived, they can also help you track when your ancestors *didn't* really move. Boundaries for towns, districts, and even states have changed over time. Additionally, for towns and counties to change names wasn't unheard of. Knowing whether your ancestors really moved or just appeared to move because a boundary or town name changed is important when you try to locate records for them.

To determine whether a town or county changed names at some point, check a gazetteer or historical text on the area. (Gazetteers are discussed earlier in this chapter, in the section, "Where is Llandrindod, anyway?") Finding boundary changes can be a little more challenging, but resources are available to help you. For example, historical atlases illustrate land and boundary changes. You can also use online sites that have maps for the same areas over time, and a few sites deal specifically with boundary changes in particular locations. A couple of examples are

✔ The Boundaries of the United States and the Several States site:

    www.ac.wwu.edu/~stephan/48states.html

✔ The Counties of England, Scotland, and Wales Prior to the 1974 Boundary Changes site:

    www.genuki.org.uk/big/Britain.html

You can also use software designed specifically to show boundary changes over time. Programs like these can help you find places that have disappeared altogether:

✔ The Centennia Historical Atlas tracks boundary changes in Europe. Its Web site is

    www.clockwk.com

✔ AniMap Plus tracks boundary changes in the United States (a demonstration version is included on the CD-ROM accompanying this book). Its Web site is

    goldbug.com/store/page1.html

Figure 6-4:
A map generated at TopoZone.com.

Here's a quick walk-through using the AniMap Plus demonstration to see how some counties have changed over time:

1. **Open the demonstration version of AniMap Plus that you installed from the CD-ROM that accompanies this book. (For installation instructions, see Appendix C.)**

   AniMap opens to a 1683 map that shows the 12 original counties of New York. All counties are named in the upper-left corner of the map. Abbreviations of each are explained in the County Codes box; you can see the county boundaries on the map.

2. **Double-click Start Demo in the upper-left corner of the screen.**

3. **Click Next to advance to the next map of New York to see changes that took place between 1683 and 1686.**

   The box in the upper-left corner briefly explains the changes that took place and which counties still existed in New York in 1686.

4. **You can advance through the maps in sequential order by clicking the Next button or you can skip to other years by double-clicking the years identified in the Go To box.**

Positioning your family: Using global positioning systems

After learning the location of the final resting place of great-great-great grandpa Nimrod (yes, that is the name of one of April's ancestors), you just might get the notion to travel to the cemetery. Now, finding the cemetery on the map is one thing, but often finding the cemetery "on the ground" is a completely different thing. That is where global positioning systems come into play.

A *global positioning system* (GPS) is a device that uses satellites to determine the exact location of the user. While the technology is pretty sophisticated, in simple terms, satellites send out radio signals that are collected by the GPS receiver — the device that you use to determine your location. The receiver then calculates the distances between the satellites and the receiver to determine your location. These receivers can come in many forms, ranging from vehicle-mounted receivers to those that fit in your hand. (We frequently use a GPS receiver mounted inside Matthew's cell phone for quick readings.)

While on research trips, we not only use GPS receivers to locate a particular place, but we also use them to document the location of a specific object within that place. For example, when we visit a cemetery, we take GPS readings of the gravesites of ancestors and then enter those readings into our genealogical databases. That way, if the marker is ever destroyed, we still have a way to locate the grave. As a final step, we take that information and plot the specific location of the sites on a map, using geographical-information-systems software. (See the following section for more details on geographical information systems.)

We should also mention that a new project is under way that combines genealogy with the use of GPS devices. The U.S. GeoGen project (geogen.org) was established to create county-level pages with coordinates of some places of interest to genealogists (such as cemeteries, mines, homesteads, and historical post offices). At present, these resources are being developed for 22 states.

Plotting against the family

While finding the location where your ancestors lived on a map is interesting, it is even more exciting to create your own maps that are specific to your family history. One way genealogists produce their own maps is by plotting land records: They take the legal description of the land from a record and place it into land-plotting software, which then creates a map showing the land boundaries. A popular program for plotting boundaries is DeedMapper by Direct Line Software (users.rcn.com/deeds/factsht.htm). There are also a number of commercial plotting programs that can be found using a search engine such as Google (www.google.com).

Another way to create custom maps is through geographical information systems (GIS) software. GIS software allows you to create maps based upon layers of information. For example, you may start with a map that is just an outline of a county. Then you might add a second layer that shows the township sections of the county as they were originally platted. A third layer might show the location of your ancestor's homestead based upon the legal description of a land record. A fourth layer might show watercourses, or other terrain features within the area. The resulting map can give you a great appreciation of the environment in which your ancestor lived.

To begin using GIS resources, you first have to acquire a GIS data viewer. This software comes in many forms, including free software and commercial packages. One popular piece of free software is ArcExplorer available on the ESRI site at www.esri.com/company/free.html. Then you download (or create) data to use with the viewer. There are a number of sites that contain data, both free and commercial. Starting points for finding data include Geography Network (www.geographynetwork.com) and GIS Data Depot (data.geocomm.com). For more information on GIS software, see GIS.com at www.gis.com.

You can also use maps from other sources and integrate them into a GIS map. For example, when visiting cemeteries, we like to use GIS resources to generate an aerial photograph of the cemetery and plot the location of the grave markers on it. When we get back home, we use the aerial photograph as the base template and then overlay the grave locations on it electronically to show their exact positions.

Using our example of grave-hunting in the German Reformed Cemetery (discussed earlier in the chapter), we generated an aerial view by going to TerraServer USA (`terraserver-usa.com`, or you can get to the site through a link marked <u>View USGS Digital Orthophoto Quadrangle</u> on the GNIS results page that we generated in the section titled, "Where is Llandrindod, anyway?").

You can produce an aerial map from GNIS coordinates in the following way:

1. **Using your Web browser, go to TerraServer USA at** `terraserver-usa.com`.

2. **Select the Advanced Find link from the menu in the left column.**

   This takes you to the Advanced Find page.

3. **Choose the link called <u>Geographic</u>.**

4. **Enter the GNIS coordinates into the appropriate fields and click on the button marked Geographic Search.**

   The aerial photograph should appear on-screen. You can zoom in by clicking an area of the photograph.

Figure 6-5 shows the photograph at its maximum zoom (one-meter resolution). The cemetery is the slightly darker, triangular gray area near the center of the photograph (it's bordered on the west by the highway and on the east by a grove of trees). This view of the cemetery helps a lot when we try to find it "on the ground."

From the photograph, we know it's right off of the highway, in between two farms, and across from a triangular lake (although we have to keep in mind that the aerial photograph was taken in 1998 — some things might have changed since then).

After plotting the gravestone locations based on GPS readings at the cemetery, we generated the picture in Figure 6-6. We store that picture in our genealogical database so it's easy to find gravestones at that cemetery should we (or anyone else) wish to visit it in the future.

Figure 6-5:
An aerial
map gener-
ated at the
TerraServer
USA site.

Figure 6-6:
An aerial
map on
which we
plotted
family
gravestones
that we
visited and
for which
we gathered
GPS
readings.

There's No Place Like Home: Using Local Resources

A time will come (possibly early in your research) when you need information that's maintained on a local level — say, a copy of a record stored in a local courthouse, confirmation that an ancestor is buried in a particular cemetery, or just a photo of the old homestead. So how can you find and get what you need?

Overview of the USGenWeb Project

The USGenWeb Project provides a central resource for genealogical information (records and reference materials) pertaining to counties within each state. USGenWeb offers state-level pages for each state within the United States that have links to pages for each county, as well as links to other online resources about the state. At the county level, the pages have links to resources about the county.

In addition to links to other Web sites with genealogical resources that are geographic-specific, most of the county-level pages have query sections in which you can post or read queries (or questions) about researching in that county. Some of the county-level pages offer other services in addition to the query section, such as a surname registry for anyone researching in the county and a look-up section that identifies people who are willing to look up information for others.

Although some states have uniform-looking county pages with the same standard resources for each county, other states don't. The content and look of USGenWeb state and county pages vary tremendously from state to state.

In addition to state- and county-level pages, the USGenWeb Project includes special projects

that cross state and county lines. Some of these projects include the following:

- A project to collect and transcribe tombstone inscriptions so genealogists can access the information online.

- An undertaking to transcribe all federal census data for the United States and make it available online.

- The Pension project — an attempt to transcribe pensions for all wars prior to the year 1900.

- A lineage project to provide resources for individuals researching all descendants of a particular ancestor.

- The Digital Map Library project is designed to provide free, high-quality digital maps to researchers.

- The Kidz Project, a resource page for kids interested in genealogy.

The various pages and projects that make up the USGenWeb Project are designed and maintained by volunteers. If you're interested in becoming involved, visit the USGenWeb home page (www.usgenweb.org).

Finding this information is easy if you live in or near the county where the information is maintained — you decide what it is you need and where it's stored, and then go get a copy. Getting locally held information isn't quite as easy if you live in another county, state, or country. Although you can determine what information you need and where it may be stored, finding out whether the information is truly kept where you think it is and then getting a copy is another thing. Of course, if this situation weren't such a common occurrence for genealogists, you could just make a vacation out of it — travel to the location to finish researching there and get the copy you need while sightseeing along the way. But unfortunately, needing records from distant places is a common occurrence, and most of us can't afford to pack the bags and hit the road every time we need a record or item from a faraway place, which is why it's nice to know that resources are available to help.

From geographic-specific Web sites to local genealogical and historical societies to libraries with research services to individuals who are willing to do lookups in public records, a lot of resources are available to help you locate local documents and obtain copies. Some resources are totally free, others may charge you a fee for their time, and still others will bill you only for copying or other direct costs.

Geographic-specific Web sites

Geographic-specific Web sites are those pages that contain information only about a particular town, county, state, country, or other locality. They typically provide information about local resources, such as genealogical and historical societies, government agencies and courthouses, cemeteries, and civic organizations. Some sites have local histories and biographies of prominent residents online. Often, they list and have links to other Web pages that have resources for the area. Sometimes they even have a place where you can post *queries* (or questions) about the area or families from there, in the hope that someone who reads your query will have some answers for you.

How can you find geographic-specific Web sites, you ask? Doing so is easy:

1. **Using your Web browser, go to the Genealogy Toolbox at** www.genealogytoolbox.com.

   Note: For more information on using a browser, see Appendix A.

2. **Select the Places link.**

   The Places link takes you to a list of continents, major geographical areas, and some popular countries.

3. **Click the country or geographic link that interests you.**

   Doing so brings up a list of links to general sites or to states/provinces.

4. **Click the state or province of your choice.**

   This takes you to a page that lists all Internet sites pertaining to the state or province you selected that are indexed in the Genealogy Toolbox. Each entry includes a brief abstract of the site and a link to that site; you can select sites that sound promising.

You can find several good examples of geographic-specific Web sites:

- ✔ **The USGenWeb Project** (www.usgenweb.org) conveys information about the United States. The USGenWeb Project is an all-volunteer online effort to provide a central genealogical resource for information (records and reference materials) pertaining to counties within each state. (See the sidebar "Overview of the USGenWeb Project" in this chapter for more information.)

- ✔ **GENUKI: UK + Ireland Genealogy** (www.genuki.org.uk) is an online reference site containing primary historical and genealogical information in the United Kingdom and Ireland. It links to sites containing indexes, transcriptions, or digitized images of actual records. All of the information is categorized by locality — by country, then county, then parish.

- ✔ **The American Local History Network** (www.alhn.org) organizes its resources by state and by topic.

- ✔ **The WorldGenWeb project** (www.worldgenweb.org) attempts the same type of undertaking as USGenWeb, only on a global scale. For more information about WorldGenWeb, see The *Genealogy Online For Dummies* Internet Directory in this book.

Genealogical and historical societies

Most genealogical and historical societies exist on a local level and attempt to preserve documents and history for the area in which they are located. Genealogical societies also have another purpose — to help their members research their ancestors whether they lived in the local area or elsewhere. (Granted, some surname-based genealogical societies, and even a couple of virtual societies, are exceptions because they aren't specific to one particular place.) Although historical societies usually don't have a stated purpose of aiding their members in genealogical research, they are helpful to genealogists anyway. Often, if you don't live in the area from which you need a record or information, you can contact a local genealogical or historical society to get help. Help varies from look-up services in books and documents the society maintains in its library to volunteers who actually locate records for you and get copies to send you. Before you contact a local genealogical or historical society for help, be sure you know what services it offers.

Many local genealogical and historical societies have Web pages and identify exactly which services they offer to members and nonmembers online. To find a society in an area you're researching, try this:

1. **Using your Web browser, go to Genealogy Resources on the Internet: World Wide Web at** `www-personal.umich.edu/~cgaunt/gen_int1.html`.

   Note: For more information on using a browser, see Appendix A.

2. **Select the link for World Wide Web sites and scroll down (if necessary) and click a link for *[Insert Place Name Here]* Resources, using the location where you're looking for an association or society as the place name.**

   For example, if you're looking for a genealogical or historical society in Belgium, scroll down and click the <u>Belgium Resources</u> link. This action takes you to a page that identifies and links to all sorts of genealogical sites pertaining to Belgium.

3. **Look through the list of links to see if any associations or societies exist for the area you are interested in. If so, click the link to visit the site.**

   Visit the group or society home page to see what services that group or society offers to members and nonmembers. If the group or society offers a service you need (lookup, obtaining copies of records, and so on), use whatever contact information the site provides to get in touch and request help.

You can also use a search engine to effectively locate genealogical and historical societies. Typically, typing in the name of the location you're looking for, followed by either "genealogical society" or "historical society," is all you need to be successful. Keep in mind, however, that you may need to search on the county name rather than the town name — some societies are formed at the county level rather than the town level.

Libraries and archives

Often, the holdings in local libraries and archives can be of great value to you — even if you can't physically visit the library or archive to do your research. If the library or archive has an Internet site, go online to determine whether that repository has the book or document you need. (Most libraries and archives that have Web pages or other Internet sites make their card catalogs or another listing of their holdings available online — and some are even adding indexes or images of actual documents online.) After seeing whether the repository has what you need, you can contact it to borrow the book or document (if they participate in an interlibrary loan program) or to get a copy of what you need. (Most libraries and archives have services to copy information for people at a minimal cost.)

To find online catalogs for libraries in particular places, follow these steps:

1. **Using your Web browser, go to LibDex: The Library Index at** www. libdex.com.

   Note: For more information on using a browser, see Appendix A.

2. **Click the Country link.**

   This brings up a Geographic Index of links sorted by country.

   For example, you can look for the National Library of Australia to see whether its collection has books that would help your Australian research.

3. **Scroll down and click the link for Australia.**

   Clicking the link for Australia takes you to a page that lists regions in Australia.

4. **Click a region and browse through the list to find a library of interest.**

   Depending on the link you select, you are taken to a page for that particular location. For example, selecting the Australian Capital Territory link takes us to the Geographic: Countries: Australia: Australian Capital Territory page, where we can scroll through a list of catalogs.

5. **Click the National Library of Australia link in the Government section.**

   Selecting the National Library of Australia link under Government takes you to a description page with a link to the National Library's Catalogue. The main Web page for the Catalogue explains its purpose and collection and provides specific information on how to search the site for particular publications or other works.

   From this point on, follow the site's instructions to search for books of interest and applicability to your particular research.

Professional researchers

Professional researchers are people who research your genealogy — or particular family lines — for a fee. If you're looking for someone to do all the research necessary to put together a complete family history, some do so. If you're just looking for records in a particular area to substantiate claims in your genealogy, professional researchers can usually locate the records for you and get you copies. Their services, rates, experience, and reputations vary, so be careful when selecting a professional researcher to help you. Look for someone who has quite a bit of experience in the area in which you need help. Asking for references or a list of satisfied customers isn't out of the question. (That way you know who you're dealing with before you send the researcher money.) Chapter 10 provides a list of questions we recommend you ask when looking for a professional researcher to hire, as well as provides some steps to follow in finding a professional researcher online.

Looking at directories and newspapers

If you have a general idea of where your family lived at a particular time, but no conclusive proof, city and county directories and newspapers from the area may help. (Census records, which we discuss in Chapters 1 and 5, are quite helpful for this purpose, too.) Directories and newspapers can help you confirm whether your ancestors indeed lived in a particular area and, in some cases, they can provide even more information than you expect. A friend of ours has a great story — morbid as it is — that illustrates just this point. He was looking through newspapers for an obituary about one of his great-uncles. He knew when his great-uncle died but could not find mention of it in the obituary section of the newspaper. As he set the newspaper down (probably in despair), he glanced to the front page — only to find a very graphic description of how a local man had been killed in a freak elevator accident. And guess who that local man was? That's right, he was our friend's great-uncle! The newspaper not only confirmed for him that his great-uncle lived there, but also gave our friend a lot more information than he ever expected.

Directories

Like today's telephone books, the directories of yesteryear contained basic information about the persons who lived in particular areas, whether the areas were towns, cities, districts, or counties. Typically, the directory identified at least the head of the household and the location of the house. Some directories also included the names and ages of everyone in the household and occupations of any members of the household who were employed.

Unfortunately, no centralized resource on the Web contains transcriptions of directories or even an index to all directories that may exist on the Internet. But don't be discouraged. Some sites can direct you to directories for particular geographic areas, but they are by no means universal. You can find a list of city directories available on microfilm at the Library of Congress for nearly 700 American towns and states through the U.S. City Directories on Microfilm in the Microform Reading Room Web page (www.loc.gov/rr/microform/uscity). Another list of city directories can be found at the City Directories of the United States of America site (www.uscitydirectories.com). This site contains the years of the city directories and which repositories house them. Right now, the site only contains information on the collections in twenty repositories; however, the site is still growing. You can also often find lists of city directories on the Web sites of local and state libraries.

Some individuals have also posted city directories in their areas. An example of this is the Fredericksburg, Virginia City Directory 1921 page at

`departments.mwc.edu/hipr/www/fredericksburg/1921directory.htm`

And a commercial effort from Ancestry.com is attempting to recreate the 1890 Census through city directories. For more information on this subscription-based project, see its Web site at

`www.ancestry.com/search/rectype/census/1890sub/main.htm`

For tips on using city directories, see the article "City Directories," by Brian Andersson at

`www.ancestry.com/library/view/news/articles/2011.asp`

Some societies and associations have made a commitment to post on the Web the contents of directories for their areas or at least an index of what their libraries hold so that you know before you contact them whether they have something useful to you. To help you find out whether such a project exists for an area you're researching, use the location-specific search engine at GenealogyPortal.com (`www.genealogyportal.com`). This tool enables you to search the full text of several genealogical Web sites at once.

Newspapers

Unlike directories that list almost everyone in a community, newspapers are helpful only if your ancestors did something newsworthy — but you'd be surprised at what was considered newsworthy in the past. Your ancestor didn't necessarily have to be a politician or a criminal to get his picture and story in the paper. Just like today, obituaries, birth and marriage announcements, public records of land transactions, advertisements, and gossip sections were all relatively common in newspapers of the past.

Finding copies online of those newspapers from the past is a challenge. Most of the newspaper sites currently on the Web are for contemporary publications. Although you can read about wedding anniversaries and birthdays in England and Sweden today, you can't necessarily access online information about your ancestor's death in one of those countries in the 1800s. Many researchers are beginning to recognize the potential that the Web holds for making historical information from newspapers available worldwide. However, the lack of committed resources (time and money, primarily) prevents them from doing so as quickly as we'd like.

Here's what you're likely to find online pertaining to newspapers:

✔ **Indexes:** A variety of sites serve as indexes of newspapers that are available at particular libraries, archives, and universities. Most of these list the names and dates of the periodicals that are held in the newspaper or special collections. Examples of index sites include the following:

- **The Newspapers at the National Library of Canada page:**

  www.nlc-bnc.ca/services/enews.htm

- **The Newspaper Collections at the State Library of Victoria, Australia:**

  www.slv.vic.gov.au/slv/newspapers/

- **New England Old Newspaper Index Project of Maine:**

  www.rootsweb.com/~megenweb/newspaper/project

- **The Online Newspaper Indexes Available in the Newspaper and Current Periodical Reading Room of the Library of Congress:**

  lcweb.loc.gov/rr/news/npindex2.html

✔ **Transcriptions:** A few sites contain actual transcriptions of newspaper articles, entire issues, and/or excerpts. Typically, the contents at these sites are limited to the topic and geographic interests of the person who transcribed the information and posted it for public access on the Web. Here are a couple of examples:

- **Old Newspaper Articles of Henderson County Texas:**

  www.rootsweb.com/~txhender/Newspapers.htm

- **The Knoxville Gazette:**

  www.rootsweb.com/~tnnews/kgmain.htm

- **Ireland Old News:**

  www.irelandoldnews.com

✔ **Collectors' issues for sale:** Although they don't provide information directly from the newspaper online for you to use in your genealogical pursuits, these sites can help you find out about collectors' editions of newspapers and possibly even buy them online. The sites that sell old newspapers generally market their papers as good gift ideas for birthdays and anniversaries. For the services to be really useful to you as a genealogist, you have to know the date and place of the event you want to document (and a newspaper name helps, too), as well as be willing to pay for a copy of that paper. Here are a couple of newspaper collector sites to check out:

- **History Buff's Home Page by the Newspaper Collectors Society of America:**

  www.historybuff.com

- **Historic Newspaper Archives:**

  www.historicnewspaper.com

✔ **Online newspaper projects:** Many people are beginning to recognize the important role newspapers play in recording history and the value of putting newspaper information on the Web. We've seen an increasing number of online projects to catalog or transcribe newspapers — some of the projects are organized on a state level, and others are for cities or particular newspapers. The Web sites for these projects explain the purpose of the project, its current status, and how to find the newspapers if they've been transcribed or digitized and placed online. Here are a couple of examples:

• **The New York State Newspaper Project (see Figure 6-7):**

   www.nysl.nysed.gov/nysnp/

• **Martin's General Store, Old Newspaper Clippings:**

   wrkhome.northstarnet.org/hmca/c_indx.htm

• **NewspaperArchive.com:**

   www.newspaperarchive.com

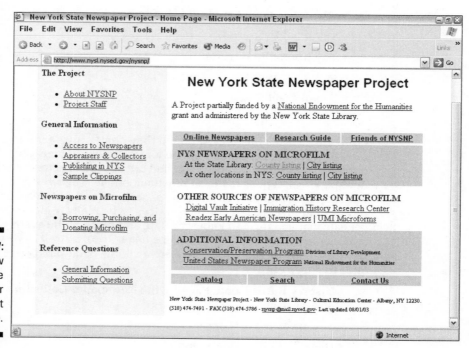

Figure 6-7:
The New York State Newspaper Project Web site.

Now you know what newspaper resources you may find online but how do you find these sites? One option is to use a geographic category in a comprehensive genealogical site (though most may not list newspaper transcriptions if the transcriptions are buried under a larger site). A better option may be to use a genealogically focused search engine, or even a general Internet search engine — especially if you know the location and time frame for the newspaper.

Localizing your search

To find a lot of detail about a specific area and what it was like during a particular time frame, local histories are the answer. Local histories often contain information about when and how a particular place was settled and may have biographical information on earlier settlers or principal people within the community who sponsored the creation of the history.

Online local histories can be tucked away in geographical specific Web sites, historical society pages, library sites, and Web-based bookstores. There are also a few sites that feature local histories. For example, HeritageQuestOnline (`www.heritagequestonline.com`) contains over 25,000 works in its family and local history collection. The site, which is produced by ProQuest Information and Learning Company, is offered mainly to libraries. You can access its contents through the subscription Genealogy.com Family and Local histories collection (`www.genealogy.com/hqosub.html`). A collection of Canadian local histories is available at Our Roots/Nos Racines (`www.ourroots.ca`).

Hit the Road, Jack! (Planning Your Genealogy Travels Using the Web)

A wealth of information is available to help you plan your travels — and it's all at your fingertips! You can surf the Web to check out hotels/motels, car-rental places, airlines, local attractions, and a host of other things related to research trips and vacations. Two sites that provide links to all sorts of travel-related information are MapQuest (`www.mapquest.com`) and the Yahoo! Travel section (`dir.yahoo.com/recreation/travel`). Each has sections for transportation, lodging, dining, and a variety of other things you need while traveling. You can even use MapQuest to plan your route if you're driving in North America (see "Mapping your ancestor's way," earlier in this chapter).

Follow these steps to get driving directions from MapQuest:

1. **Using your World Wide Web browser, open the MapQuest site (**www.mapquest.com**).**

2. **Click the Driving Directions icon.**

   The Driving Directions page appears, offering two columns of boxes to complete and some option buttons you can choose (in the right column).

3. **In the first column, complete the four fields indicating where you're starting your journey.**

   You can type an actual street address in the Address or Intersection field.

   Type the city from which your journey will begin in the City field.

   Type the state or province from which you'll begin your trip in the State/Prov field.

4. **In the second column, complete the four fields indicating your destination (where you want to go).**

   The four destination fields are titled just like the starting fields and accept the same sort of information.

5. **Click the Get Directions button.**

   MapQuest determines the directions from your starting point to your destination. If MapQuest can't determine a route for you, it provides an explanation and recommends trying your Driving Directions transaction again.

Chapter 7

Ethnic Research

. . . .

In This Chapter

▶ Discovering African ancestry

▶ Finding American Indian sites

▶ Identifying Hispanic roots

▶ Researching European ethnic groups

. . . .

Researching ethnic groups can often be frustrating. Even though every ethnic group has records that are unique to it, a particular ethnic group may have been very mobile — making records for it hard to find. And in some cases, records were destroyed during periods of war. Despite the difficulties in finding some of these records, ethnicity-based research can be very rewarding. By looking for records specific to ethnic groups, you get a clearer picture of your ancestor's part in history and find unique sources of information that can add color to your family's story. This chapter examines some of the online resources available to assist you in finding ethnic-specific records.

 If you're looking for a good reference resource that covers ethnic research, we recommend *The Source: A Guidebook of American Genealogy,* edited by Loretto Dennis Szucs and Sandra Hargreaves Luebking (published by Ancestry, Inc.). *The Source* is available in print and on CD-ROM (as part of the Ancestry Reference Library).

Researching African Ancestry

It's a common misconception that tracing African ancestry is impossible. In the past decade or so, much has been done to dispel that perception. If your ancestors lived in the United States, you can use many of the same research techniques and records (census schedules, vital records, and other primary resources) that genealogists of other ethnic groups consult back to 1870. Prior to 1870, your research resources become more limited, depending on whether your ancestor was a freedman or a slave. To make that determination, you may want to interview some of your relatives. They often possess oral traditions that can point you in the right direction.

If your ancestor was a slave, try consulting the slave owners' probate records (which you can usually find in local courthouses), deed books (slave transactions were often recorded in deed books — which you also find in local courthouses), tax records, plantation records, Freedman's Bureau records, and runaway-slave records. These types of records can be helpful because they identify persons by name.

Although your first inclination may be to turn to a slave schedule in the U.S. Census (slave schedules show the owner's name and the age, sex, and color of slaves), such schedules are not as useful as other sources in your research because the *enumerators* who collected the census information didn't record the names of slaves, nor did the government require them to do so. This fact doesn't mean that looking at slave schedules is a total waste of time; the schedules simply don't identify your ancestor by name. You need to find other resources that name your ancestor specifically.

If your ancestors served in the American Civil War, they may have service and pension records. You can begin a search for service records in an index to Civil War records of the United States Colored Troops or, if your ancestor joined a state regiment, in an Adjutant General's report. (An *Adjutant General's report* is a published account of the actions of military units from a particular state during a war; these reports are usually available at libraries or archives.) A good place to begin your search for Civil War records is the Civil War Soldiers and Sailors System at www.itd.nps.gov/cwss/.

Two other sources of records to keep in mind are the Freedmen's Bureau and the Freedmen's Savings and Trust:

- ✔ **The Freedmen's Bureau** (its full name was the Bureau of Refugees, Freedmen and Abandoned Lands) was established in 1865 to assist ex-slaves after the American Civil War. For more on the Bureau, see the article at

  www.nara.gov/publications/prologue/everly.html

  The Freedmen's Bureau Online offers examples of Freedmen's Bureau records:

  www.freedmensbureau.com

  The Freedman's Savings and Trust Company was also established in 1865 as a bank for ex-slaves. For more information, see the article at

  www.archives.gov/publications/prologue/summer_1997_
  freedmens_bureau_records.html

Several of the bank's contributors were members of the United States Colored Troops during the American Civil War. Although the company failed in 1874, its records are now kept at the National Archives and Records Administration, along with the records for the Freedmen's Bureau. You can also find information on the Freedman's Bank Records CD-ROM available from the FamilySearch.org store:

```
www.ldscatalog.com/webapp/wcs/stores/servlet/Category
Display?catalogId=10001&storeId=10001&categoryId=100107&
langId=-1&parent_category_rn=100102&bcname=Miscellaneous%
20Databases&top=&resetCat=N&replBC=subcatlist100102
```

✔ **The National Archives and Records Administration** provides information about Freedman's Savings records (and their availability on microfilm) at

```
www.archives.gov/research_room/federal_records_guide/
bureau_of_refugees_freedmen_and_abandoned_lands_rg105.html
```

For more information on using records to research your African ancestry, try the following resources:

✔ *The Source: A Guidebook of American Genealogy,* edited by Loretto Dennis Szucs and Sandra Hargreaves Luebking (published by Ancestry, Inc.). In particular, see Chapter 15, "Tracking African American Family History," written by David Thackery.

✔ *Black Roots: A Beginners Guide to Tracing the African American Family Tree,* written by Tony Burroughs (published by Fireside).

✔ *Black Studies: A Select Catalog of National Archives Microfilm Publications*, available in the National Archives in Washington, D.C., and online at
```
www.archives.gov/publications/microfilm_catalogs/black_
studies/black_studies.html.
```

✔ *Slave Genealogy: A Research Guide with Case Studies,* written by David H. Streets (published by Heritage Books).

Mailing lists focusing on African research

When you look for key records that are specific to African ancestral research, it's a good idea for you to interact with other researchers who may already be knowledgeable about such resources. One place to start is the *AfriGeneas* mailing list. This mailing list focuses primarily on African genealogical research methods. On the Web page for the mailing list (www.afrigeneas.com), you find the following resources (see Figure 7-1):

- A beginner's guide to researching genealogy
- Links to census schedules and slave data on the Internet
- A digital library of transcribed resources
- A link to a database of African American surnames and their corresponding researchers

Here's how you subscribe to the AfriGeneas mailing list:

1. **Start your favorite e-mail program.**

   How you start your e-mail program depends on which one you use. Generally, you can begin the program by double-clicking the program's icon (or, in Windows 95 and later versions, by opening the program from the Start button). If you're not sure how to start your e-mail program, see the documentation that came with the program. (You also can take a look at Appendix A for more information on using e-mail.)

2. **Create a new e-mail message.**

   Normally you create a new e-mail message by clicking an icon in your e-mail program's toolbar or by using a menu. If you don't know how to create a new e-mail message, consult the documentation that came with the program.

3. **Type** majordomo@msstate.edu **in the To line.**

   Make sure that you type *only* majordomo@msstate.edu in the To line. You subscribe to AfriGeneas at this listserv e-mail account. If you type anything more, your e-mail message won't be delivered, and your attempt to subscribe fails.

4. **Make sure that your e-mail address is in the From line.**

   Most e-mail programs automatically fill in your e-mail address in the From line. In that case, just make sure that it's correct. Otherwise, type the e-mail address where you want to receive postings to the AfriGeneas mailing list.

5. **In the body of the message, type** subscribe afrigeneas **or** subscribe afrigeneas-digest.

   Use **subscribe afrigeneas-digest** if you want to receive fewer e-mail messages a day from the list. In the digest form, the listserver compiles all the messages that people post throughout the day into one e-mail. For example, if April subscribes to the mailing list in its regular format, where each posting arrives separately, she'd type **subscribe afrigeneas** in the body of her message. Again, don't type anything more than this line in the message body, or you confuse the automatic program that adds you to the mailing list — and it rejects your attempt to subscribe.

6. **Send the e-mail message.**

Your e-mail program probably features a Send button that sends the message after you click it. If you don't see a Send button or a Send command in one of the drop-down menus, consult your e-mail program documentation for details on sending a message.

Another resource is the Ethnic-African Mailing Lists page at

```
lists.rootsweb.com/index/other/Ethnic-African
```

This page identifies more than 80 mailing lists of interest to those conducting African-ancestored research. For mailing lists with a little broader focus, see the list at Genealogy Resources on the Internet at

```
www.rootsweb.com/~jfuller/gen_mail_african.html
```

Figure 7-1:
The AfriGeneas site aids with finding African-ancestored roots.

Genealogical resource pages on the Web

In addition to the AfriGeneas Web site, a number of online resources are available to assist you in finding your African ancestry.

One site that identifies several of these resources is Christine's Genealogy Web site located at `ccharity.com` (see Figure 7-2). Here you find the following:

- ✔ A list of Web pages that are of interest to genealogists
- ✔ Transcriptions of records from the Freedmen's Bureau (a government entity established to assist former slaves) arranged by state
- ✔ Lists of ex-slaves who emigrated to Liberia from 1820 to 1843
- ✔ Sites that contain transcribed wills that name slaves or mention them within the wills
- ✔ Transcriptions of *manumission* papers (documents giving slaves their freedom)

For a brief list of resources that you can use offline, see the University of Pennsylvania African Studies Center bibliography page at

`www.africa.upenn.edu/Bibliography/menu_Biblio.html`

Figure 7-2: Christine's Genealogy Web site includes several unique databases.

Transcribed records pertaining to ancestors with African roots

Many genealogists recognize the benefits of making transcribed and digitized records available for other researchers. However, limited resources prohibit most of these genealogists from being able to do so. A few Web sites have transcribed records that are unique to the study of African ancestry online. Following are some examples:

- **Cemetery records:** For a transcribed list of cemeteries, see African American Cemeteries Online at

  www.prairiebluff.com/aacemetery/

- **Freedman's Bureau records:** You can find transcribed Freedman's Bureau records at the Freedman's Bureau Online at

  www.freedmensbureau.com/index.htm

- **Manumission papers:** For examples of manumission papers, see Christine Charity's site at

  ccharity.com/slavesearch.php

- **Registers:** At the Valley of the Shadow site, you can view transcribed Registers of Free Blacks in Augusta County, Virginia, at

  valley.vcdh.virginia.edu/govdoc/free.html

- **Slave Schedules:** You can find transcriptions of slave schedules (lists of slave owners and the number of slaves owned by them) at the African American Census Schedules Online site at

  www.afrigeneas.com/aacensus/

  Although some of these schedules don't identify ancestors by name, they're useful if you know the name of the slave owner.

- **Wills and Probate records:** Slaves were often mentioned in the disposition of wills. A list of slaves mentioned in probate records of Noxubee County, Mississippi, can be found at

  earphoto.tripod.com/SlaveNames.html

The preceding sites are a few examples of transcribed records that you can find on the Internet. To see whether online records exist that pertain specifically to your research, visit a comprehensive genealogical site and look under the appropriate category.

Special ethnic pages about African ancestry

Many Web sites include information on a particular subset of individuals of African ancestry. Here are some you may want to visit:

- ✔ The African-Native Genealogy home page provides details on the Estelusti, a tribe of Black Indians in Oklahoma (www.african-nativeamerican.com).

- ✔ You can find a brief article on the Free People of Color and Creoles Web site (www.neworleansonline.com/tours-attractions/multicultural/fpc.html).

To find additional sites containing unique information about researching your African ancestry, visit a comprehensive genealogical site and look under the appropriate category to review a list of links to such sites or use a genealogical search engine. (For a list of comprehensive genealogical sites and search engines, see The *Genealogy Online For Dummies* Internet Directory in this book.)

American Indian Resources

Tracing your American Indian heritage can be challenging. Your ancestor may have moved frequently and, most likely, few written records were kept. However, your task isn't impossible. With a good research strategy, you may be able to narrow down your search area and find primary resources to unlock some of the mysteries of your ancestors.

One key to your research is old family stories that have been passed down from generation to generation. Interviewing your family members is a good way to find out what tribe your ancestor belonged to and the geographic area in which that ancestor lived. After you have this information, a trip to your local library is well worth the effort to find a history of the tribe and where it migrated throughout time. From this research, you can then concentrate your search on a specific geographic area and gain a much better chance of success in finding records of genealogical value.

Fortunately, the government of the United States did compile some records on American Indians. For example, you can find annual census lists of American Indians, dating from 1885 to 1940, in the National Archives. You can also find probate and land records at the federal level, especially for transactions occurring on reservations. You can also find in federal repositories school records for those who attended schools on reservations. Additionally, the Bureau of Indian Affairs has a vast collection of records on American Indians.

For more information about American Indian resources available from the National Archives and Records Administration, visit

`www.archives.gov/research_room/alic/reference_desk/native_american_links.html`

You may also be able to find records on your ancestor in one of the many tribal associations in existence. To find out how to contact tribes recognized in the United States, go to the American Indian Tribal Directory at

`www.indians.org/Resource/FedTribes99/fedtribes99.html`

For more information about researching American Indian records, see the following resources:

- ✔ *The Source: A Guidebook of American Genealogy,* edited by Loretto Dennis Szucs and Sandra Hargreaves Luebking (published by Ancestry, Inc.). In particular, see Chapter 14, "Tracking Native American Family History," written by Curt B. Witcher and George J. Nixon.

- ✔ *Native American Genealogical Sourcebook,* edited by Paul K. Byers and published by Gale Research

- ✔ *Guide to Records in the National Archives of the United States Relating to American Indians,* written by Edward E. Hill and published by the National Archives and Records Services Administration

Where to begin looking for information about American Indians

For a general look at what Internet resources are available on American Indians, see the NativeWeb site (`www.nativeweb.org`). NativeWeb includes a resource center with hundreds of links to other Internet sites on native peoples around the world.

If you want to know whether the United States officially recognizes a particular tribe, visit the official list (categorized by tribe, state, and city/state) at the American Indian Tribal Directory:

`www.indians.org/Resource/FedTribes99/fedtribes99.html`

To survey the types of records on American Indians available at the National Archives, see

`www.archives.gov/research_room/alic/reference_desk/native_american_links.html`

When you're ready to dive into research, you may want to join the INDIAN-ROOTS-L mailing list, which is devoted to discussing American Indian research methods. To subscribe to the list, type **SUB INDIAN-ROOTS-L *your first name your last name*** in the body of an e-mail message and send it to listserv@listserv.indiana.edu.

Another resource worth exploring is the National Archives and Records Administration's Archival Research Catalog (ARC) at

www.archives.gov/research_room/arc/index.html

ARC contains indexes to a small portion of the archive's holdings. Among the Native American collections in ARC are the following:

- Images of the Index to the Final Rolls of the Citizens and Freedmen of the Five Civilized Tribes in Indian Territory

- Images of the Index to Applications Submitted for the Eastern Cherokee Roll of 1909 (Guion Miller Roll)

- Records of the Bureau of Indian Affairs Truxton Canon Agency

- Record of Applications under the Act of 1896 (1896 Citizenship Applications) received by the Dawes Commission

- Descriptions for records of the Cherokee Indian Agency and the Seminole Indian Agency

- Descriptions for records of the Navajo Area Office, Navajo Agency, and the Window Rock Area Office of the Bureau of Indian Affairs

- Some images of Cherokee, Chicasaw, Creek, and Seminole Applications for Enrollment to the Five Civilized Tribes (Dawes Commission)

- Images of the Kern-Clifton Roll of Cherokee Freedmen

- Images of the Wallace Roll of Cherokee Freedmen in Indian Territory

- Surveys of Indian Industry, 1922

- Classified Files of the Extension and Credit Office, 1931–1946

- Selected Documents from the Records of the Bureau of Indian Affairs, 1793–1989

- American Indians, 1881–1885

To search ARC, try this:

1. **Go to** www.archives.gov/research_room/arc/index.html.

   Note: See Appendix A for more information about using your Web browser.

2. **Click the Search button located near the ARC logo.**

   This link takes you to the ARC Basic Search interface.

3. **Type the name or keyword you're looking for and click the Go button.**

   For example, if April is looking for a person with the name Annie Abbott, she simply types **Annie Abbott** in the blank text box and then clicks the Go button. After you submit the search, you are taken to the ARC Search Results page. Each result contains the title of the document, creator, type of material, description level, and physical location.

4. **Click the link to see the full record description.**

   This takes you to a screen displaying the available information on the document, including a description of its content.

At this point, ARC contains descriptions of only 20 percent of the Archives total holdings. So, if you don't find something in it, that does not mean it does not exist.

For general information on how to begin researching American Indian resources, see the article "How-To Guide for Native Americans" at

`members.aol.com/bbbenge/page12.html`

A brief outline of tracing American Indian ancestry is found on the U.S. Department of the Interior site (`www.doi.gov/ancestry.html`). Another page that you may want to visit is Tawodi's American Indian Genealogy site (`members.aol.com/tawodi/`). It contains a how-to guide, a list of American Indian texts online, and links to several tribal and American Indian pages.

American Indian resource pages on the Web

Researching American Indian roots would be much easier if some sites were dedicated to the genealogical research of specific tribes. If your ancestor's tribe passed through the state of Oklahoma, you may be in luck. Volunteers with the Oklahoma USGenWeb project developed the Twin Territories site at

`www.rootsweb.com/~itgenweb/index.htm`

(For more information about USGenWeb, see Chapter 4.) Here are some links to various tribes available on the World Wide Web:

- ✔ Cherokee Nation Indian Territory at

   `www.rootsweb.com/~itcherok/`

- ✔ Cherokee Archival Project at

   `www.rootsweb.com/~cherokee/`

- NC Cherokee Reservation Genealogy at

  `www.rootsweb.com/~ncqualla/index.htm`

- Cheyenne-Arapaho Lands Indian Territory at

  `ww.rootsweb.com/~itcheyen/`

- Chickasaw Nation, Indian Territory 1837–1907 at

  `www.rootsweb.com/~itchicka/`

- Choctaw Nation, Indian Territory at

  `www.rootsweb.com/~itchocta/`

- Kiowa, Comanche, Apache Lands Indian Territory at

  `www.rootsweb.com/itkiowa/`

- Muscogee (Creek) Nation of Oklahoma at

  `www.rootsweb.com/~itcreek/index.htm`

- Native Genealogy People of the Three Fires (Chippewa, Ottawa, and Potawatomi) at

  `www.rootsweb.com/~minatam/`

- Osage Nation Genealogical Web site at

  `www.rootsweb.com/~itosage/`

- Quapaw Agency Lands Indian Territory at

  `www.rootsweb.com/~itquapaw/index.htm`

- Seminole Nation in Indian Territory at

  `www.seminolenation-indianterritory.org/`

- Sovereign Nation of the Kaw at

  `www.rootsweb.com/~itkaw/KanzaNation.html`

Transcribed American Indian records

There are some Web sites that have transcribed records that are unique to researching American Indian roots. Here are some examples:

- **The Chickasaw Historical Research Page:** This page contains transcriptions of marriage records, a partial census roll of 1818, land sale records, court records, and treaty letters, all at

  `www.flash.net/~kma/`

✔ **1851 Census of Cherokees East of the Mississippi:** This site provides a transcription of the census, including names, family numbers, ages, and relationships to head of household, all at

```
members.aol.com/1redtail/siler.htm
```

✔ **South Dakota Native American Genealogy page:** You can find several transcribed records at

```
www.geocities.com/Heartland/Plains/8430/
```

These records include marriage lists, agency rolls, and links to cemetery records.

Many families have legends that they are descended from famous American Indians. These claims should always be researched carefully and backed up with appropriate proof. One of the most prolific legends is descent from Pocahontas. If that legend runs through your family, you may want to visit the Pocahontas Descendants page for resources that can help you prove your heritage. You can find it at

```
www.geocities.com/Broadway/1001/poca_desc.html
```

Hispanic Roots

A growing number of genealogists are researching their Hispanic roots. If you have Hispanic ancestors, you can use several different types of records to pursue your genealogy, depending on when your ancestor immigrated.

If your ancestor immigrated in the nineteenth or twentieth century, look for vital records, military records, photographs, passports, church records, passenger lists, naturalization papers, diaries, or other items that can give you an idea of the birthplace of your ancestor. For those ancestors who immigrated before the nineteenth century, you may want to consult Spanish colonial records after you exhaust any local records in the region where your ancestor lived.

For more information on researching Hispanic records, see the following:

✔ *The Source: A Guidebook of American Genealogy,* edited by Loretto Dennis Szucs and Sandra Hargreaves (published by Ancestry, Inc.). In particular, see Chapter 16, "Tracking Hispanic Family History," written by George Ryskamp.

✔ *Hispanic Family History Research in the L.D.S. Family History Center,* written by George R. Ryskamp (published by Hispanic Family History Research).

Where to begin searching for genealogical information on Hispanic ancestors

If you aren't sure where to begin your research, check out the messages that people post to the GEN-HISPANIC-L mailing list at

`lists.rootsweb.com/index/intl/ESP/GEN-HISPANIC.html`

If your genealogical interests lie in a specific country or ethnic subgroup, you may want to join one of the following mailing lists:

- **Basque-L:** This list discusses Basque culture and periodically includes genealogical postings. To subscribe to the mailing list, type **SUBSCRIBE BASQUE-L** *your first name your last name* in the body of an e-mail message and send it to `listserv@cunyvm.cuny.edu`.

- **Columbia:** COLEXT is a general mailing list on Columbia. To subscribe to the mailing list, type **SUBSCRIBE COLEXT** *your first name your last name* in the body of an e-mail message and send it to `listserv@cuvmb.columbia.edu`.

- **Costa Rica:** This mailing list is devoted to people who have a genealogical interest in Costa Rica. To subscribe to the mailing list, send a message to `costa-rica-l-request@rootsweb.com` with only the word *subscribe* in the body of the message.

- **Cuba:** This mailing list is devoted to people who have a genealogical interest in Cuba. To subscribe to the mailing list, send a message to `cuba-l-request@rootsweb.com` with only the word *subscribe* in the body of the message.

- **Dominican Republic:** This mailing list is for people with a genealogical interest in the Dominican Republic. To subscribe to the mailing list, send a message to `republica-dominicana-l-request@rootsweb.com` with only the word *subscribe* in the body of the message.

- **Ecuador:** This mailing list is devoted to people who have a genealogical interest in Ecuador. To subscribe to the mailing list, send a message to `ecuador-l-request@rootsweb.com` with only the word *subscribe* in the body of the message.

- **El Salvador:** This mailing list is devoted to people who have a genealogical interest in El Salvador. To subscribe to the mailing list, send a message to `elsalvador-l-request@rootsweb.com` with only the word *subscribe* in the body of the message.

✔ **Guatemala:** This mailing list is devoted to people who have a genealogical interest in Guatemala. To subscribe to the mailing list, send a message to `guatemala-l-request@rootsweb.com` with only the word *subscribe* in the body of the message.

✔ **Honduras:** This mailing list is devoted to people who have a genealogical interest in Honduras. To subscribe to the mailing list, send a message to `honduras-l-request@rootsweb.com` with only the word *subscribe* in the body of the message.

✔ **Mexico:** This mailing list is for anyone with an interest in genealogy in Mexico. To subscribe to the mailing list, send a message to `mexico-l-request@rootsweb.com` with only the word *subscribe* in the body of the message.

✔ **Nicaragua:** This mailing list is devoted to people who have a genealogical interest in Nicaragua. To subscribe to the mailing list, send a message to `nicaragua-l-request@rootsweb.com` with only the word *subscribe* in the body of the message.

✔ **Paraguay:** This mailing list is for anyone with an interest in genealogy in Paraguay. To subscribe to the mailing list, send a message to `paraguay-l-request@rootsweb.com` with only the word *subscribe* in the body of the message.

✔ **Spain:** This list is devoted to people who have a genealogical interest in Spain. Send a message to `spain-l-request@ rootsweb.com` with only the word *subscribe* in the body of the message to subscribe to the list.

✔ **Venezuela:** This mailing list is for anyone with an interest in genealogy in Venezuela. Send a message to `venezuela-l-request@rootsweb.com` with only the word *subscribe* in the body of the message to subscribe to the mailing list.

Hispanic resource pages on the Web

The Hispanic Genealogy Center (`www.hispanicgenealogy.com`) is a Web page that the Hispanic Genealogical Society of New York maintains to promote genealogy among Hispanic Americans. A companion site for Puerto Rican researchers is found at `www.prroots.com`. America Online also features a Hispanic forum (`users.aol.com/mrosado007/index.htm`), which includes a newsletter, surname list, and links to other Hispanic resources on the Internet. For a list of Hispanic resources by location, the Puerto Rican/Hispanic Genealogical Society maintains a page of links to genealogical resources at `www.rootsweb.com/~prhgs/` (see Figure 7-3).

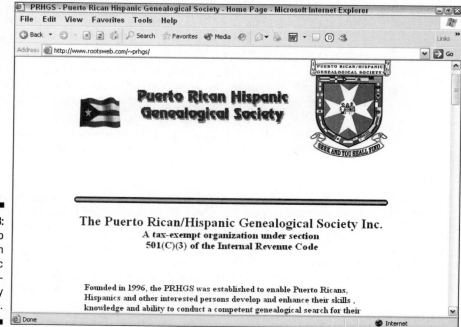

Figure 7-3:
The Puerto
Rican
Hispanic
Genealogi-
cal Society
home page.

The National Society of Hispanic Genealogy (www.hispanicgen.org) also maintains a Web site dedicated to people researching ancestors in the Southwest area of the United States (formerly known as New Spain). For resources specific to a country or area, see the following sites:

- Argentina WorldGenWeb at www.rootsweb.com/~argwgw/
- Genealogia de El Salvador at www.rootsweb.com/~slvwgw/
- Genealogía de Venezuela at www.geocities.com/Heartland/Ranch/2443/
- Genealogical Research in South America at www.saqnet.co.uk/users/hrhenly/latinam1.html
- Genealogie d'Haiti et de Saint-Domingue at www.rootsweb.com/~htiwgw/
- GuatemalaGenWeb at www.rootsweb.com/~gtmwgw/
- Honduras GenWeb at www.rootsweb.com/~hndwgw/honduras.html
- La Genealogia de Puerto Rico at www.rootsweb.com/~prwgw/index.html
- Mexican GenWeb Project at www.rootsweb.com/~mexwgw/
- Panama GenWeb at www.rootsweb.com/~panwgw/Panama_home.htm
- Peru — The WorldGenWeb Project at www.rootsweb.com/~perwgw/

Transcribed records for Hispanic ancestors

Transcribed records are also available on sites that focus on Hispanic ancestors. Here are a couple of typical examples:

✔ You can view transcribed records from the 1757, 1780, 1791, 1823, and 1860 Censuses of the village of Guerrero in Mexico (along with baptismal records) at the following site:

`members.aol.com/gallegjj/viejo.html`

✔ Selected Parish Registers from Uruguay and Argentina are available at the Genealogical Research in South America site:

`www.saqnet.co.uk/users/hrhenly/latinam1.html`

Other transcribed records are available online; visit a comprehensive genealogical site if you're interested in discovering whether other sites pertain more specifically to your research. For example, you can choose from a long list of ethnic groups at the Genealogy Toolbox's Ethnic/Religious Groups page:

`www.genealogytoolbox.com/people.html`

European Resources

If your ancestors came from Europe, you may want to consult information on one of the continent's many ethnic groups. Your level of genealogical success with European ethnic records depends greatly on the history of the group and the areas in which your ancestors lived. There may be fewer surviving records for ancestors from places that weathered several wars and border changes than for those who lived in a more stable environment. Here is a sampling of European ethnic-research sites:

✔ **Austrian:** AustriaGenWeb (`www.rootsweb.com/~autwgw/`)

✔ **Belarusian:** Belarusian Genealogy (`www.belarusguide.com/genealogy1/index.html`)

✔ **Belgian:** Genealogie in België (`users.skynet.be/sky60754/genealbe/`)

✔ **Bosnia-Herzegovina:** Bosnia-Herzegovina Web Genealogy Project (`www.rootsweb.com/~bihwgw/`)

✔ **Bulgarian:** Bulgarian GenWeb (`www.rootsweb.com/~bgrwgw/`)

✔ **Croatian:** CroatiaGenWeb (`www.rootsweb.com/~hrvwgw/`)

✔ **Czech:** Czech Republic Genealogy (`www.rootsweb.com/~czewgw/`)

✔ **Danish:** DIS Danmark (`www.dis-danmark.dk/index.asp`)

- **Dutch:** DutchGenealogy.com (`www.dutchgenealogy.com/`)

- **Estonian:** Estonian GenWeb (`www.fortunecity.com/meltingpot/estonia/200/genweb.html`)

- **Federation of East European Family History Societies (FEEFHS):** If you're looking for research guides for Eastern Europe, start here. The federation's pages (`feefhs.org`) have information on the Albanian, Armenian, Austrian, Belarusian, Bohemian, Bulgarian, Carpatho-Rusyn, Croatian, Czech, Danish, Finnish, Galician, German, Hutterite, Hungarian, Latvian, Lithuanian, Polish, Moravian, Pomeranian, Romanian, Russian, Silesian, Slavic, Slavonian, Slovak, Slovenian, Transylvanian, Ukrainian, and Volhynian ethnic groups.

- **Finnish:** Family History Finland (`www.open.org/~rumcd/genweb/finn.html`)

- **French:** Francogene (`www.francogene.com/`) focuses on genealogy of French-speaking groups, including French Canadians, Acadians, Cajuns, Belgians, and Swiss.

- **German:** The German Genealogy Pages (`www.genealogy.net/gene/genealogy.html`) focus on research of German, Austrian, Swiss, Alsatian, Luxemburger, and Eastern European genealogy. Also, Ahnenforschung.net (`www.ahnenforschung.net`) is a search engine dedicated to German genealogy.

- **Greek:** GreeceGenWeb (`www.rootsweb.com/~grcwgw/`)

- **Hungarian:** HungaryGenWeb (`www.rootsweb.com/~wghungar/`)

- **Icelandic:** Iceland Genealogy (`www.rootsweb.com/~islwgw/`)

- **Irish:** Irish Ancestors (`www.ireland.com/ancestor/`) provides guides on sources of genealogical information in Ireland, a list of county heritage centers, record sources, and useful addresses.

- **Italian:** The Italian Genealogy Homepage (`www.italgen.com`) covers many topics including medieval genealogy, tips for researching in Italy, records repositories, common surnames, and history.

- **Latvian:** LatvianGenWeb (`www.rootsweb.com/~lvawgw/`)

- **Liechtenstein:** LiechGen (`www.rootsweb.com/~liewgw/`)

- **Luxembourg:** Luxembourg Home Page (`www.rootsweb.com/~luxwgw/`)

- **Maltese:** MaltaGenWeb (`www.rootsweb.com/~mltwgw/`)

- **Moldava:** MoldavaGenWeb (`www.rootsweb.com/~mdawgw/`)

- **Norwegian:** Norway Genealogy (`www.rootsweb.com/~wgnorway/`)

- **Polish:** PolandGenWeb (`www.rootsweb.com/~polwgw/polandgen.html`)

- **Romanian:** Romania World GenWeb (`www.rootsweb.com/~romwgw/index.html`)

- **Russian:** RussiaGenWeb (`www.rootsweb.com/~ruswgw/`)

- **Serbian:** SerbiaGenWeb (`www.rootsweb.com/~serwgw/`)

- **Slovak:** Slovak Republic Genealogy (`www.rootsweb.com/~svkwgw/`)

- **Slovenia:** Genealogy and Heraldry in Slovenia (`genealogy.ijp.si/`)

- **Spanish:** Espana GenWeb (`www.genealogia-es.com/`)

- **Swedish:** Sweden Genealogy (`www.rootsweb.com/~wgsweden/`)

- **Swiss:** Swiss Genealogy on the Internet (`www.eye.ch/swissgen/gener-e.htm`)

- **UK and Ireland Genealogical Information Service (GENUKI):** GENUKI (`www.genuki.org.uk`) includes details on English, Irish, Scottish, Welsh, Channel Islanders, and Manx ethnic groups

- **Ukrainian:** Ukraine World GenWeb (`www.rootsweb.com/~ukrwgw/index.html`)

To find information on European ethnic groups, your best bet is to consult a comprehensive genealogy site. The following steps provide an example of how to conduct such a search:

1. **Go to the Genealogy Resources on the Internet site:**

   `www.rootsweb.com/~jfuller/internet.html`

   In the first paragraph of the home page, you see a list of resources including mailing lists, Usenet newsgroups, anonymous File Transfer Protocol (FTP), Gopher, World Wide Web, Telnet, and e-mail.

2. **Click the <u>World Wide Web</u> link.**

   This link takes you to an alphabetical listing of categories of genealogical Web sites.

3. **Click a geographic location or name of an ethnic group.**

   We're interested in finding information on individuals of Dutch ancestry, so we choose the Dutch Resources link. This brings up a page with a list of Dutch-related links.

4. **Choose a link from the list that interests you.**

Asian Resources

If your ancestors came from Asia or the Pacific Rim, your success at finding records depends greatly on the history of the ancestor's ethnic group and its recordkeeping procedures. Currently, there isn't much online genealogical information that pertains to these areas and peoples. Here's a sampling of Asian and Pacific Rim resources:

- **Australia:** AustraliaGenWeb at `www.australiagenweb.org/`
- **Bangladesh:** Bangladesh Genealogy at `www.rootsweb.com/~bgdwgw/`
- **Bhutan:** Bhutan Genealogy at `www.rootsweb.com/~btnwgw/`
- **China:** ChinaGenWeb at `www.rootsweb.com/~chnwgw/`
- **India:** Family History in India at `www.ozemail.com.au/~clday/`
- **Japan:** Japan GenWeb at `www.rootsweb.com/~jpnwgw/`
- **Lebanon:** Lebanon GenWeb at `www.rootsweb.com/~lbnwgw/`
- **Melanesia:** MelanesiaGenWeb Project at `www.rootsweb.com/~melwgw/`
- **Philippines:** Philippines Genealogy Web Project at `www.geocities.com/Heartland/Ranch/9121/`
- **Polynesia:** PolynesiaGenWeb at `www.rootsweb.com/~pyfwgw/`
- **Saudi Arabia:** Saudi Arabia GenWeb at `www.angelfire.com/tn/BattlePride/Saudi.html`
- **South Korea:** South Korea GenWeb at `www.rootsweb.com/~korwgw-s/`
- **Sri Lanka:** Sri Lanka GenWeb at `www.rootsweb.com/~lkawgw/`
- **Syria:** Syria GenWeb at `www.rootsweb.com/~syrwgw/`
- **Taiwan:** TaiwanGenWeb at `www.rootsweb.com/~twnwgw/`
- **Tibet:** TibetGenWeb at `www.rootsweb.com/~tibetwgw/`
- **Turkey** Turkish Genealogy at `www.rootsweb.com/~turwgw/`
- **Various:** Genealogical Gleanings (genealogies of the rulers of India, Burma, Cambodia, Thailand, Fiji, Tonga, Hawaii, and Malaysia) at `www.uq.net.au/~zzhsoszy/index.html`
- **Vietnam:** Vietnamese Genealogy at `www.rootsweb.com/~vnmwgw/`

Chapter 8

Records Off the Beaten Path

Many people who are familiar with genealogy know to use census records, vital records, tax lists, and wills to find information on their ancestors. These records tend to take historical "snapshots" of an individual's life at particular points in time. But as a family historian, you want to know more than just when your ancestors paid their taxes — you want to know something about them as people.

For example, one time April was looking through some pictures, and she came across a photograph of her great-great-grandfather. He was dressed in a uniform with a sash and sword and was holding a plumed hat. As far as April knew, her great-great-grandfather hadn't been in the military, so she decided to dig for some information about the uniform. Although part of the picture was blurry, she could make out three crosses on the uniform. One was on his sleeve, the second was on the buckle of his belt, and the third was a different kind of cross that was attached to his sash. April suspected that the symbols were Masonic. She visited a few Masonic sites on the World Wide Web and found that the crosses indicated that her great-great-grandfather had been a member of the Order of the Temple within the Masonic organization. Of course, she would never have known that he was a member of that organization had she depended solely upon the usual group of records used by genealogists.

This chapter looks at some examples of unique or hard-to-find records that can be quite useful in family history research. These records include those kept by religious groups and fraternal orders, photographs, and adoption records.

Religious Group Records

In the past, several countries required attendance at church services or the payment of taxes to an ecclesiastical authority. Although your ancestors may not have appreciated those laws at the time, the records that were kept to ensure their compliance can benefit you as a genealogist. In fact, before governments started recording births, marriages, and deaths, churches kept the official records of these events. For those places where no such laws were in effect, you can use a variety of records kept by church authorities or congregations to develop a sketch of the everyday life of your ancestor.

Some common records that you may encounter include baptismal records, parish registers, marriage records, death or burial records, tithes, welfare rolls, meeting minutes, and congregation photographs. Each type of record may include several different bits of information. For example, a baptismal record may include the date of birth, date of baptism, parents' names, and where the parents lived.

Several sites provide general information and links to all sorts of resources that pertain to specific religions and sects. Here are a few examples:

- **Anabaptists:** www.gty.org/~phil/anabapt.htm

    The Hall of Church History — The Anabaptists site has an introduction to the beliefs of the Anabaptists and links to Anabaptist resources on the Internet.

- **Catholic:** home.att.net/~Local_Catholic/

    The Local Catholic Church History & Genealogy Research Guide includes links to information on diocese and genealogy, categorized by location.

- **Church of Scotland:** www.scotlandspeople.gov.uk

    The General Register Office for Scotland site features searchable indexes of births/baptisms and banns/marriages from the Old Parish Registers dating from 1553 to 1854.

- **Huguenot:** huguenots-france.org/english.htm

    The Huguenots of France and Elsewhere site contains genealogies of several Huguenot families.

- **Hutterite:** feefhs.org/hut/frg-hut.html

    The Hutterite Genealogy HomePage gives an introduction and links to resources for this denomination found in Austria, Bohemia, Moravia, Slovakia, Hungary, Romania, Canada, the United States, and the Ukraine.

✔ **Jewish:** www.jewishgen.org

JewishGen has information about the JewishGen organization and frequently asked questions about Jewish genealogy, as well as indices of other Internet resources, including searchable databases, special interest groups, and JewishGen family home pages.

✔ **Lutheran:** www.aal.org/LutheransOnline/Gene_Ex

The Lutheran Roots Genealogy Exchange has a registry of researchers looking for information about Lutheran ancestors and a message board to which you can post questions about your research.

✔ **Mennonite:** www.ristenbatt.com/genealogy/mennonit.htm

The Mennonite Research Corner features general information about Mennonites and a collection of online resources for researchers.

✔ **Methodist:** rylibweb.man.ac.uk/data1/dg/text/method.html

The Methodist Archives and Research Centre contains information on its collections and a guide to using the archives for family history research (under "Guides and Catalogues").

✔ **Moravian Church:** www.moravian.org

The Moravian Church home page includes information on one of the oldest Protestant denominations. You can also find links to various Moravian resources on the Internet.

✔ **Quaker:** www.rootsweb.com/~quakers

The Quaker Corner contains a query board, a list of research resources, and links to other Quaker pages on the World Wide Web.

✔ **United Church of Canada Archives:** vicu.utoronto.ca/archives/archives.htm

The United Church Archives page has information on the holdings of the archives and a page on genealogical research. The archives contain records for the Presbyterian Church (Canada), Methodist Church (Canada), Congregational Union of Canada, Local Union Churches, and the Evangelical United Brethren Church.

A few church organizations have online descriptions of their archives' holdings. These two, for example, identify the specific resources available at their locations, including databases, original records, rare books and periodicals, and old photographs:

✔ The Center for Mennonite Brethren Studies in Fresno, California:

www.fresno.edu/affiliation/cmbs/geneal.htm

✔ The Catholic Archives of Texas:

www.onr.com/user/cat

Of course, at some point you may want to find sites with indices or actual records online. Finding religious records on the Internet can be quite challenging. We recommend that you start by using one of the larger comprehensive genealogy sites listed in The *Genealogy Online For Dummies* Internet Directory found in this book, or visit some of the specialty religious sites, or look at the sites referenced on personal genealogy pages. To find religious sites, try this:

1. **Open your Web browser and go to the Genealogy Toolbox at**

   www.genealogytoolbox.com

   Note: If you need a refresher on operating a browser, see Appendix A.

2. **Click the People category, and select Ethnic/Religious Groups.**

3. **Under Ethnic/Religious Groups, select the religious group that interests you.**

   For example, we're interested in finding out information on Quakers, so we click the Quakers link.

4. **Click a link on the religious group's page to visit related pages on the Internet.**

   After you select a religious group, you see links to sites on the Web about that group. You may want to read the abstracts to determine whether the site may contain the information you're looking for.

If you're curious about what types of information for religious groups are available on the Internet, here are a few examples:

✔ **Baptism Records:** You can find a list of those baptized at St. Peter's Anglican Church in Upper Island Cover, Newfoundland at

   www.genweb.ca/nfdata/065/parish/3/uic_ang_bap1.htm

✔ **Cemetery Records:** The Quaker Burying Ground Cemetery, Galesville, Anne Arundel County, Maryland, site is

   www.interment.net/data/us/md/anne_arundel/quaker.htm

   It's part of the Cemetery Records Online site, provides transcribed burial information, including the person's name and dates of birth and death, as well as some other information. (See Figure 8-1.)

✔ **Genealogical Services:** A list of information that the American Baptist-Samuel Colgate Historical Library might be able to provide researchers. The page includes a church records search request form. It is located at

   www.crds.edu/abhs/genealogy.htm

✔ **Marriage Records:** The Moravian Church, Lititz Marriages 1742–1800 page contains a list of marriage dates along with the names of the bride and groom performed in the church located in Lancaster County, Pennsylvania. Here's where you find it:

```
searches1.rootsweb.com/usgenweb/archives/pa/lancaster/
church/moravianlititz.txt
```

✔ **Parish Directories:** The Holy Trinity Church, Boston, Massachusetts, site has a searchable 1895 parish directory, an ongoing project to identify and post information about church members who served in the Civil War, and a list of church members who served in World War I. Here's the URL:

```
homepages.rootsweb.com/~mvreid/bgrc/htc.html
```

Of course, in addition to some sites that focus specifically on one type of record, you may run across sites like the Genline Project (`www.genline.com/start.php`), which collects digitized copies of all sorts of records pertaining to a particular church. The goal of the Genline Project is to place all digital copies of Swedish church records online.

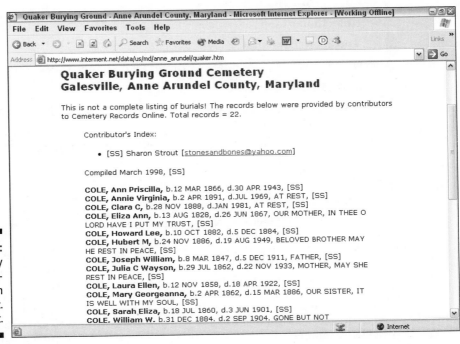

Figure 8-1: A cemetery transcription from Interment. net.

Fraternal Orders and Service Clubs

Were any of your ancestors members of fraternal orders or service clubs? Many such organizations are out there, and chances are, you have at least one ancestor who was a member of an order or club. Although most of the more commonly known organizations are for men, affiliated organizations for women exist, too. Here are a few general information sites on fraternal orders and service clubs:

- **DeMolay International:** www.demolay.org/home/index.shtml
- **Elks (Benevolent Protective Order of the Elks):** www.elks.org
- **Freemasonry:** e-m@son (www.freemasonry.org) and A Page About Freemasonry (web.mit.edu/dryfoo/www/Masons/index.html)
- **Job's Daughters (International Order of Job's Daughters):** www.iojd.org
- **Kiwanis International:** www.kiwanis.org
- **Knights of Columbus:** www.kofc.org
- **Lions Clubs:** LionNet (www.lionnet.com)
- **Moose International:** www.mooseintl.org
- **Odd Fellows (Independent Order of Odd Fellows):** www.ioof.org
- **Optimist International:** www.optimist.org
- **Order of the Eastern Star (Grand Chapter Order of the Eastern Star):** www.easternstar.org
- **Rainbow for Girls (International Order of the Rainbow for Girls):** www.iorg.org
- **Rebekahs:** www.ioof.org/rebekahs.htm
- **Rotary International:** www.rotary.org
- **Shriners (The Shrine of North America):** www.shriners.com

Most of the online sites related to fraternal orders provide historical information about the clubs and current membership rules. Although the sites may not provide you with actual records (membership lists and meeting minutes), they do give you an overview of what the club is about and an idea of what your ancestor did as a member. The sites also provide you with the names and addresses of local chapters — you can contact them to see if they have original resources available for public use or if they can send you copies of anything pertaining to your ancestor.

An important thing to note is that having information about a fraternal order doesn't necessarily make a particular site the organization's *official* site. This is particularly true for international organizations. You may find Web pages for different chapters of a particular club in several different countries, and although each site may have some general club information in common, they are likely to have varying types of information specific to that chapter of the organization.

If you're looking for sites containing information on fraternal organizations, you may want to try some of the comprehensive genealogy sites. If you can't find sufficient information there, try one of the general Internet search engines. You can find a list of both types of sites in The *Genealogy Online For Dummies* Internet Directory in this book. To find information on fraternal orders through a general Internet search engine, try this:

1. **Open your Web browser and go to the AltaVista search engine page** (www.altavista.com) **or substitute the address of your favorite search engine.**

   Note: For more information on using browsers and search engines, check out Appendix A.

2. **Type the name of a fraternal organization in the Search box and click the Find button.**

   We're interested in finding information about the Knights of Columbus, so we type that phrase in the Search box.

3. **Click a link that interests you from the search results page.**

   After you click the Search button, you see a page with the results of your search. Each result has the site's title and a brief abstract taken directly from the page. You can use these to determine whether the site contains information that you're interested in before visiting it.

A Photo Is Worth a Thousand Words

In Chapter 1, we discuss the value of photographs in your genealogical research. But a lot of us don't have photographs of our family beyond two or three generations, though it sure would be great to find at least an electronic copy of a picture of your great-great-grandfathers. Actually, a picture of your great-great-grandfather may exist. Another researcher may have posted it on a personal site or the photograph may be part of a collection belonging to a certain organization. You may also be interested in pictures of places where your ancestors lived. Being able to describe how a certain town, estate, or farm looked at the time your ancestor lived there adds color to your family history.

You can find various types of photographic sites on the Internet that can assist you with your research. Some of these sites explain the photographic process and the many types of photographs that have been used throughout history, some sites contain collections of photographs from a certain geographic area or time period in history, and some sites contain photographs of the ancestors of a particular family. Here are some examples:

✔ **General Information:** City Gallery has a brief explanation of the types of photography used during the nineteenth century, a photography query page, and a gallery of photographs from one studio of the period. (See Figure 8-2.) The Web site is `www.city-gallery.com/learning`

✔ **Photograph Collections:**

You can find images of the American West and Civil War at

`www.treasurenet.com/images/`

Here's the site for American Memory: Photographs, Prints, and Drawings:

`memory.loc.gov/cgi-bin/query/S?ammem/collections:@field (FLD003+@band(origf+Photograph)):heading=Original+Format%3 a+Photos+&+Prints`

The Florida Photographic Collection also has digitized photographs:

`www.floridamemory.com/PhotographicCollection`

✔ **Photograph Identification:**

The DeadFred Genealogy Photo Archive contains over 30,000 photographs at

`www.deadfred.com`

Each photograph includes descriptive information including where the photograph was taken, the names of the subjects, and an approximate time frame. (see Figure 8-3.)

✔ **Personal Photographs:**

The Harrison Genealogy Repository site is an example of a personal Web site with a photo gallery:

`freepages.genealogy.rootsweb.com/~harrisonrep/Photos/ harrphot.htm`

The gallery includes the likenesses of several famous Harrisons, including Benjamin Harrison V, President William Henry Harrison, and President Benjamin Harrison.

To find photographic sites, you may want to visit one of the comprehensive genealogy sites or general Internet search engines mentioned in The *Genealogy Online For Dummies* Internet Directory in this book.

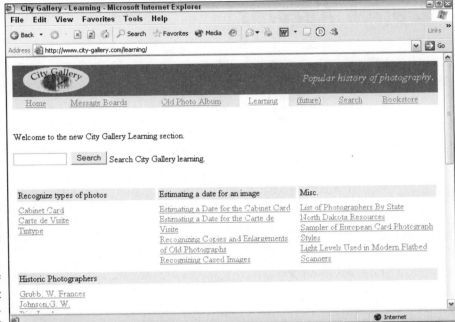

Figure 8-2:
Learn about photo-graphic methods of the past at City Gallery.

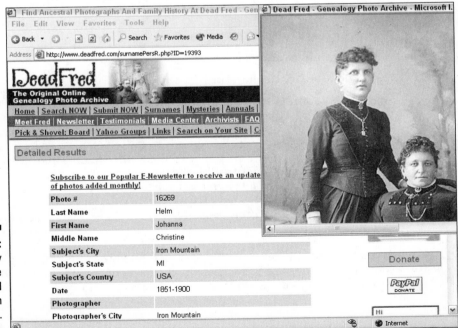

Figure 8-3:
An entry on the Dead Fred photograph archive site.

Adoption Records

Adoption records are of interest to a lot of genealogists, including those who were adopted themselves, those who gave up children for adoption, and those who have ancestors who were adopted.

If you fall into the first two groups (you were adopted or gave up a child for adoption), some online resources may help you find members of your birth family. The online resources include registries, reference materials, advice and discussion groups, and information on legislation pertaining to adoption. Registries enable you to post information about yourself and your adoption with the hope that a member of your birth family may see the posting and contact you. (Likewise, if you're the birth parent of an adoptee, you can post a message with the hope that the adoptee sees it and responds.)

Unfortunately, you won't find online sites that contain actual adoption records — for legal reasons, generally. Instead, you need to rely on registries and other resources that point you toward more substantial information about adoption. If you have a successful reunion with your birth parent(s) by registering with an online site, then with any luck you can obtain information about their parents, grandparents, and so on — so you know where to begin your genealogical pursuit of that family line.

Here are some online sites that have adoption registries, reference materials, advice and discussions, and/or legislative information:

- ✔ **Adoptees Internet Mailing List:** www.aiml.org
- ✔ **AdoptioNetwork:** www.adoption.org
- ✔ **AdoptionLinks.com:** links.adoption.com
- ✔ **Reclaiming My Roots Registry Database:** www.geocities.com/ Heartland/Hills/2638/

If you're interested in adoption records because you have ancestors who were adopted, you may have a more difficult time finding information. We have yet to discover any sites specifically designed to aid in research for adopted ancestors. In fact, you may have to rely on the regular genealogical resources — particularly query pages and discussion groups — and the kindness and knowledge of other researchers to find information about your adopted ancestors.

If you're searching for general types of adoption resources, using a general Internet directory like Yahoo! may be the best course of action. To find resources using Yahoo!, try this:

1. **Open your Web browser and go to Yahoo! at** www.yahoo.com.

   Note: If you need a refresher on operating a Web browser, see Appendix A.

2. **Click the <u>Society And Culture</u> link, and click the <u>Families</u> link.**

   A second way to find items in Yahoo! (this may be a lot faster): You can type a search term in the box near the top of the screen and have Yahoo! search for the topic. For example, you can type **Adoption** in the box and click the Search button, which produces a results page that has links to take you directly to the appropriate page in Yahoo! containing adoption links.

3. **Under the Families category, click the <u>Adoption</u> link.**

   This takes you directly to the adoption page — even though it's a couple of levels down in the directory's hierarchy.

4. **Click a link to another subdirectory in Yahoo! or a link to an Internet site containing information that interests you.**

   Descriptions follow most of the links in Yahoo! to give you an idea of what kind of information is on the sites. Figure 8-4 shows an example of a Yahoo! page.

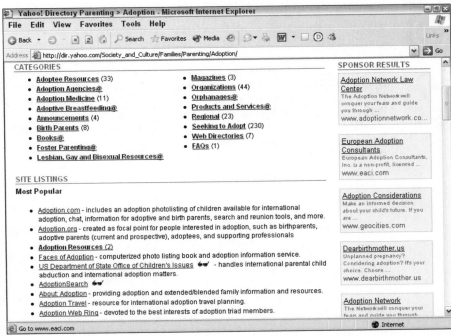

Figure 8-4:
The Adoption subcategory page at Yahoo!.

It's in the Genes: Molecular Genealogy

Just think of the possibilities — one of these days genealogical research will be as simple as rubbing a cotton swab in your mouth and submitting it to a lab that compares your DNA to that of other researchers from around the world. The lab would then send you a report showing your ancestors eight or more generations back.

While this entire scenario is not yet possible, *molecular* (or *genetic,* if you prefer) *genealogy* is an area that has captured the imagination of researchers over the past few years. Private companies now provide tests that can be used by genealogists to help determine ancestor relationships. Some are even encouraging researchers to establish surname project groups where the DNA results from several people are used to map their relationships to ancestors with the same surname (and, as a result, to each other).

The following Web sites contain more information on DNA services.

✔ **Family Tree DNA:** www.familytreedna.com

✔ **Oxford Ancestors:** www.oxfordancestors.com

The About.com Genetic Genealogy page (genealogy.about.com/cs/geneticgenealogy) contains a list of testing services, as well as articles on tracing family trees using DNA and tracing medical histories.

Of course, you can trace medical histories without sampling your relatives' DNA — all you have to do is ask about health problems or conditions and look for health-related records when you're digging through the attic. Once you've gathered some health-related information, you can store it in your genealogical database or in a program that was created specifically for holding medical information. We include a demo of just such a program — Geneweaver — on the CD-ROM that accompanies this book.

The *Genealogy Online For Dummies* Internet Directory

The 5th Wave   By Rich Tennant

"The good news is that I've located Pinocchio's natural mother. The bad news is she's part of the parquet flooring at a bowling alley in upstate New York."

In this directory . . .

*L*ooking for an overview of the types of sites you can find online? Well, look no further. This directory identifies some of the sites you'll find on the Internet and gives a brief abstract of what you find at each site. We also provide some descriptive narratives telling you why these types of sites are useful to you. Among our examples are all sorts of search engines (genealogically focused and otherwise), comprehensive genealogical sites, and resources that are surname-related, government-sponsored, geographic-specific, or commercial in nature. We organized the examples in the directory according to the following order:

- ✔ Booksellers and publishers
- ✔ Comprehensive genealogical Web sites
- ✔ Hard-to-find records
- ✔ Professional researchers
- ✔ Search engines
- ✔ Software information
- ✔ Surname-related Web pages

Recognizing Micons

For each site, we provide the name of the site, the URL (Web address), and a brief description of what you can find there. Also, the mini icons (*micons,* as we like to call 'em) tell you at first glance what kinds of resources the site offers. Here's a list of the micons and what each one means:

Queries: At this site, you can post genealogical questions pertaining to surnames, geographic locations, or research in general, or read and respond to queries left by other researchers.

Online database: This site includes an online database of genealogical information. By online database, we mean a collection of data that may include any of the following: information known about a family or surname, indexes, and other such collections of information.

Online records: Here you find transcribed and/or digitized records with genealogical value. The information at this site is either in the form of transcriptions from actual records (such as vital records, military personnel files, census returns, and so on) or digitized (scanned) copies of actual records.

FAQs: Find answers to those Frequently Asked Questions about a particular aspect of genealogical research at this site.

Searchable: This site has a search engine you can use to look for keywords and/or surnames.

Index: This site includes a section listing genealogical resources (including other genealogical sites, types of records, and information from actual records).

GEDCOM: This software supports GEDCOM, the standard for sharing data between genealogical programs.

Post to Web: This software enables you to take information from the database and post it directly to the Web.

On the CD: A version of this software is included on the CD-ROM that accompanies this book.

Book: This software has features that enable you to put together your own genealogical book containing charts, forms, photographs, and reports you generate using the data you enter into that software.

Online ordering: Here you can place online orders for genealogical books or supplies.

Multimedia: This software supports the use of photographs, sound, or video in your genealogy.

Download: You can download software at the URL indicated.

Charge for Services: You must pay a fee to use some or all of the services at this site (or described at this site).

Booksellers and Publishers

Sometimes a specific book about a particular surname, geographic location, or event in history can be difficult to find. After all, not all local bookstores or libraries have the best collections of genealogical books and supplies. In fact, most of the bookstores we've been to carry somewhere around 10 to 20 titles on genealogy, and that's about it.

When you can't find that certain book you're looking for in the local bookstore or library, online bookstores and publishers come in handy. These online resources identify books and other products that they publish and/or sell, and most of them tell you how you can order from them. (Even if you can't order online from them, their Web sites tell you how you can order by mail or phone.) Following is a list of some online bookstores and publishers that specialize in genealogy-related materials. If you want to see a more extensive listing of genealogy bookstores, visit a comprehensive genealogy Web site. (See the next section for more information about comprehensive sites.)

Ancestry.com

shops.ancestry.com

Ancestry.com is best known as the publisher of *The Source: A Guidebook of American Genealogy,* and the two magazines *Ancestry* and *Genealogical Computing.* Its Web site contains information about books and electronic products that are available for online purchase. Other parts of the Ancestry.com site offer resources for genealogists, including searchable databases, informational columns by well-known genealogists, and message boards. Although a decent number of Ancestry.com's online services are free, some of its online services are restricted to subscribers. The Web site provides detailed information about what's restricted to subscribers and how to subscribe.

Family History Network

www.familyhistorynetwork.net

The Family History Network is what used to be known as Everton Publishers, the long-time publisher of the popular *Everton's Genealogical Helper* magazine, which is now called *Family History Magazine.* Family History Network is also the publisher of many books, including *The Handybook for Genealogists.* The Web site provides detailed information about the Family History Network's products and services. Also, it has a members-only section (called Online Helper) that offers discounts on orders, access to professional researchers, an annual subscription to *Family History Magazine,* and searchable access to articles from past issues.

Frontier Press Bookstore

www.frontierpress.com/frontier.cgi

Frontier Press Bookstore specializes in providing genealogical and historical books, CD-ROMs, and audio tapes. The Frontier Web site has an online catalog you can browse by subject, as well as listings of new publications that are available and a bargain basement where you can find special deals. After you determine which books you'd like, you can order by e-mail, mail, phone, or fax.

Genealogical.com

www.genealogical.com

Genealogical.com is the online storefront for the Genealogical Publishing Company, a large publisher of genealogical books, and Clearfield Company (a publisher of family histories for individuals). This Web site provides a catalog of books that are published by and available from Genealogical Publishing Company, as well as a listing of releases on CD-ROM. You can search the site using keywords or browse through the many categories of offerings, and then order a product that captures your interest (whether online, by fax, mail, e-mail, or phone).

GenealogyDirect.com

www.genealogydirect.com

GenealogyDirect.com provides an online source for all sorts of genealogical books, maps, and CD-ROMs. In particular, it is an outlet for its sister-site's digital images of microfilmed records — those produced for online use at Sources2Go.com. Once you find the particular product you need, you can order it online or by mail.

GlobalGenealogy.com, Inc.

www.globalgenealogy.com

GlobalGenealogy.com is the Internet-based shopping experience for all things genealogical. The site offers books, videos, software, CD-ROMs, maps, microfilm, and archival and *scrapbooking* supplies (items for preservation of documents and photos) for purchase online. The online store has a sister-operation that's a physical store in Milton, Ontario — called the Global Genealogy & History Shoppe. Global Heritage Press (GlobalHeritagePress.com) is the publishing arm of GlobalGenealogy.com and prints genealogical and historical books. GlobalGenealogy.com also offers a free online newsletter — called *The Global Gazette* — for genealogical research in Canada (GlobalGazette.net).

Heritage Books, Inc.

www.heritagebooks.com

Heritage Books, Inc., publishes genealogical and historical books and CD-ROMs, as well as an e-mail newsletter called *The Heritage Town Crier*. Its Web site provides information about all of its publications and supports online shopping for its products. Heritage Books, Inc. is also the parent company of Willow Bend Books (www.willowbendbooks.com), an online store and a physical-store that sells over 13,000 genealogical products.

Heritage Quest

www.heritagequest.com

Heritage Quest publishes a variety of resources on book and CD-ROM. It also offers all of its genealogical products for sale online. In addition to information about titles for sale, Heritage Quest's Web site includes information about the U.S. federal censuses, Genealogy 101 (an Internet-based tutorial on genealogy), and a query section where you can post messages.

The Institute of Heraldic and Genealogical Studies Family History Bookshop

www.ihgs.ac.uk/institute/bookshop.html

The Institute of Heraldic and Genealogical Studies Family History Bookshop is physically located in England. It has books that are geographic-specific in nature (covering England, Scotland, Wales, and Ireland), as well as heraldic titles and books specifically for beginners to genealogy as well as for advanced researchers. Its Web site includes a list of publications available from the Family History Bookshop. The Bookshop also offers research aids including maps, charts, and pamphlets, along with visual-aid kits for use in teaching others about genealogy.

Comprehensive Sites

A *comprehensive* genealogical site is one that identifies a large number of other sites of interest to genealogists, especially those containing information on surnames, families, locations, or a variety of other subjects. Most comprehensive sites have the names and URLs indexed in some manner — usually broken down into categories. Some people refer to these comprehensive sites as large genealogical *indexes* or *listings*.

Most comprehensive sites are relatively easy to navigate because they categorize and cross-index their links to other genealogical sites. As long as you know the topic you're looking for, you can glance through the listing and see what's available. For example, if you're looking for American Revolutionary War records for the state of Massachusetts, you can visit a comprehensive site and look in its sections pertaining to the American Revolution, military records, and the state of Massachusetts.

Some comprehensive sites make searching even easier through the use of a search engine. Rather than clicking through the hierarchy of categories and subcategories to find a list of links pertaining to the topic in which you're interested, you can enter a keyword into a form and let the search engine do the work for you. Typically, the search engine returns the results in the form of a list of possible matches to your keyword; from that abbreviated list, you pick sites to visit.

Here are a few of the comprehensive genealogical sites you can find online, along with descriptions of their features.

Cyndi's List of Genealogy Sites on the Internet

www.cyndislist.com/

This popular site by Cyndi Howells has over 204,000 links indexed and cross-indexed by topic in more than 150 categories. The categories are based on ethnic groups, religious groups, geographic locations, products (such as books and software), types of records, learning resources (such as beginner information, how-to, and writing a family history), and other interests (for example, adoption, reunions, royalty, and travel).

Genealogy Home Page

www.genealogyhomepage.com

The Genealogy Home Page was the very first comprehensive genealogical site. It classifies Internet genealogical sites in 15 areas, including Genealogy Help and Guides, Internet Genealogy Guides, Religious Genealogy Resources, and Upcoming Genealogy Events. Two unique aspects of Genealogy Home Page are the FTP site and the "What's New" sections. The Genealogy Anonymous FTP Site is a collection of downloadable freeware, shareware, archived ROOTS-L files, and other FTP files. And in the "What's New" and "What's Really New in WWW Genealogy Pages" sections, you can find frequently updated lists of new sites on the Web or sites that are newly listed in the Genealogy Home Page.

Genealogy Resources on the Internet

www-personal.umich.edu/~cgaunt/gen_int1.html

Christine Gaunt and John Fuller work together to bring you Genealogy Resources on the Internet. This comprehensive site identifies online resources by type of resource. It includes sections on mailing lists, USENET newsgroups, anonymous FTP, Gopher, World Wide Web, Telnet, and e-mail. The Web resources are sorted by various topics including geographic-specific, ethnic, and descriptive. Several sections not only identify and link to resources, but also explain in detail what each resource is and how to use it.

Helm's Genealogy Toolbox

www.genealogytoolbox.com

Helm's Genealogy Toolbox started simply as a list of links on Matthew's first Web page in the fall of 1994 and became the second comprehensive genealogical index when he moved the links to their own site in early 1995 — at that time, there were 134 links. Now the index is part of a larger, integrated site (still known as Helm's Genealogy Toolbox) and contains links divided into seven top-level categories: Computers, How-To and Help, Media, People, Places, Supplies and Services, and Original Records. The index is completely searchable (along with the other parts of the site) using the Global Search function.

Elusive Records

Some unique records and resources can be of great value to you in your genealogical pursuits. Some records pertain to a particular group of people; others are commonly-thought-of records that are just hard to find because of past disasters (fire, war, and government changes). Here are some examples of sites that fit the bill.

Cemeteries in and around Gunning Shire, New South Wales

gundaroo.alphalink.com.au/genealogy/cemeteries/

Graeme Challinor visited and cataloged graves and memorials at cemeteries in and around Gunning Shire in New South Wales, Australia. For each cemetery that he visited, he includes the exact coordinates (longitude and latitude), the size of the cemetery, miscellaneous information about the cemetery or its surroundings, an area diagram, and transcriptions of the inscriptions on every gravestone in the cemetery. In all, he provides information on 28 cemeteries.

Chicago City Council Proceedings Files Index, 1833–1871

www.sos.state.il.us/departments/archives/data_chi.html

The Illinois State Archives, in conjunction with the University of Illinois at Chicago, provide an online index of the more than 35,000 files that document the Chicago City

Council Proceedings between 1833 and 1871. These files, thought to have been lost in the Great Fire in 1871 until they were rediscovered in 1983, contain the working papers and documents of the city council. You can search this index by subject term or by date. For each record identified in the index, there's a file title, calendar and/or fiscal year for the file, file number, and filing month and date. If you find the index for a file in which you're interested, you can then use the control number to write to the Illinois Regional Archives Depository to get a copy.

Gold Rush

www.calgoldrush.com/index.html

This Gold Rush site is published by *The Sacramento Bee* and accompanies a series that the paper ran. The information is divided into three parts:

Part 1: Gold! An Era Remembered: This part provides a general overview of the Gold Rush and the California lands in which gold was discovered.

Part 2: At Work and Play: This part has articles describing California society during the Gold Rush and includes information about the legal system, religion and culture, and even the food that was popular in the area at that time.

Part 3: Chasing a Dream: This part describes the people who played a part in the Gold Rush including those who were Mexican, American Indian, African American, Chinese, Japanese, and female.

Green County, Arkansas Poor Farm

www.rootsweb.com/~argreene/
　grecpofa.htm

This site contains historical information about the county-government-run farm in

Green County, Arkansas, where some poor people were sent to live and work. In addition to the historical narrative, there are articles that appeared in nearby newspapers and transcribed census listings for 1900, 1910, 1920, and 1930, and a couple of photographs of the farm.

Inmates of the Ohio State Penitentiary

www.witsend.org/gen/marion/
　badguys.htm

This site contains abstracts of information about inmates serving time in the Ohio State Penitentiary in Columbus, Ohio, during the years 1834 through 1875. Each abstract includes the inmate's name, county information, record and volume number, sentence, status, age, birthplace, occupation, physical description of the offender, and general information about the offender and his family.

Searching for Birth Relatives

www.adoptions.com/aecsearch.html

This is an online article at the Adoptions.com Web site. It provides sources where you can get help when researching an adopted relative's birth family, as well as some general information about adoption research.

Seeking Birth Parents

www.genealogytoday.com/adoption/

Part of the Genealogy Today Web site, this page provides a free database where adoptees can post messages with the hopes that their birth parents will see them. It also offers articles with information about how to research adoptions, as well as links to some other adoption-related sites.

Ethnic Records

If your ancestors were members of a particular ethnic group, you probably want to find online sites that have records and information pertaining specifically to that group. Although not as prevalent as surname-related and geographic-specific Web sites, some ethnic resources are now available to help you. Here are a few sites geared to particular ethnic groups.

AfriGeneas

www.afrigeneas.com/

The AfriGeneas Web site is closely associated with and complements the AfriGeneas mailing list, which was created as a place to discuss family history research and promote genealogy, particularly as it pertains to African ancestry. A look at the site map shows the many resources, including a beginner's guide, slave data, a surname registry, and information about various projects. There is also a forum/chat area and information about the AfriGeneas mailing list and how to subscribe.

Christine's Genealogy Website

ccharity.com

Christine's Genealogy Website is a collection of online resources for African American genealogical research. It contains transcriptions of documents, indexes to records, historical information, and links to many other resources. You can read through the index of online resources, or you can search the site using keywords or names.

Civil War Soldiers & Sailors System

www.itd.nps.gov/cwss/

This well-designed and interesting Web site contains a searchable database of more than 5 million names of soldiers and sailors who served during the Civil War. (The database also includes the names of soldiers who served in the United States Colored Troops.) To use the database, click the link for the category in which you wish to search: Soldiers, Sailors, Regiments, Cemeteries, Battles, Prisoners, Medals of Honor, or National Parks. The site then walks you through how to search that particular area of the database, and returns a list of results based on your search terms.

The Genealogy of Mexico

members.tripod.com/~GaryFelix/
    index1.htm

The Genealogy of Mexico is an interesting site that contains historical information and lists of conquistadors, early settlers, members of expedition parties, and personal genealogical findings for several families.

Indians.org

www.indians.org./index.html

In addition to a section recommending how to research American Indian heritage, this site offers information about current efforts. Also, under the Resource Directory link, the American Indian Resource Directory contains a list of all the American Indian tribes recognized by the United States government. The list is sorted by geographic area of the country.

National Archives and Records Administration: African American Research

www.archives.gov/research_room/geneal
ogy/research_topics/african_american_
research.html

The National Archives and Records Administration (NARA) offers several online lessons and copies of publications for researching African American ancestors. NARA provides FAQs and online catalogs of its traditional resources, as well as explains how and where you can get copies of records, publications, and microfilms.

National Archives and Records Administration: Native American Research

www.archives.gov/research_room/geneal
ogy/research_topics/native_american_
records.html

The National Archives and Records Administration (NARA) offers several online lessons and copies of publications for researching American Indian ancestors. NARA provides FAQs and online catalogs of its traditional resources, as well as explains how and where you can get copies of records, publications, and microfilms.

NativeWeb

www.nativeweb.org

NativeWeb is a cooperative effort to provide a community on the Internet for aboriginal or native persons of the world. Click the Resource Center link to get a list of the categories of information at the site.

Family Associations

Sometimes distinguishing between one-name studies and family-association sites is difficult because their content is usually similar (see "One-Name Studies," later in this directory). However, generally every family association has an underlying organization; one-name studies do not. Formal family associations may focus on a surname as a whole or on a particular branch and, as a result, the association's Web site has the same focus. Similarly, projects that the family association is undertaking (such as writing a book or putting together a comprehensive database of information from all members) may carry over to the Web site. The most distinguishable characteristic is that the Web site may require you to be a member of the family association before you can fully participate at the site or access some of the information online.

MacDermot Clan Homepage

www.macdermot.com

The MacDermot Clan Homepage provides online family trees and a notice board where you can post messages about your genealogical research on a MacDermot or variations of that surname. Also, the site has all sorts of membership information, including how to join and some of the benefits that are limited to members. Some of these benefits are an online registry of all members and their e-mail addresses and receipt of the official clan journal.

The National Blue Family Association

members.tripod.com/blue_family/

In addition to a list of descendants of John Blaw (died 1757 in New Jersey), this site offers information about others with the surname Blue, Blu, Blew, Blau, Blawen, and Blaw. You'll also find information about joining the association, a listing of all known Blue/Blaw family reunions and past reunion photos, transcriptions from the Richard and Susanna Blue family Bible, and a registry of researchers with their e-mail addresses.

Peacock Family Association of the South

www.peacockfamily.org/

Regardless of its name, membership in this family association is open to anyone who's interested in the surname Peacock. The Web site identifies resources available from the association, including information about reunions and membership, photographs of some ancestors (and pictures from past reunions), GEDCOM files pertaining to Peacocks, and various downloadable files.

The Rutledge Family Association

www.rootsweb.com/~rutledge

Here, you can find information about membership in the Rutledge Family Association, and instructions for meeting others in the Rutledge Chat room to discuss your genealogical research. Also, you can find pages with Frequently Asked Questions, online Family Group Sheets submitted by other Rutledge researchers, photographs, a list of association members and their e-mail addresses, and queries.

Watkins Family History Society

www.watkins.org.au/index.shtml

The Watkins Family History Society collects and organizes genealogical information on all Watkins worldwide. You can download a copy of the Watkins Family Newsletter, or submit your research to the family tree project. Also the Association offers mailing lists, a message board where you can post queries, and links to other Watkins Web sites.

Genealogically Focused Search Engines

There are search engines specific to genealogy that employ technology similar to the general search engines; we think you'd find them useful. They cover significantly fewer links than do general search engines, limiting the number of indexed sites that aren't related to a genealogy focus for your search.

GenealogyPortal.com

www.genealogyportal.com

A joint project by The Genealogy Home Page and Helm's Genealogy Toolbox, GenealogyPortal.com features eight different genealogically focused search engines. Each search engine focuses on a particular subject area, including Archives and Libraries, Guides to Research, Historical Sites, Location-Specific Research, Names and Personal Sites, Primary Records, Research Supplies, and Software and Utilities.

Origin Search

www.originsearch.com/help/about.aspx

 $

Origin Search is a fee-based search engine that focuses on searching for individual ancestors by name. It currently indexes over 434 million names and allows users to save searches (so that they can be notified when new search results appear).

General Search Engines

You've probably been hearing about the Big Guys (the major search engines, that is) ever since you first ventured online. *Search engines* are programs that search large indexes of information gathered by online robots (sometimes called *spiders*) sent out to catalog resources on the Internet. Typically, the search engine has an interface form where you can enter keywords to search for in the index. The engine then searches its index and returns its findings to you online with links directly to the pages where the search engine's robot identified the keywords.

Although we don't recommend starting your online genealogical research using one of the major search engines (see Chapter 4 for the reasons), they may be the only place left to go for some leads if you hit a brick wall in your research. Maybe the comprehensive sites didn't identify enough resources pertaining to a particular religious or ethnic group, and the searchable genealogical pages had only surname information. Where do you turn? To the Big Guys, of course.

Because a search on one name or word likely will result in thousands — even hundreds of thousands — of results, follow the particular engine's instructions for narrowing your search. Typically this means using more than one word in your search and

avoiding really common words altogether. (For example, if you're using a common surname, such as Johnson, you should narrow your list by including other details you know — such as the first name, a known or suspected location for that person, and/or dates. Also, you don't want to include *the, a,* and *of* in your search, or you get an unmanageable number of results if the search engine doesn't automatically ignore those words.) Reviewing the information that the search engine site provides online is a good idea and a quick way to learn new methods of narrowing your searches.

AltaVista

www.altavista.com

Using the main search box on AltaVista searches its index of Internet sites. Check out the Help section — or customize your settings — to narrow your search results. If you prefer not to search, you can find links of interest by clicking through the categories listed in the AltaVista directory of categories. And if you'd like to focus your search on information from or about a particular country — or in a language other than English — click the <u>Settings</u> link and follow the instructions.

Ask Jeeves

www.ask.com

At Ask Jeeves, you can either enter a keyword, search term, or an actual question to submit for your search. You can also limit your search to particular areas of the search engine site, such as searching only pictures or news. There's also a section set aside specifically for kids (appropriately called Ask Jeeves Kids), which includes educational reference tools (like a dictionary, thesaurus, world atlas, and math help).

Excite

www.excite.com

Excite has a directory of subjects from which you can choose to look for sites of interest to you. Like the other search engines with directories, you click the subject of interest that takes you to a submenu where you can select a more specific topic to get down to links to actual sites on that topic. Or you can use the search engine to look for particular keywords in Excite's databases of Web sites.

Google

www.google.com

The Google search engine is a no-nonsense sort of site. Its main page is simple — you notice the search interface field, two buttons from which to choose, the total number of Web sites that Google has indexed, and a few links to other parts of the Google site. Simply enter your search term in the field, and click Google Search. (Of course, if you're optimistic that Google will find the perfect site you're looking for, you may choose to select the I'm Feeling Lucky button instead.) To narrow your search, check out the Advanced Search function and follow the instructions. If you prefer to use the search engine's directory of links instead, click the Directory link. Or if you're interested in checking out the latest on various newsgroups, click the Groups link.

Lycos

www.lycos.com

Lycos allows you to click through a list of subjects and their submenus to locate sites of interest, or you can use the search engine to look for keywords. It even offers Parental Controls on its search function so younger or sensitive users in your household can have restricted searches in which certain types of sites are weeded out of the results list. You may want to check out the Advanced Search feature to narrow your searches. And although this main Lycos page is in English, Lycos offers its pages in several other languages. (You can select the language you want from the list at the bottom of the page.)

WebCrawler

www.webcrawler.com

WebCrawler is a one-stop shop for searching other major search engines and Internet directory sites, including Google, Yahoo!, AltaVista, Ask Jeeves, About, and LookSmart.

Government Resources

If you're like us, you probably groan and grumble about paying taxes and sometimes even wonder what exactly the government is using your good tax dollars for. Maybe you're lucky, and all you have to do is go down to your local library or courthouse where you find efficient operations and friendly government employees who give you the assurance your tax dollars are being well spent. With the increasing popularity of the Internet, it is now a little easier for some of us to see our tax dollars at work — helping spread useful information along the superhighway. Here are some sites — either created by government entities or containing government-related information and records — that contain helpful information for genealogists.

Social Security Death Index

ssdi.genealogy.rootsweb.com

The United States government (through the Social Security Administration) assigns a unique nine-digit number to everyone who lives and works in the United States. The purpose of this number is to track who's eligible for Social Security benefits (sort of a supplemental retirement income) after they reach a certain age.

Whenever a claim for death benefits is filed with the Social Security Administration, the government adds the person's name and some other information to the Master Death Index. If your ancestors lived and worked in the United States, the Social Security Death Index can be useful in your genealogical pursuits, and RootsWeb's online interface to search the index makes it easy to check and see whether your ancestors are included.

To search the database of over 71 million names, go to the search site, enter your ancestor's name, and click Search. (Only the last name is required, but knowing the first name can be helpful.) Also, to narrow the search, you may want to complete any other fields on the form for which you have information. After you complete the form and click Search, you get a list of persons matching your search. Besides the person's name, the list includes the Social Security number, date born, date died, residence, Zip code to which the person's last Social Security benefit was sent, state in which the person's Social Security card was issued, and date that the card was issued.

Archives of Mechelen (Belgium)

www.mechelen.be/archief/

This site provides general information about the hours and holdings of the Archives of Mechelen. Some of the records held by the archives include birth, death, marriage, population, and parish registries, property records, tax lists, and a registry of abandoned children.

National Archives of Australia

www.naa.gov.au

The mission of the Australian Archives is to preserve Commonwealth records and make them accessible to the public. Some of the Archives' services include public reference, an archival library, and maintaining personnel records of those Australians who served in World War I. The Web site provides information about the Archives' collections, publications, and exhibitions.

Other Australian Sites to Check Out

State Records: New South Wales
www.records.nsw.gov.au

Queensland Government State Archives
www.archives.qld.gov.au

State Records of South Australia
www.archives.sa.gov.au

Archives Office of Tasmania
www.tased.edu.au/archives

Public Record Office of Victoria
www.prov.vic.gov.au/

State Library of Western Australia
www.liswa.wa.gov.au

Northern Territory Archives Service
www.nt.gov.au/nta

Bureau of Land Management, Eastern States, General Land Office, Official Land Patents Records Site

www.glorecords.blm.gov

The Bureau of Land Management, General Land Office site contains a searchable database and digitized Federal land patent records for 33 states. Simply click the Search Land Patents link in the upper left corner of the main page, provide your Zip code, and follow the instructions to complete the online form to search the land patents database. (If you need additional help, there's a Search Tips page you can access from a link at the bottom of the search form.) The system returns a list of potential matches for your search criteria, from which you can choose to see more details and a digitized copy of the land record.

Canadian Archival Resources on the Internet

www.usask.ca/archives/menu.html

Canadian Archival Resources on the Internet provides just that — an index of archives in Canada that have Web sites. In addition to some basic information about the types of archives, this site has links to each of the archival resources identified. The various archives are categorized as provincial, university, municipal, religious, medical, and other. They're also cross-categorized by region (western, central, eastern, and national).

Danish State Archives

www.sa.dk

The Danish State Archives home page is, as you would expect, in Danish. It is also available in an English version. It provides general information about the Archives, as well as a Genealogy section that provides a genealogical dictionary and information about various types of records, naming traditions, and handwriting techniques.

General Register Office (Northern Ireland)

www.groni.gov.uk/

The General Register Office (GRO) maintains statutory registers of vital events — births, deaths, and marriages. Although the registers themselves aren't available for public use, you can order copies of certificates that contain information from the registers. This site explains in detail exactly what is available, how to order copies of

certificates, what you must include when requesting certificates, and the costs for doing so.

General Register Office (Scotland)

www.gro-scotland.gov.uk/

The General Register Office (GRO) is the government agency responsible for registering births, deaths, marriages, divorces, and adoptions in Scotland. It's also responsible for conducting censuses of Scotland's population. The GRO Web site is well organized and easy to use. Clicking the Searching Historical Records under the Family Records section brings you to a helpful list of Frequently Asked Questions (FAQs). You can find an alphabetical index identifying records and how to use them, annual reports and statistical information about the GRO, and services that the GRO offers (including evening visits for genealogical groups).

Library of Congress

www.loc.gov

Although not officially recognized as the national library of the United States, this is what the Library of Congress has become since its inception in 1800. The Library now holds approximately 19 million books, 56 million manuscripts, 12 million photographs, 4.8 million maps, and 2.6 million recordings. The Library of Congress Web site explains its many research tools, including searchable Library of Congress catalogs; country studies and area handbooks; a database with information pertaining to U.S. military personnel who were killed, missing in action, or imprisoned in Southeast Asia during the Vietnam conflict; and U.S. Copyright Office records from 1978 to the present. Of special interest is the American Memory: Historical Collections section. Part of the Library of Congress

National Digital Library Program, American Memory provides digitized and transcribed historical documents you can view on the Internet.

National Archives and Records Administration: United States

**www.archives.gov/research_room/
genealogy/index.html**

The mission of the National Archives and Records Administration (NARA) is to provide access to evidence documenting the rights of American citizens, actions of federal officials, and the national experience. Among the resources at NARA's Web site are a couple of sections of special interest to genealogists. The Genealogy Page provides information about records held by NARA pertaining directly to individuals — including census returns, military service records, and passenger lists. The section explains how to use NARA and its resources in your genealogical research. You may also find interesting the section containing information about historical records for government agencies, particularly if events surrounding or prompted by one of these agencies had a direct impact on your ancestors and/or the area in which they lived. NARA has regional facilities across the United States, containing microfilmed copies of the records of interest to genealogists. Their Web sites (which provide their hours and locations and identify resources held by the branch) can be found at the following addresses:

Northeast Region: Boston
www.archives.gov/facilities/ma/
boston.html

Northeast Region: Pittsfield, Massachusetts
www.archives.gov/facilities/ma/
pittsfield.html

Northeast Region: New York City
www.archives.gov/facilities/ny/new_york_
city.html

Mid Atlantic Region: Philadelphia
www.archives.gov/midatlantic/index.html

Southeast Region: Atlanta
www.archives.gov/facilities/ga/
atlanta.html

Great Lakes Region: Chicago
www.archives.gov/facilities/il/chicago.html

Great Lakes Region: Dayton
www.archives.gov/facilities/oh/
dayton.html

Central Plains Region: Kansas City
www.archives.gov/facilities/mo/kansas_
city.html

Southwest Region: Fort Worth
www.archives.gov/facilities/tx/fort_
worth.html

Rocky Mountain Region: Denver
www.archives.gov/facilities/co/denver.html

Pacific Region: Laguna Niguel, California
www.archives.gov/facilities/ca/laguna_
niguel.html

Pacific Region: San Francisco (San Bruno)
www.archives.gov/facilities/ca/san_
francisco.html

Pacific Alaska Region: Seattle
www.archives.gov/facilities/wa/
seattle.html

Pacific Alaska Region: Anchorage
www.archives.gov/facilities/ak/
anchorage.html

National Personnel Records Center: St. Louis
www.archives.gov/facilities/mo/
st_louis.html

National Archives of Canada

www.archives.ca

The National Archives of Canada is tasked with preserving the memory of the nation and government of Canada and enhancing a sense of national identity. The Web site provides information about researching on location and contains detailed descriptions of the types of records held by the Archives. Among the many resources are civil registrations of births, marriages, and deaths dating from the nineteenth century, passenger manifests from 1865, immigration documents for people who arrived in Canada from U.S. borders, some naturalization records dating from 1828 to 1850, and petitions for land. Of particular interest to those with ancestors who served in the military is an online index of about 620,000 personnel folders for the citizens who enlisted in the Canadian Expeditionary Force (CEF) during World War I. The personnel folders contain various documents, including attestation and enlistment papers, medical records, discipline and pay records, and discharge papers. You can search the index online; if your search is successful, you can order copies of the documents from the personnel folder. The Web site explains how to do all this.

National Archives of Ireland

www.nationalarchives.ie/

The National Archives of Ireland Web site contains information to help you prepare to research in the Archives. It covers how to research on site, what records it has available to the public, and how to obtain copies. There are also indexes to record sets you can search online.

National Archives (United Kingdom)

www.nationalarchives.gov.uk/

Founded in 1838, the Public Records Office (PRO) served as the national archives for England, Wales, and the United Kingdom. In 2003, it was merged with the Historical Manuscripts Commission and the resulting agency became known as the National Archives. The National Archives is responsible for documents relating to British history, including records of the government and the courts, census information, and historical manuscripts of all sorts.

Public Record Office of Northern Ireland

proni.nics.gov.uk

The Public Record Office of Northern Ireland (PRONI) is the official depository for records of government agencies, courts, and other public offices, as well as for records contributed by businesses, institutions, churches, and individuals. The PRONI's Web site provides general information about the office, its resources and how to use them, publications, and exhibitions and events.

Local Connections

Most official information about your ancestors was recorded at a local level — in the towns, counties, parishes, or states where they lived. Online sites can help you whether you live near to or far from the areas where your relatives hailed. Sites that have a local flavor to them typically contain information (and, in some cases, records) specific to a geographical area. Here are some examples.

Australasian-Genealogy Web Resources: Australasia

home.vicnet.net.au/~AGWeb/agweb.htm

The Australasian-Genealogy Web (AGWeb) links together and provides access to regional genealogical resources. In addition to providing links to sites that are members of the network, AGWeb links to nonmember sites that have information pertaining to Australia. Of special interest to genealogists researching ancestors from the area is its section on Categories and Records, which contains transcribed files you can view online or download for use. The categories that have files associated with them include aborigines; civil registration; convicts; directories and almanacs; land records; local government records; manuscripts, letters, and diaries; newspapers; occupational records; passenger arrivals and departures; family histories and biographies; local histories; research directories and indexes; shipping; and genealogy-related.

CanadaGenWeb Project

www.rootsweb.com/~canwgw

The CanadaGenWeb Project helps researchers find the enormous amount of Canadian information available through the Internet. It is modeled after the USGenWeb project and has links to each of the main pages for the provinces/territories of Canada. Each territorial page has links for county/district pages, which provide links to resources for those areas. Additionally, the CanadaGenWeb page has a historical timeline of Canada, information about famous Canadians, and some facts and trivia about the country.

CaribbeanGenWeb Project

www.rootsweb.com/~caribgw

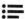

CaribbeanGenWeb has Web sites set up or planned for each island in order to provide information about and links to genealogical resources on the Internet that pertain to that particular island. Additionally, the main CaribbeanGenWeb page provides links to some resources that pertain to the Caribbean in general.

EuropeGenWeb Project

www.britishislesgenweb.org/
www.rootsweb.com/~ceneurgw
www.rootsweb.com/~easeurgw
www.mediterraneangenweb.com/

EuropeGenWeb is actually four sites:

BritishIslesGenWeb Project
(www.britishislesgenweb.org/)

CenEuroGenWeb Project
(www.rootsweb.com/~ceneurgw/)

EastEuropeGenWeb
(www.rootsweb.com/~easeurgw/)

MediterraneanGenWeb
(www.mediterraneangenweb.com/).

Each section provides information about and links to the WorldGenWeb pages for countries that are located in that particular area. Each WorldGenWeb page for such countries then provides information and links to genealogical resources on the Internet that pertain to that country, as well as links to any state/county/province pages that fall under the heading of the particular country.

GENUKI: UK + Ireland Genealogy

www.genuki.org.uk

The GENUKI service is intended to be a "virtual reference library" of primary historical and genealogical information in the United Kingdom and Ireland. The creators of GENUKI provide a comprehensive information service that covers all aspects of genealogy in the United Kingdom and Ireland, yet remains coherent and easy to use. Its structure is a four-level hierarchy corresponding to locality — from the British Isles as a whole down to each country within, to each county, to each parish. Its links are to sites that contain actual primary information, indexes of such information, or transcriptions or electronic images of actual records. Some of the subjects covered in GENUKI are archives and libraries, cemeteries, census, church records, civil registrations, colonization, heraldry, military, probate records, and taxation.

International Internet Genealogical Society

www.iigs.org

This site is available in 11 languages. The International Internet Genealogical Society (IIGS) helps the genealogy community find new and better ways to preserve and present records and information on the Internet to share with others. This site explains in detail the services and resources that are available from IIGS. Two ongoing projects include an IIGS University, which holds online classes about genealogical research, and an Internet Relay Chat, where genealogists can go to discuss research and ideas.

Middle EastGenWeb Project

www.rootsweb.com/~mdeastgw/

Middle EastGenWeb provides information about and links to the WorldGenWeb pages for countries that are located in the Middle East. Each page for these countries then provides information and links to genealogical resources on the Internet that pertain to that country, as well as links to any state/county/province pages that fall under the particular country.

Perry-Castañeda Library Map Collection

www.lib.utexas.edu/Libs/PCL/Map_collection/Map_collection.html

The Perry-Castañeda Library Map Collection at the University of Texas at Austin has online copies of various continent, country, state/territory/province, and county outline maps. This main Web page provides links to pages for several continents and countries, as well as outline county maps for the state of Texas. It also has historical maps and city maps.

South AmericanGenWeb Project

www.rootsweb.com/~sthamgw

The South AmericanGenWeb Project provides information about and links to the WorldGenWeb pages for countries that are located in South America. Each WorldGenWeb page for such countries then provides information and links to genealogical resources on the Internet that pertain to that country, as well as links to any state/county/province pages that fall under the heading of the particular country.

United States Internet Genealogical Society

www.usigs.org/

The United States Internet Genealogical Society (USIGS) is just that — an online genealogical society. Its Web site provides a history of the organization and explains its current projects.

USGenWeb Project

www.usgenweb.org

The USGenWeb Project provides Web sites for every county in every state in the United States. Each Web site is tasked with identifying genealogical resources that are available on the Internet for its particular county. This main site provides links to all the state pages, which, in turn, provide links to existing county pages. It also contains information about the USGenWeb's Archives project and explains how you can become involved in the USGenWeb.

World Factbook

www.odci.gov/cia/publications/factbook/
index.html

The Central Intelligence Agency's World Factbook site provides information on every country and ocean in the world. The country pages are accessible from this main page through the pull-down menu at the top. Each country page includes a map and the geographical location of the country, as well as detailed information about the country's flag, geography, people, government, economy, transportation, communication, and defense. The pages for the oceans contain a map and geographical location, as well as information about the ocean's geography, economy, and transportation.

WorldGenWeb Project

www.worldgenweb.org

The goal of the WorldGenWeb Project is to have a Web site for every country in the world that would contain information about and links to genealogical resources on the Internet. Although many of the countries have pages, more still need volunteers.

One-Name Studies

Unlike personal Web pages, which provide you with detailed information about an individual's research and particular branch of a family, one-name studies give you a wide range of information on one particular surname. Usually the information presented at these sites is not constrained by geographic boundaries — in other words, the site may have information about the surname in several different countries. One-name studies typically have information that includes histories of the surname (including its origins), variations in spelling, heraldry associated with the name, and databases and queries submitted by researchers worldwide.

Chicken Family Histories

ourworld.compuserve.com/homepages/
Chicken_Matthews/homepage.htm

Chicken Family Histories is "intended to be a focus for ALL Chickens and their descendants across the world." The Master Coop tells you about the origins of the Chicken surname, and the Chicken Scratchings section has information about some better-known Chickens. Geoff Matthews, the site's creator, also provides a narrative genealogy on his Matthews-Chicken ancestors and the surnames of some of his other ancestors. The various poultry graphics and play-on-words at this site make it fun to visit even if you're not a "Chicken-chaser!"

The Gyllenhaal Family Tree Project

www.gyllenhaal.org/

This is an international effort to collect and share as much information as possible on the Gyllenhaal surname. There's lots of information about Gyllenhaal descendants in Sweden and North America. A growing database is available for viewing at the site, as well as information on the surname and Coats of Arms. You can also find online biographies and photographs of some Gyllenhaals, and transcriptions (in Swedish and English) of the letter ennobling Nils Gunnarsson Gyllenhaal in 1672.

Kelton Family HomePage

www.kelton.org/

The Kelton Family HomePage is an online repository for any information pertaining to families with the surname Kelton. It has an exchange section where you can post questions and general information about your Kelton ancestors. Additionally, it has sections with stories about some Keltons, family registers, information about Keltons in census records, and links to other sites of interest to those researching the Kelton name. This site is easy to navigate and has online forms you can use to submit any information you have on Kelton ancestors.

Thompson One-Name Study

www.geocities.com/Athens/2249

The Thompson One-Name Study site focuses on collecting and making available for users information about all Thompsons (and variations of the surname). The site includes some downloadable records for some Thompsons from the United Kingdom, as well as information about the origins of the surname, Coats of Arms, the one-name study project in general, and researchers of the Thompsons. You can also find several online histories of various Thompsons.

Walsh Family Genealogy

homepages.rootsweb.com/~walsh/

Walsh Family Genealogy is a site dedicated to sharing information about the Walsh surname and families worldwide. You can register as a researcher and identify the Walsh ancestors you're researching, post messages and queries about your research, and join the Walsh-L mailing list to participate in discussions. The site also has sections with some online Walsh family trees, searchable indexes and lists of information (cemetery, marriage, passenger lists, and land records), and information about the origins of the surname and Coats of Arms.

Personal Web Sites

Personal Web sites usually provide information about one individual's or family's specific research interests, and they're the most common type of surname-related sites you will find. Generally, a personal Web site has information about a particular branch of a family. The format and presentation of this information can vary greatly. Some personal Web pages merely list the surnames that the site maintainer is researching; others contain the GEDCOM file of the site maintainer. And others have narrative histories about the family and areas in which they lived.

Given that thousands and thousands of personal Web pages exist, we had a difficult time narrowing our choices for this directory. A lot of good personal pages contain detailed and useful information. We chose these sites because they each provide a variety of information about the maintainer's interests and research, they are well organized and easy to use, and they show that the maintainer cares a lot about genealogical research and sharing information with others.

Ashworth Family Page

www.murrah.com/gen/ashworth.htm

Lee Murrah's Ashworth Family Page provides a narrative about the descendants of James Ashworth of Craven County, South Carolina. Included in the narrative are the surnames of some other families that married into the Ashworths, information about the Ashworths' role in the American Revolution, and their moves to South Carolina, Louisiana, and Texas. The controversy surrounding the Ashworths' race provides for very interesting reading at this site. You can find excellent explanations of and references to other sites with more information about Melungeons, Lumbee Indians, and Redbones.

Chenoweth Family Site

chenowethsite.com/

This site has extensive resources on the Chenoweth family, including an online database of the descendants of John Chenoweth and Mary Calvert, and some Descendant reports, too. You can find background information on the genealogy itself and the Coat of Arms, discussions about disputes among researchers over information that is presented online, and explanations of areas in which Jon Egge (the site creator) is looking for information. The site also has sections with specific information about Chenoweths who served in the Civil War and other wars. You can find snail-mail (regular mail) and e-mail addresses for other researchers interested in Chenoweths. We found it quite nice to see a section that graciously cites the sources of the information contained on the Web site.

Jeff Alvey Genealogy and Other Good Stuff

www.fred.net/jefalvey

Jeff Alvey shares an index of the persons contained in his genealogical database, as well as historical information about various Alveys and the origins of the surname. Two unique resources at this site are an informative section about heraldry and an index of names that appear in the book, *The Chronicles of Newgate,* which has information about inmates and others associated with the Newgate prison in London.

The Mabry Family

homepages.rootsweb.com/~mabry/

Don Collins, the creator of the Mabry Family Web site, shares with you lots of information about the Mabry (and various spellings) family in America. It also has information about various Mabrys who fought in the American Revolution and Civil War, a chronology of events in which Mabrys were involved, information about the Mabry Family newsletter, and several online photographs of Mabrys. You can also find a list of various spellings of the surname and a history of the Mabry Mill in Virginia, as well as several resources to help you research your Mabry family — including queries, a list of books, and a schedule of family reunions.

Mike Schwitzgebel's Genealogy Pages

homepages.rootsweb.com/~mschwitz/

Mike Schwitzgebel offers a variety of resources on his Web site. He includes an online photo album, database of his research findings, and information about the origins of his surname and a Coat of Arms. He also identifies the main goals of his current research for you to review to see whether you have any information that may help him and other researchers — they are listed under the Wanted section of his site. We are impressed with Mike's open and gracious acknowledgments of work by other researchers from whom he's received information about the Schwitzgebels, and of those who have helped him put his information on the Internet in one form or another. This is an excellent example of citing one's sources and giving credit where credit is due.

Professional Researchers

At some point, you may need to hire a professional researcher to pursue a particular family line's genealogy. Maybe you've exhausted all your leads on that family line, or you no longer have the time to devote to research, or the records you need are in a distant land, and you have neither the time nor the money to travel there just to look for paper. A lot of research services are available — some from reputable companies, others from individuals who just want to help others.

The following is a list of just a few professional research services that are available in different parts of the world. Chapter 10 provides more information about finding and choosing professional researchers.

Adelaide Proformat

www.users.on.net/proformat/ proformat.html

$

Formed in 1994, Adelaide Proformat specializes in helping Australians with their genealogical research and researching Australian resources for those who do not live there or cannot travel there to do their own research. Adelaide Proformat offers a variety of services — which include researching, obtaining copies of documents, preparing family histories, drawing family trees, and delivering presentations on genealogical research.

Family Tree - Családfa

www.familytree.hu

$

Family Tree – Családfa is a genealogical and probate research bureau that was formed in Hungary in 1988. Its researchers work in Hungary, Slovakia, Austria (Burgenland), Transylvania (part of Romania), Croatia, Slovenia, the former Yugoslavia (Banat), and the Ukraine (Sub-Carpathia), and speak English, Hungarian, French, German, Russian, Romanian, Polish, Czech, Slovak, and Serbo-Croatian. The Web site explains how the bureau researches in various places and provides historical information about Hungary, as well as details about Jewish genealogy and probate searches in the area.

Lineages, Inc.

www.lineages.com/store/searches.asp

$

Lineages, Inc., was founded in 1983 to provide genealogical research services and products nationwide in the United States. The Lineages Web site provides detailed information about using the organization's research services, including what you can expect upon hiring it to the costs of its services. One of the things you can expect if you do hire Lineages to conduct some research for you is an extensive report explaining how it researched your ancestors, copies of records it used, and Ancestry charts and Family Group Sheets reflecting your line of descent.

Scottish Family Research

www.scottishfamilyresearch.co.uk/

$

Scottish Family Research uses base information you provide (birth, marriage, or death details about a Scottish ancestor), researches many genealogical sources in Scotland, and puts together a report for you. The service includes using civil registrations, census returns, and old parish registers. The Scottish Family Research home page provides detailed information about the services, what information about your ancestor is initially required, costs of the services, and what you can expect to get in the report.

Threshold Concepts, Inc.

www.xmission.com/~tconcept/
    genhome.htm

$

Threshold Concepts, Inc., specializes in research services in Salt Lake City, Utah, and Washington, D.C. Its Web site explains what research services it offers, as well as its other services: restoring and preserving photographs and documents, and preparing and publishing family histories, among others. Threshold's Web site lists the costs for each of its services.

Compiled Genealogical Databases

Much like the compiled genealogies published in book form, compiled genealogical databases typically contain a lot of information about various family lines all in one place. They show other researchers' findings in a neatly organized, published format. Unlike compiled genealogies in book form — which often are not indexed thus requiring you to dig through the pages looking for the names in which you're interested — these compiled genealogical databases are searchable. Chapter 4 delves into compiled genealogical databases and identifies others you may want to check out.

FamilySearch

www.familysearch.org

The FamilySearch Internet Genealogy Service is the official research site for the Church of Jesus Christ of Latter-day Saints (LDS). It actually contains several of the LDS databases, including the Ancestral File, International Genealogical Index, Family History Catalog, Research Guidance, and census records.

Gendex

www.gendex.com/gendex

Gendex is a site with a server that indexes hundreds of Web pages containing genealogical data. The index contains some 40 million names and brief biographical information about those persons for whom information is available. You can use the Gendex search engine to search the database by surname, or you can click through the alphabet to find surnames. Access to use Gendex is available on two levels: unregistered users (free access) and registered users (pay for use). Registered users are given priority access for searching Gendex, search filters that enable them to customize their searches, and the option of modifying how the data that results from a search is displayed on their computers.

WorldConnect

worldconnect.rootsweb.com

The WorldConnect project is a RootsWeb.com compilation of GEDCOM files submitted by researchers like you. It contains over 300 million names you can search. The WorldConnect home page provides an excellent list of FAQs with information about the project and GEDCOMs in general.

Genealogical Databases

Over the past few years, we've seen major expansion in the area of genealogical software — from commercial databases to mapping programs to freeware and software that lets you manipulate your GEDCOM. Whether you want to buy your first genealogical organization program, upgrade to a program that is more powerful, or make some sort of enhancement to your genealogical files, you're probably interested in what software is available and what it has to offer you. Here's a list of genealogical software databases and a few specialty-type programs you may want to check out.

Ancestral Quest

www.ancquest.com

Ancestral Quest is available for Windows 95 or later. You can enter information using various views, and the software produces many standard reports/family trees.

Ancestry Family Tree

aft.ancestry.com/

Ancestry Family Tree runs on Windows 95 or later systems. The software enables you to search the Ancestry.com site automatically — and you can download files directly to the software.

Brother's Keeper

ourworld.compuserve.com/homepages/
   Brothers_Keeper

Brother's Keeper is available for Windows 95 or later and MS-DOS. Reports include

ahnentafel, Pedigree charts, Family Group Sheets, and a timeline. Version 6 enables you to store information on up to 10 million individuals. It is available in English, French, Norwegian, Danish, German, and Dutch.

Cumberland Family Tree

www.cf-software.com

Cumberland Family Tree is available for Windows 95 or later. Thirty-one types of reports are available, including ahnentafel, Pedigree charts, Family Group Sheets, and Descendant charts. Each database can hold 1 million individuals. Reports can be generated in Danish, Dutch, Finnish, French, German, Italian, Norwegian, Portuguese, Spanish, and Swedish.

EZITREE

www.ram.net.au/users/ezitree

EZITREE is available for Windows 95 or later. Reports include Ancestor charts, Descendant charts, and Family Group Sheets. The number of individuals allowed per database is 99,999.

Family Historian

http://www.family-historian.co.uk/

Family Historian is available for Windows 95 or later. It has customizable reports and a search engine that queries the database for the specific information for which you are looking. With this program, you can generate standard reports, including Ancestor and Descendant charts, as well as an All Relatives report.

Family Matters

www.matterware.com/

Family Matters is available for Windows 95 or later. Reports include Pedigree and Descendant charts. The software has Soundex, relationship, and birth/age calculators.

Family Reunion

www.famware.com

Family Reunion is available for Windows 95 or later. Reports include Pedigree, Descendant, and Family Group Sheets.

Family Tree Legends

www.familytreelegends.com/

Family Tree Legends is available for Windows 95 or later. It offers a large selection of charts and reports you can generate, including standard reports, a fact usage report, and statistics report.

Family Tree Maker

www.familytreemaker.com

This is one of the most popular genealogical programs ever, and there's a copy on the CD accompanying this book so you can try it out. Family Tree Maker is available for Windows 98 or later. Reports include Ancestor, Descendant, Kinship, Calendar, and Family Group Sheets.

GEDitCOM

www.geditcom.com/

This is a Macintosh program that enables you to manipulate GEDCOM files. With it, you can set up your own interface or use the default one. You can use it to generate Web-based charts, including a standard Web site or Pedigree chart. And there's a feature with which you can query the database for statistical information.

Gene

www.ics.uci.edu/~eppstein/gene

Gene is available for the Macintosh platform. Reports include Ancestor, Calendar, and Relationship charts.

Genealogical Information Manager

www.gimsoft.com/

Genealogical Information Manager is available for MS-DOS. Reports include Family Group Sheets, Pedigree, and Descendant charts.

Genius

www.gensol.com.au/genius.htm

Genius is available on the Windows 95 or later platform. You can generate eight types of reports, including Descendant, Pedigree, Individual Information Sheet, and Family Group Sheets. You can have 15,000 individuals per database. The software includes built-in backup.

Généatique

www.cdip.com/geneatiq.htm

Généatique is designed for Windows 95 or later. Reports include Ancestor and Descendant charts. The program only comes in French.

Heredis

www.heredis.com

Heredis is available for Windows 98, ME, NT4, 2000, or XP, or Macintosh OS X. Available reports include ahnentafel, Descendant, Pedigree, and Anniversary lists. The program is available in English, French, and German.

Heritage Family Tree

www.individualsoftware.com/new/
consumer/details/fd2_details.htm

Heritage Family Tree is available for Windows 98 or later. Two of its research-aiding tools are a Web collaboration feature and research manager function. It generates several standard reports, including Pedigree, Descendant, Family Group Sheets, and ahnentafels.

KinQuest

www.orelle.com/Kinquest/kinquest.htm

Kinquest is available for MS-DOS. Reports include ahnentafel and Family Group Sheets. You can store up to 2 billion names in each database.

Kith and Kin Pro/Of That Ilk Pro

www.spansoft.org/

Kith and Kin Pro, which is known as Of That Ilk Pro in some countries, is available for Windows 95 or later. It supports Structured Query Language (SQL) searching for producing custom reports and files.

Legacy Family Tree

www.legacyfamilytree.com

Legacy Family Tree is available for Windows 95 or newer. You can choose the view you wish to use for entering information and you can open up to eight Family/Pedigree View windows at one time. The software has a To Do List, as well as standard reports including Ancestor, ahnentafel, Descendant, Pedigree, Family Group Sheets, Calendar, Timeline, and Individual.

LifeLines

lifelines.sourceforge.net/

There are several versions of LifeLines available for different platforms, including UNIX, MS-DOS, Macintosh, and Windows 95 or later. All have been developed and are supported by different individuals; however, this Web site directs you to information about — and downloadable copies of — each. Information in the database is stored in the GEDCOM format.

The Master Genealogist

www.whollygenes.com

The Master Genealogist is available for Windows 98 or later. It is best known for being a powerful genealogical database and for its selections of excellent reports. Another feature is its ability to directly import files from other genealogical programs without the use of GEDCOM.

Oedipus II

www.lamain.nl/oedipus.htm

Oedipus II is available for Windows 95 or later. Reports include Ancestor, Descendant, and Family Group Sheets. The software is in Dutch.

Parentèle

us.parentele.com/

Parentèle is available for Windows 95 or later. You can choose from three views in which to enter information into the database. This software allows you to customize your organization and reports, as well as generates 80 types of reports.

Personal Ancestral File

www.familysearch.org

Personal Ancestral File runs on Windows 95 or later. It is distributed by the Church of Jesus Christ of Latter-day Saints. It has a feature that allows you to customize the interface through which you enter information. And it generates standard reports, such as Pedigrees, Family Group Sheets, and lists.

Pocket Genealogist

www.northernhillssoftware.com/
mainframe.htm

Pocket Genealogist is a program for personal digital assistants (PDAs) and runs under Windows CE. It is compatible with and can read data directly from several genealogical software programs that run under Windows 95 or later.

Reunion

www.leisterpro.com

Reunion is a well-known genealogical database available for Macintosh computers. There are versions available for those running Mac OS X and earlier Mac OS systems. It has non-gender specific relationship descriptions (for example, use of grandchild in reports instead of grandson or granddaughter when gender is unknown). Also, it generates a nice selection of reports, including Pedigree, Family Group Sheets, Register, Timeline, and ahnentafel.

RootsMagic

www.rootsmagic.com/

RootsMagic is the newest genealogical database produced by FormalSoft. It is available for Windows 95 or later. It has three views through which you can enter information, and it can handle an unlimited number of people and events. With it, you can create standard reports, various pre-designed narrative reports, or custom reports.

Windows into PAF

ourworld.compuserve.com/homepages/
phoenix/WIPafhom.htm

Windows into PAF, which is also called
WIPaf, is a Windows interface for data from
older versions of Personal Ancestral File
(PAF). It is available for Windows 3.1.
Reports include Pedigree, Family Group
Sheets, ahnentafel, and Descendant.

Miscellaneous Utilities

Clooz

www.clooz.com

Clooz is a utility that helps you organize
and store all of the various sources you
use during research.

DeedMapper

www.ultranet.com/~deeds/factsht.htm

Direct Line Software produces DeedMapper,
which is a program that enables you to
transfer information from land records
to maps you can see and use on your
computer.

GCFiler

www.orelle.com/Kinquest/kinquest.htm

This utility converts GEDCOM files into
comma-delimited ASCII file you can import
into a spreadsheet or database for use, or
the reverse (ASCII to GEDCOM).

GED2HTML

www.gendex.com/ged2html

GED2HTML is Gene Stark's popular program
for converting your GEDCOM file into an
HTML file you can post on the Web.

GED2WWW

www.lesandchris.com/ged2www/

GED2WWW is Leslie Howard's freeware to
convert GEDCOM files to HTML so you can
post your information on the Web.

GEDClean

www.raynorshyn.com/gedclean

GEDClean is Tom Raynor's shareware that
helps you strip your GEDCOM file of information on living persons or certain other
types of information you specify.

Gedpage

www.frontiernet.net/~rjacob/
gedpage.htm

Gedpage converts your GEDCOM files to
HTML for posting on the Web. Rob Jacob
wrote this program that provides output in
the form of Family Group Sheets. The software is available for Windows and
Macintosh.

Genelines

www.progenysoftware.com/
genelines.html

Genelines is a fun utility that creates historical bar charts from the data contained in
Personal Ancestral File, Family Tree Maker,
Legacy, Ancestral Quest, and Ancestry
Family Tree, or a GEDCOM file. It runs
under Windows 95 or later. It produces
seven types of charts including the two
biographical and five relationship charts
you can customize to include timelines,
historical events, and/or personal or family
events.

Sparrowhawk

www.bradandkathy.com/genealogy/
sparrowhawk.html

Sparrowhawk is Bradley Mohr's GEDCOM
to HTML converter for the Macintosh.

Surname-Related Resources

You're probably wondering how to find
sites that pertain to the specific surnames
in which you're interested. Wonder no
more! Here are some sites that index surname resources with explanations of what
each resource has to offer. And if these
sites don't pan out for you, we have a
couple of other suggestions. First, run a
search on the surname you're researching
at a genealogically focused search engine.
(See the "Genealogically Focused Search
Engines" section earlier in this directory.)
Second, take a look back at some comprehensive genealogical sites — some of
which are identified, appropriately enough,
in the "Comprehensive Sites" section in
this directory.

The Guild of One-Name Studies

www.one-name.org

The Guild of One-Name Studies site is liter-
ally a guild of groups and online sites that
have registered as repositories for information pertaining to particular surnames.
The site's Register of One-Name Studies is
searchable here. Additionally, you will find
general information about the Guild and
how to join.

Online Genealogical Database Index

www.gentree.com/gentree.html

The Online Genealogical Database Index
provides brief information about and links
to genealogical databases on the Web.
Most of the databases were created using
GEDCOM files that have been converted to
HTML. The index itself is organized alphabetically by the main surname of the database and does not include a complete
listing of all surnames in the database.

Yourfamily.com

www.yourfamily.com

Among other services, Yourfamily.com
provides a free, searchable index of family
home pages. By entering the surname you
want to search and clicking the Search
button, the search engine produces a list
of links to pages that may meet your name
specification. You can then look through
the list and any accompanying comments
about the sites to pick home pages to visit.
Additionally, if you have a family home page
you want to register with Yourfamily.com,
this is the place to do it.

Part IV
Share and Share Alike

The 5th Wave   By Rich Tennant

"Tell the boss the `Begets' aren't cutting it.
The people are demanding online access!"

In this part . . .

Discover how to maximize your online research by effectively using as many resources as possible. This part also addresses sharing information with others using reports, GEDCOMs, and Web pages that you create yourself, as well as how to coordinate your research efforts with those of others. Along the way, you also find out a little history about GEDCOM and the best way to respect others' privacy and copyrights.

Chapter 9

Storing and Organizing Information in Your Computer

. . . .

In This Chapter

▶ Getting started with genealogical software

▶ Producing genealogical reports

▶ Selecting accessories for your computer

. . . .

After organizing your paper records and photographs, put your computer to work storing and manipulating your family history. We think that a computer may be your best friend when it comes to storing, organizing, and publishing your genealogical information.

With your computer, you can use genealogical software to maintain information on thousands of individuals, access CD-ROMs containing indexes to and digital images of valuable genealogical records, scan images to preserve your family heritage, and share information with researchers throughout the world via the Internet. This chapter examines genealogical database software and what it can do for you and looks at some gadgets that may enhance the capabilities of your computer.

Finding and Running Genealogical Software

Several kinds of software programs enable you to track your ancestors easily and successfully. You can store facts and stories about your relatives, attach files containing scanned photographs of them with their biographical information, and generate numerous reports at the click of a button. Some programs even enable you to store audio and video recordings. (This capability is especially wonderful if you want to put together a multimedia presentation on your genealogy to share at a reunion or conference.)

Most currently available genealogical software programs have many features and system requirements in common. To ensure that you make the most of your computer and software, look closely at the specific system requirements on the container (box or CD case) of the software before you buy.

In general, the following list is what we recommend as the minimum requirements for your computer system to run most genealogical software adequately. However, keep in mind that if you want additional accessories for your computer to assist your genealogical effort (such as scanners, digital cameras, other software, and so forth) — or if you want to store electronic images — you may need to have a higher-end system: a faster microprocessor, more random-access memory (RAM), and more hard-drive space.

If you have a PC, you need at least the following:

- A Pentium processor
- Windows 95, 98, 2000, ME, or XP
- A CD-ROM drive
- 500 megabytes of free hard-drive space
- 64 megabytes of RAM
- VGA display with at least 256 colors
- A Microsoft-compatible mouse

If you have a Macintosh computer, you need at least the following:

- A PowerPC processor
- Mac OS 8.5 or newer
- A CD-ROM drive
- 500 megabytes of free hard-drive space
- 64 megabytes of RAM

Finding a Research Mate (Of the Software Variety)

You may think you already have the perfect research mate — that special person who accompanies you to every library, cemetery, and courthouse as you research, right? Wrong! The research mate we're referring to comes on CD-ROMs or is downloadable from the Internet; you install it on your computer and then let it perform all sorts of amazing tasks for you.

Several software programs can store and manipulate your genealogical information. They all have some standard features in common; for instance, most serve as databases for family facts and stories, have reporting functions to generate pre-designed charts and forms, and have export capabilities so you can share your data with others. Each software program also has a few unique features (for example, the capability to take information out of the software and generate online reports at the click of a button) that make it stand out from the others. Here's a list of the features you want to look for when evaluating different software packages:

- ✔ **How easy is the software to use?** Is it reasonably intuitive graphics-wise so that you can see how and where to enter particular facts about an ancestor?

- ✔ **Does the software generate the reports you need?** For instance, if you're partial to Family Group Sheets, does this software support them?

- ✔ **Does the software allow you to export and/or import a GEDCOM file?** *GEDCOM* is a file format that's widely used for genealogical research. For more info about GEDCOM, see the "GEDCOM: The genealogist's standard" sidebar later in this chapter.

- ✔ **How many names can this software hold?** Make sure that the software can hold an adequate number of names (and accompanying data) to accommodate all the ancestors about whom you have information.

Keep in mind that your genealogy continues to grow over time.

- ✔ **Can your current computer system support this software?** If the requirements of the software cause your computer to crash every time you use it, you won't get very far in your genealogical research.

- ✔ **Does this software provide fields for citing your sources and keeping notes?** Including information about the sources you use to gather your data — with the actual facts, if possible — is a sound genealogical practice. Take a look at Chapter 11 for more information about the importance of citing sources and how to do so.

Sharing Your Genealogical Success with Others

After you organize all your paper documents and enter as much information possible into your genealogical software, you can share what you've gathered and organized with others — or you can generate notes to take with you on research trips. (If you haven't organized your information yet, Chapter 3 can help you.)

GEDCOM: The genealogist's standard

As you probably already discovered, genealogy is full of acronyms. One such acronym that you hear and see repeatedly is *GEDCOM (GEnealogical Data COMmunication)*. GEDCOM has become the standard for individuals and software manufacturers for exporting and importing information to or from genealogical databases. Simply put, GEDCOM is a file format intended to make data transferable between different software programs so people can share their family information easily.

The Church of Jesus Christ of Latter-day Saints first developed and introduced GEDCOM in 1987. The first two versions of GEDCOM were released for public discussion only and not meant to serve as the standard. With the introduction of Version 5.*x* and later, however, GEDCOM was accepted as the standard.

Having a standard for formatting files is beneficial to you as a researcher because you can share the information that you collect with others who are interested in some (or all) of your ancestors. It also enables you to import GEDCOM files from other researchers who have information about family lines and ancestors in whom you're interested. And you don't even have to use the same software as the other researchers! You can use Reunion for Macintosh and someone with whom you want to share information can use Family Tree Maker;

having GEDCOM as the standard in both software programs enables each of you to create and exchange GEDCOM files.

To convert the data in your genealogical database to a GEDCOM file, follow the instructions provided in your software's manual or Help menu. You can create the GEDCOM file relatively easily; most software programs guide you through the process with a series of dialog boxes.

In addition to creating GEDCOM files to exchange one-on-one with other researchers, you can generate GEDCOM files to submit to larger cooperatives that make the data from many GEDCOM files available to thousands of researchers worldwide via the World Wide Web and e-mail. Here are a couple of cooperatives that you may want to check out:

- **GenServ:** www.genserv.com
- **The WorldConnect Project at RootsWeb:** worldconnect.rootsweb.com

You can also convert your GEDCOM file to HTML so that you can place the data directly on the World Wide Web for others to access. Software utilities are available (such as GED2HTML) that make it a snap to convert your GEDCOM file to HTML. (For more information on generating Web pages using GED2HTML, see Chapter 12.)

Your genealogical software can help you by generating printed reports reflecting the information that you collected and entered. Most genealogical software packages have several standard reports or charts in common, including a Pedigree chart (also called an Ancestor chart), Descendant chart, Outline of Descendants, Family Group Sheet, and Kinship report.

In this section, we examine the different types of reports and explain how to generate them using Family Tree Maker. For more information about entering information into (and using) this program, please flip back to Chapter 3.

Pedigree charts (or Ancestor Trees)

Family Tree Maker calls its *Pedigree chart* an *Ancestor Tree*. Flowing horizontally across a page, it identifies a primary person by that person's name, date and place of birth, date and place of marriage, and date and place of death. The chart uses lines to show the relationship to the person's father and mother, then each of their parents, then their parents, and so on until the chart runs off the page. See Figure 9-1 for an example of an Ancestor Tree generated using Family Tree Maker.

Descendant charts

A *Descendant chart* contains information about an ancestor and spouse (or spouses if more than one exists), their children and their spouses, grandchildren and spouses, and so on down the family line. (Family Tree Maker calls this type of chart a Descendant Tree.) A Descendant chart usually flows vertically on a page, rather than running horizontally across the page like a Pedigree chart (Ancestor Tree). See Figure 9-2 for an example of a Descendant Tree generated by Family Tree Maker.

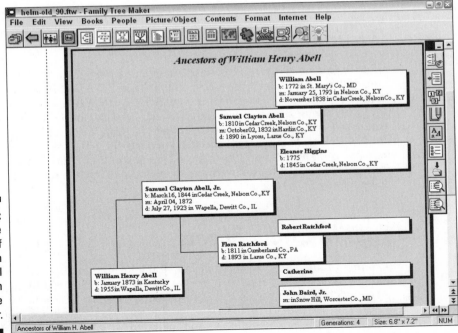

Figure 9-1:
A Pedigree chart of William Henry Abell generated in Family Tree Maker.

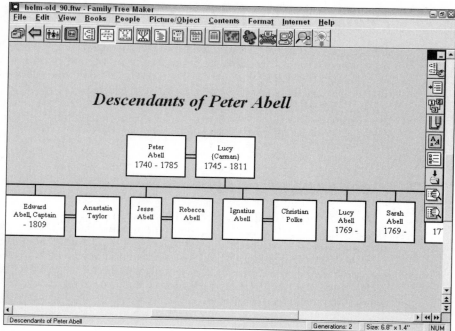

Figure 9-2: Part of a Descendant chart for Peter Abell.

Outline reports

A family *Outline* is a list of the descendants of a particular ancestor. (Family Tree Maker calls it an Outline Descendant Tree.) The first numbered line contains the name (and sometimes the years for birth and death) of the primary ancestor. The next line shows the name of a spouse, followed by the next numbered line, which contains the name of the ancestor and spouse's first child. If that child is married and has children, the name of the child's spouse follows, as do names and information for each of that child and spouse's children. See Figure 9-3 for an example of an Outline Descendant Tree generated using Family Tree Maker.

Family Group Sheets

A *Family Group Sheet* is a summary of vital information about a particular family. At the top of the page, it shows the *Husband,* followed by the *Wife,* and then any children of the couple, as well as biographical information (such as dates and places of birth, marriage, and death). However, information on the children's spouses and children isn't included on this Family Group Sheet; you can generate a separate Family Group Sheet for each child's family (if applicable). See Figure 9-4 for an example of a Family Group Sheet generated by Family Tree Maker.

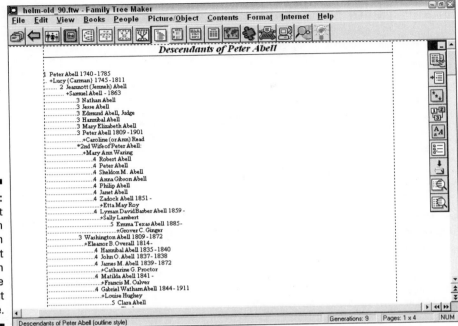

Figure 9-3:
Descendant
information
provided in
a different
form — an
Outline
Descendant
Tree.

Kinship reports

A *Kinship report* is a list of family members and how they relate directly to one particular person. This report includes the name of the family member, the person's relationship to the primary ancestor, and the Civil and Canon Codes reflecting the degree of relationship between the two people. See

Figure 9-5 for an example of a Kinship report generated by Family Tree Maker.

Civil and Canon Codes explain the bloodline relationship in legal terms — in other words, they identify how many *degrees of separation* (or steps) are between two people who are related by blood. Civil law counts each step between two relatives as a degree, so two people who are first cousins have a degree of separation equal to four, which is the total of two steps between one cousin and the common grandparent — and two steps between the *other* cousin and the common grandparent. Canon law counts only the number of steps from the nearest common ancestor of both relatives, so the degree of separation between two first cousins is two. Two steps separate the grandparent from each of the cousins.

Figure 9-4:
A Family Group Sheet generated from Family Tree Maker.

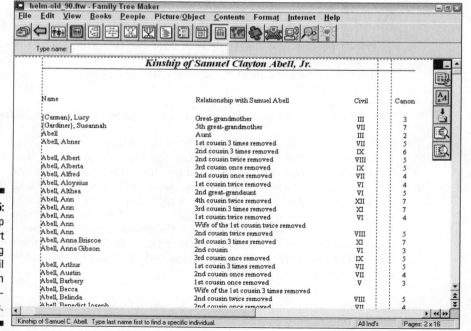

Figure 9-5:
A Kinship report showing both civil and canon relationships.

Generating charts and reports using Family Tree Maker

See the "Completing the Family Page" section in Chapter 3 for details on how to fill out a Family Page entry for each of your family members. When you have at least a few Family Pages completed, follow these steps to create any of the five charts/reports that we discuss in the preceding paragraphs:

1. **Open Family Tree Maker.**

2. **Under the View drop-down menu, select the Index of Individuals.**

   This action brings up a box that lists all the individuals entered in your database, in alphabetical order.

3. **Scroll through the index and select the person for whom you want to generate a chart/report by double-clicking the name or highlighting the name and clicking OK.**

   This takes you to the Family Page for the person you selected.

   For example, if Matthew wants to produce a Pedigree chart for his ancestor Samuel Abell, he highlights Samuel Abell in the index and clicks OK.

4. **Place your cursor in the person's name field.**

   Move your cursor into the Husband, Wife, or Children field to select the exact person on whom you want to generate a chart/report.

   Matthew places the cursor in the Husband field, which reflects the name Samuel Abell.

5. **Click the appropriate button in the toolbar at the top of the Family Tree Maker screen, or choose View⇨[Type of tree or report].**

   You can find buttons for Ancestor Trees, Descendant Trees, Outline Descendant Trees, and Family Group Sheets. Or if you use the drop-down menu, the charts/reports appear as Ancestor Tree, Descendant Tree, Outline Descendant Tree, Kinship Report, and Family Group Sheet. (You can generate other reports using Family Tree Maker, but these are the most common types and the five types that we discuss in this chapter.)

   Family Tree Maker generates the requested chart/report for the person that you selected.

   Matthew clicks the button that says Ancestor Tree or uses the View drop-down menu to select Ancestor Tree. Family Tree Maker automatically generates a Pedigree chart for Samuel Abell. (To see what this Pedigree chart looks like, refer to Figure 9-1.)

6. **Look at the chart on the screen, copy it to your word processor to save it, or print it out to share with others.**

   For more information about moving reports into your word processor, see Chapter 11.

Formatting and customizing charts and reports

Keep in mind that you can control exactly what to include in each of the Family Tree Maker charts or reports — by telling the program how many generations to include, to exclude particular ancestors, to change the types of information to include, or to customize the appearance (borders and fonts). Here are some quick references to help you when manipulating the content of these reports in Family Tree Maker:

- ✓ **To control the number of generations included on the chart or report:** Choose Contents⇨# of Generations to Show.
- ✓ **To change the format:** Choose Format⇨Tree Format (or Report Format if you're working with a report).
- ✓ **To change boxes, lines, and borders:** Choose Format⇨Box, Line, & Border Styles.
- ✓ **To change the fonts:** Choose Format⇨Text Font, Style, & Size.

Other genealogical software programs enable you to manipulate your charts and reports in a similar manner. When you use other programs, simply take a look at the manual or Help files, or follow the tutorial (if it has one) for precise guidance when creating charts and reports.

Let's Talk Hardware: Is Your Computer Equipped?

As you grow more accustomed to using the information you store in your computer, you may want to consider adding other hardware and peripheral equipment to your system to enhance your genealogy research and the reports that you generate. You may want to start including electronic images of some of the photographs and original documents that you have in your paper filing system. You may think about adding audio of your grandmother reminiscing, or video of your grandchild greeting people at the family reunion. As you find additional documents, you may want to add images of them to your main database as well. So what kind of computer hardware or other equipment do you need in order to include images and other enhancements with your genealogical information?

You should consider several pieces of equipment as you prepare to enhance your genealogy with audio and video. These include writable CD-ROM or DVD drives, sound cards, video-capture boards, scanners, digital cameras, and extra hard drives.

Writable CD-ROM or DVD drives

If you're looking to solve both the space needs of files and mobility issues when you'd like to take your database on the road, then you may want to consider getting a writable CD-ROM drive. With it, you can cut your own data CDs — filling them with family photos (which typically take up a lot of space on your computer) or family files that you want to share at the family reunion — or some of both. Writable CD-ROM drives are available in internal and external varieties. Similar to writable CD-ROM drives are the newer-to-the-market writable DVD drives. They can hold more data than a CD-ROM. CD-Rs, the discs you use with a writable CD-ROM drive, can hold around 650–700 megabytes. DVD-Rs, the discs you use with writable DVD drives, can hold around 4.7 *gigabytes*.

Sound cards

A *sound card* is an internal device that is a standard feature on most computers today. It allows you to hear any audio that comes on software (particularly games) or audio files that you download off the Internet. In most cases, the card also enables you to record your own audio from your stereo, radio, video camera, or microphone — but you must have software that supports recordings. If your sound card is capable of recording and you have adequate software, you simply plug the sound source into the microphone jack (or the sound-in jack on the back of your computer), set your software to record, and go for it. After you make the recording, you can import it into your genealogical software if your genealogical software supports audio.

Video-capture boards

Similar to a sound card, a *video-capture board* enables you to grab images from your video camera or VCR. You can use moving images or still pictures, depending on the type of your video-capture board and the accompanying software. Video-capture boards aren't usually a standard feature on computers. They have varying system requirements depending on the manufacturer and the software that's included. Be sure that your computer system can handle a particular video-capture board and software before making your purchase.

Scanners

Scanners remain one of the most popular computer peripherals for genealogists. Everyone wants to include some family photos with their genealogy or preserve precious documents electronically. With the cost of scanners decreasing — and the availability of bundled software that allows you to use a scanner not only as a scanner, but also as a fax machine, and copier — adding a scanner to your equipment collection makes a lot of sense. It can make your genealogical research more colorful and more efficient without making a big dent in your wallet.

A variety of scanners are available. The most common types are snapshot, sheet-fed, and flatbed. Although they're harder to find, a few hand-held scanners are still around. You can find color scanners and scanners that capture images only in black and white. The system requirements for scanners vary greatly, so read the packaging of any scanner you're considering — very carefully. Additionally, each scanner requires software to make it work, so carefully read the software's system requirements and capabilities as well. Here's a quick rundown of the major types of scanners:

- ✔ **Photo scanners:** Useful for creating electronic images of photographs that measure 5 x 7 inches or smaller because they're designed to work primarily with that size of photograph. Photo scanners (also called snapshot scanners) are compact and come in external and internal varieties. You feed the photograph into the scanner, and then the scanner captures an image before sending the photo back out. Some photo scanners have a removable top that you can use as a hand-held scanner when you want to capture images larger than 5 x 7 inches. One caution with photo scanners: You may not want to use these with old, fragile photographs. The scanner can damage the photograph as it's fed through the scanner.

- ✔ **Film scanners:** Check out a film scanner if you'd like to produce your own photographs directly from negatives. These compact scanners can capture images in color or black and white. You manually feed the negative into the scanner. Some film scanners have optional slide feeders.

- ✔ **Document scanners:** Document scanners are also sometimes called sheet-fed scanners, appropriately enough because they are typically a little wider than a regular sheet of paper (8.5 inches across). They're still rather compact as far as scanners go, but all are external. You feed the photograph or document into the feeder on the scanner, and the scanner captures an image as the document goes through. As do some photo scanners, some document scanners have a removable top that you can use as a hand-held scanner to capture images larger than 8.5 inches across. Use caution when using these scanners with fragile photographs.

✓ **Flatbed scanners:** These scanners used to be large and bulky but are now incredibly light and compact. You lift the top of the scanner and place your document or photograph on the bed, close the lid, and tell the scanner (through software) to capture the image. Flatbed scanners are somewhat safer for photographs and old paper records than are other types of scanners. That's because photos are laid on the scanner's glass plate, not fed through the device.

✓ **Hand-held scanners:** Although these are great for genealogy because of their flexibility and mobility, they're also more difficult to find these days. You can use them not only for scanning photographs and paper documents but also for scanning books. Hand-held scanners are external and compact. They're the perfect size to carry with you when you go on-site for your genealogical research. You scan photos and other objects by holding the scanner and slowly moving it over the object while holding down a button. The quality of the scanned image depends greatly on how steady your hand is, how good the lighting is where you're scanning, and the original size of the document.

Digital cameras

Over the past few years, digital cameras have increasingly captured the interest of genealogists as well as the general public. The ability to take all your photographs with a camera that downloads the images directly to your computer is very appealing. And the fact that you can easily attach digital photos to your genealogical database (or import them in) is definitely exciting. Some digital cameras even come with a document setting, so you don't need both a scanner and a digital camera. This feature is extremely convenient when you're on the road researching your ancestors — you can use your digital camera to capture images from cemetery visits, pictures of long-lost cousins at reunions, and copies of rare documents at the local courthouse.

Depending on the model, you store the digital pictures within the memory of the camera, on compact flash cards, or on a 3½-inch disk. With the models that store the images internally or on a flash card, you must take an extra step to download the images to your computer through a serial cable. For the models that save the images to a floppy disk, you can simply insert the disk into your computer and copy the files to your database.

Coordinate your research via phone and GPS

You already know a couple of good reasons to carry your cellular phone with you on research trips, right? It enables you to call relatives in the town you're visiting, and allows you to call ahead to ensure that a record exists in a location before traveling there. And it gives you reassurance that you can reach help if something goes wrong while you're away from home. But there's another wonderful reason to carry certain types of cellular phones on genealogical jaunts. That's because some cellular phones now have Global Positioning System (GPS) receivers built in. The GPS is a satellite system

that receives and sends signals to a receiver enabling the person controlling the receiver to determine his/her exact geographical coordinates. This is a handy system to employ when recording the locations of family markers, such as burial plots and old homesteads. After all, natural markers (such as rocks and trees) and man-made markers (such as buildings) may move or disappear entirely after years and years, but the latitude and longitude of a location will remain the same. For more information about using GPS for genealogical purposes, check out Chapter 6.

As with every other computer peripheral, if you're considering purchasing a digital camera, carefully read the package and software requirements to make sure that your computer system can support the equipment.

Traveling with Your Genealogical Tools

Whether you go to a family reunion, travel a couple hundred miles to research in a particular county or province, or give a presentation at a conference, chances are you may eventually want to take your show on the road. If you're just testing the waters to see whether buying a computer for genealogical purposes is worth your time and money, you may want to consider getting a laptop or notebook computer instead of a desktop system. Portable computers give you the flexibility to take your genealogical database with you wherever you go, as well as some presentation possibilities that desktop systems don't allow because of their size.

Portable databases

As you get more involved in genealogy and begin to take research trips, you may find having your database with you to be useful. Of course, you can always print out the contents of your database, but who wants to carry around thousands of pages? One alternative is to carry a notebook computer with you.

Notebooks are quite popular, especially since they've become more affordable and more powerful over the years. Most notebook computers have capabilities similar to their desktop counterparts, but in a more convenient package.

Another group of research assistants is gaining prominence on the market — Personal Digital Assistants (PDAs), which are also often called *palmtops*. PDAs are hand-sized computers that can contain some of the same programs housed on desktop computers. You can transfer information from a PDA to your desktop or laptop PC. You can even have a scaled-down version of your genealogical database on your PDA. For example, GedStar (www.ghcssoftware.com/gedstar.htm) allows you to view and edit GEDCOM files on PDAs running the Palm OS 5 operating system. The storage capacity for GedStar is limited only by the capabilities of your PDA.

Storage on the run

If you already own a desktop system and aren't in the market to buy a notebook or palmtop, don't worry! You have other means for transporting your data and reports without spending the money on another computer.

Your database may grow too large to fit on a regular 3½-inch floppy disk. However, CD-Rs and DVD-Rs hold a lot more data and can easily accommodate your genealogical database. Buying a writable CD-ROM or DVD drive is typically a lot cheaper than buying a laptop computer. (See the "Let's Talk Hardware: Is Your Computer Equipped?" section, earlier in this chapter for more information about writable CD-ROM and DVD drives.) At your favorite computer retailer site, you can also find a number of other external storage options beyond CD-ROMs and DVDs. Of course, the drawback to using a disc to transport your data is that you need a computer on the other end that can handle the disc and accommodate the information contained on it. So before you take a CD-ROM with all your family information to that reunion at Aunt Lola's, make sure that Aunt Lola's computer has a CD-ROM drive and any necessary software to open the contents of your disc. Of course, another option is to upload your information to the Internet, so you can access it from any computer that's connected to the Internet.

One other portability issue is having a means for getting information from a computer source away from home to your computer. Most public libraries and Family History Centers have genealogical information on computers that you can access. You can use a 3½-inch floppy disk to download information that you find on computers and CD-ROMs at these research facilities. Popping a floppy disk into the computer at the library to download a few lines of information about an ancestor is much easier than hand-writing everything, and a lot cheaper than paying for each individual printout! But be careful when sending your disk in to gather data on a public computer and remember to run a virus scan on the disk when you return to your trusty machine at home — you don't want to pick up a bug on your disk and infect your faithful companion. Viruses can wreak havoc on many of the programs on your computer, including your genealogical database.

Chapter 10

Coordinating Your Attack: Getting Help from Other Researchers

You can think of genealogical research as a long journey. You may begin the journey by yourself, but before long, you discover that the journey goes a lot faster when someone else is along for the ride. In your genealogical journey, these travel partners can take various forms — a single individual researching the same family, or a research group searching for several branches of a family in which you're interested, or a genealogical society that coordinates the efforts of many people researching different families.

In the next few pages, we explore ways of finding (and keeping) research partners, as well as ways that research groups and genealogical societies can help you meet your research goals.

Putting All Your Eggs in One Basket: Relying Only on Your Research

Don't put all your eggs in one basket — so the old saying goes. A variation of this adage applies to genealogical research — don't try to do all the research yourself. As you'll discover, an awful lot of people out there are researching, and it would be a shame for you not to take advantage of the work they have done and vice versa.

We can't emphasize enough the benefits of sharing genealogical data. Sharing is the foundation on which the genealogical community is built. For example, when Matthew began researching his genealogy, he went to the National Archives, Library of Congress, and several regional libraries and archives. Along the way, he found a few books that made a passing mention of some of his ancestors, and he discovered some original records that helped him put some pieces together. It wasn't until he shared his information online that he began to realize just how many people were working on his surname. During the month following the creation of his Web site, he received messages from 40 other Helm researchers — one of whom lived in Slovenia! Although not all these researchers were working on Matthew's specific branch (only two of the 40 were directly related), he received valuable information on some of the areas that other researchers were working on. Matthew may never have known that some of these researchers existed had he not taken the first step to share his information.

By knowing the family lines and regions that other researchers are pursuing, you can coordinate your efforts with theirs — not only sharing information you've already collected, but also working together toward your common goal. Maybe you live closer to a courthouse that holds records relating to your ancestor than does a distant cousin with whom you're communicating online — but maybe the cousin lives near a family gravesite that you'd like to have a photo of. Rather than duplicating efforts to collect the court records and photographs, you can make arrangements for each of you to get the desired items that are closest to you and then exchange copies of them over the Internet or through traditional mail.

The Shotgun Approach

You're probably wondering how to find individuals with whom to share your information. Well, you could start by going through telephone books and calling everyone with the surname that you're researching.

However, given how some people feel about telemarketers, we don't recommend this as a strategy.

Similar to this telemarketing strategy is sending mass e-mails to anyone you find with your surname through one of the online white-pages sites. We refer to this mass e-mail strategy as the *shotgun approach*. You shoot out a bunch of e-mail messages aimed in various directions, with hopes of successfully hitting one or two targets. Although you may find one or two people who answer you in a positive way, a lot of people may find such unsolicited e-mail irritating. Instead of bearing the wrath of hundreds of people, go to a site that focuses on genealogy to find the names of researchers who are interested in your surname — this is a much kinder, better way to go about finding others with the same interests as you.

Also, please note that we aren't saying that e-mail directories don't have a function in genealogy (see Appendix A for details on how to use an e-mail directory). E-mail directories can be a good place to find an e-mail address that you've lost or an address of a relative who may be interested in your e-mail. You can also use e-mail directories to see the distribution of your surname in the United States and throughout the world. (See Figure 10-1.)

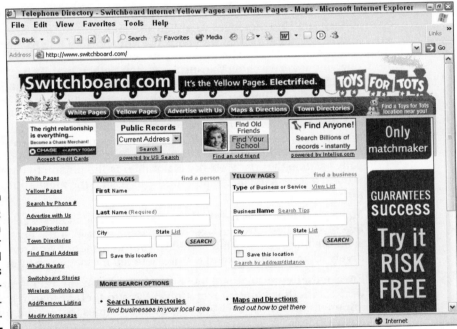

Figure 10-1: You can search for e-mail addresses at Switchboard.com.

Making Friends (And Keeping Them) Online

The best place to begin your search for others who are doing similar research is the Roots Surname List. (See Figure 10-2.) The Roots Surname List (rsl. rootsweb.com/) is one of the oldest genealogy resources on the Internet and consists of a list of individuals, the surnames they're researching, and where on the planet those surnames are found. (For more info on using the Roots Surname List, see Chapter 4.) Other places to find fellow researchers include query pages on the World Wide Web, newsgroups, and mailing lists. (If you need a refresher on using these or other surname resources, you can find more information in Chapter 4 and Appendix A.) After you identify some potential online friends, send them e-mail messages introducing yourself and briefly explaining your purpose for contacting them. Be sure to include a listing of the ancestors you're researching in your e-mail message.

Before we send you out to contact people, however, we want to give you a few pieces of advice:

- ✔ **Before sending messages to a Web-site maintainer, look around the site to see whether that person is the appropriate one to approach:** More often than not, the person who maintains a Web site is indeed the one who is researching the surnames you find on that Web site. However, it's not unusual for site maintainers to host information on their sites for other people. If they do, then typically they have separate contact addresses for those individuals and an explanation that they're not personally researching those surnames. Some even go so far as to post notices on their sites stating that they don't entertain research questions. So when you see a list of surnames on a site, don't automatically assume that the Web-site maintainer is the person to contact. Look around a little to ensure that you're addressing the most appropriate person.

- ✔ **Make your messages brief and to the point:** E-mail messages that run five or six pages long can overwhelm some people. If the person you send the message to is interested in your information and responds positively to you, you can send a more-detailed message at a future date.

- ✔ **Ensure that your message has enough detail for the recipients to decide whether your information relates to their research and determine whether they can help you:** Include names, dates, and places as appropriate.

- ✔ **Use net etiquette, or *netiquette,* when you create your messages:** Remember, e-mail can be an impersonal medium. Although you may mean one thing, someone who doesn't know you may mistakenly misinterpret your message. (For more on netiquette, see the "Netiquette: Communicating politely on the Internet" sidebar in this chapter.)

- ✔ **Don't disclose personal information that could violate a person's privacy:** Information such as address, birth dates, and Social Security numbers for living persons is considered private and should not be freely shared with other researchers. Also, we don't recommend you send out much personal information about yourself until you know the recipient a lot better — when first introducing yourself, your name and e-mail address should suffice, along with the information about the deceased ancestors you're researching.

✔ **Get permission before forwarding messages from other researchers:** Sometimes researchers may provide information that they do not want made available to the general public. Asking permission before forwarding a message to a third party eliminates any potential problems with violating the trust of your fellow researchers.

Netiquette: Communicating politely on the Internet

Part of being a fine, upstanding member of the online genealogy community is learning to communicate effectively and politely on the Internet. Online communication is often hampered by the fact that you can't see the people with whom you're corresponding, and you can't hear the intonation of their voices to determine what emotions they're expressing. To avoid misunderstandings, follow some simple guidelines — called *netiquette* — when writing messages:

✔ Don't send a message that you wouldn't want posted on a bulletin board at work. You should expect that every e-mail you send is potentially public.

✔ Make sure that you don't violate any copyright laws by sending large portions of written works through e-mail. (For more information on copyrights, see Chapter 12.)

✔ If you receive a *flame* (a heated message usually sent to provoke a response), try to ignore it. Usually, no good comes from responding to a flame.

✔ Be careful when you respond to messages. Instead of replying to an individual, you may be replying to an entire group of people. Checking the To: line before you hit the Send button is always a good idea.

✔ Use mixed case when you write e-mail messages. USING ALL UPPERCASE LETTERS INDICATES SHOUTING! The exception to this guideline is when you send a query and place your surnames in all-uppercase letters (for example, George HELM).

✔ If you participate in a mailing list or newsgroup, and you reply with a message that interests only one person, then consider sending that person a message individually rather than e-mailing the list as a whole.

✔ When you're joking, use smileys or type **<grins>** or **<g>**. A *smiley* is an *emoticon* that looks like :-). (Turn the book on its right side if you can't see the face.) *Emoticons* are graphics created by combinations of keys on the keyboard to express an emotion within an e-mail. Here are a few emoticons that you may run into:

:-) Happy, smiling

;-) Wink, ironic

:-> Sarcastic

8-) Wearing glasses

:-(Sad, unhappy

:-< Disappointed

:-o Frightened, surprised

:-() Mustache

RootsWeb Surname List Search Results: Surnames matching helm - Microsoft Internet Explorer

File   Edit   View   Favorites   Tools   Help

Back | Search   Favorites   Media | Links »

Address   http://rsl.rootsweb.com/cgi-bin/rslsql.cgi | Go

Surname	From	To	Migration	Submitter	Comment
Helm	----	1188	RUS>SWE>DNK>DEU>FRA	hhelm	
Helm	1089	1652	DEU>FRA>ENG>SCT>IRL	hhelm	
Helm	1422	1789	SCT>IRL>RI>MA>CT,USA	hhelm	
Helm	1600	1850	PA>VA,USA	ltucker9	
Helm	1600	1738	Bergen,NJ	sandia	
Helm	1641	1780	SCT>BRB>NY>NJ>PA,USA	hhelm	
Helm	1650	1820	MD	SCHUPP	
Helm	1660	1800	ENG>VA>MD>Fayette Co,KY,USA	dbelling	Leonard m. Calmes
Helm	1660	1996	ENG>FrederickCo,VA>SelbyCo,KY>Guernsey,OH>IN>IL	dregen	
Helm	1663	1810	NY>NJ>PA>VA>KY,USA	hhelm	
Helm	1667	1932	RHE-PFA,DEU>AdamsCo>MontgomeryCo,PA>MuscatineCo,IA	lpc	
Helm	1670	now	Worldwide	geohelm	
Helm	1676	? 1750	Eng,Va,	prt	
Helm	1680	1925	SCT>IRL>NY>NJ>PA,USA	hhelm	

Internet

Figure 10-2:
Example of the Roots Surname List for the Helm surname.

If you need more information on using e-mail, refer to Appendix A.

Forming Research Groups

If your relatives are tired of hearing about your genealogy research trips or the information that you found on great-uncle William, but you'd like to share your triumphs with someone, then you may be ready to join a research group.

Research groups consist of any number of people who coordinate their research and share resources to achieve success. These groups may start conducting research because they share a surname, family branch, or geographic location. Individuals who live geographically close to each other may make up a research group, or the group may consist of people who have never personally met each other. Research groups may have a variety of goals and may have a formal or an informal structure. They are quite flexible organizationally and depend entirely on the membership of the group.

A good example of an informal research group is one that Matthew discovered shortly after he posted his first Web page. An individual who was researching one of his surnames on the East Coast of the United States contacted him. After exchanging a couple of e-mails, Matthew learned that this individual was part of a small research group studying the origins of several different branches of the Helm surname. Each member of the group contributes the results of his or her personal research and provides any information that he or she has found, which may be of use to other members of the group. Additionally, the group as a whole has sponsored research by professional genealogists in other countries to discover more about their ancestors there. Several more researchers have joined the group recently (as more researchers are discovered on the Internet), and everyone communicates regularly through e-mail.

You can find an example of an online-based research group at the William Aaron Saunders Research Group site (`www.wasrg.org/`). The mission of this group is to collect and share genealogical data and stories relating to William Aaron Saunders (cir. 1735 VA to cir. 1785 NC). The site is constructed to help Saunders/Sanders researchers collaborate with each other. It has sections containing information about the research group members, family groups, stories, photos (including a section with unidentified photos), and GEDCOM files. It also has links to other Web sites that have information about some of the same ancestors that are studied through the research group.

To find research groups, your best bet is to visit a comprehensive genealogical Web site or a site that specializes in surnames, such as the GeneaSearch Surname Registry at

`www.geneasearch.com/surnameregister.htm`

or SurnameWeb at

`www.surnameweb.com`

The following steps show you how to find groups pertaining to a surname on the site:

1. **Launch your Web browser and go to the SurnameWeb site at**

   `www.surnameweb.com`

   After the page loads, you see a search field and the letters of the alphabet near the top center of the page.

2. **Choose the letter of the alphabet that's the first letter of the surname that you're researching.**

   For example, say the surname that you're researching begins with the letter *P.* Find the link to the letter *P* and click it. This action brings up a Web page with the *P* Index.

3. **Select the Po link near the top of the page.**

   This brings up a list of surname links that begin with the letters Po.

4. **Scroll through the list and select a surname link.**

   We want to find sites relating to the surname *Pollard,* so click the link for the Pollard surname, which takes us to a Results page titled "Pollard Genealogy Center."

5. **Choose a site to visit.**

   Scroll down past all of the links to search other commercial Web sites until you reach the links you're most interested in — in our case, those links that take us directly to personal and group Web pages that contain information about people named Pollard.

In addition to using comprehensive genealogy sites and specialized surname sites, you can use other strategies to identify possible research groups. One way to find research groups pertaining to surnames is to visit a one-name studies index. You can find a list of one-name studies sites at the Guild of One-Name Studies page (www.one-name.org). You can also look to existing larger groups that may have specific research components, such as genealogical societies. (The following section goes into more detail on genealogical societies.)

If you can't find an established online group that fits your interests, why not start one yourself? If you're interested in researching a particular topic, the chances are very good that others out there are interested as well. Maybe the time has come for you to coordinate efforts and begin working with others toward your common research goals. Starting an online research group can be relatively easy — just post a message stating your interest in starting a group at some key locations, such as message boards, newsgroups, or mailing lists.

Becoming a Solid Member of (Genealogical) Society

Genealogical societies can be great places to learn research methods and to coordinate your research. Several different types of societies exist. They range from the more traditional geographical or surname-based societies to newer *cyber-societies* (societies that exist only on the Internet) that are redefining the way that people think about genealogical societies.

Geographical societies

Chapter 6 introduces geography-based genealogical societies as groups that can help you discover resources in a particular area in which your ancestors lived, or as groups in your hometown that can help you discover how to research effectively. However, local genealogical societies can provide another service to their members. These societies often coordinate local research efforts of the members in the form of projects. To locate geographical societies, follow our advice in Chapter 6 or check out the site of a genealogical-society federation such as one of these:

☞ Federation of Genealogical Societies, Society Hall page, at

   `www.familyhistory.com/societyhall/`

☞ Federation of Family History Societies at `www.ffhs.org.uk`

These projects can take many forms. For example, the Illinois State Genealogical Society (`www.rootsweb.com/~ilsgs/`) is working on several projects, including creating a database of county marriage records, updating a list of Illinois pioneers, and forming a list of all cemeteries in the state. (See Figure 10-3.)

Figure 10-3:
Cemetery entries for Fayette County, Illinois, on the ISGS site.

Illinois State Genealogical Society - Projects - Fayette County Cemeteries - Microsoft Internet Explorer

File   Edit   View   Favorites   Tools   Help

Back ▾ │ Search │ Favorites │ Media │ │ Links

Address `http://www.rootsweb.com/~ilsgs/ilcemetery-al/fayette.html`   Go

Fayette County   Updated 1/16/2003

NAME	ALIAS	OL	C	R	V	ST	SEC	TOWNSHIP	LOCATION	QTR QTR	QTR SEC
Abel						DE	02	Sharon		NW	SW
Adcock	Causey or Depew or Devore or Donelson			Y	Y	IN	17	Bear Grove		SW	NW
Ambuehl				Y	Y	AC	13	Lone Grove		NE	NE
Amish					Y	IN	17	Sefton		SW	SE
Ammerman				Y	Y	DE	18	Loudon		NW	SW
Antioch			Y	Y	Y	AC	22	Bowling Green		NW	NE
Arm Prairie			Y	Y		AC	35	Otego		SW	SE
Augsburg	Immanuel Lutheran		Y	Y	Y	AC	18	Wilberton		SE	SE
Austin					Y	DE	30	Carson		SW	NW
Bails					Y	DE	?	Bowlling Green		?	?
Bear Creek				Y		AC	11	Pope		SE	SE
Beck				Y		IN	28	Ramsey		NE	NE
Beck Private	Snow			Y		IN	24	Bowling Green		SW	SW
Bethlehem	Brushy Point		Y	Y	Y	AC	07	Bear Grove		?	SE
Big Spring					Y	DE	?	Carson		?	?

Internet

Smaller groups of members sometimes work on projects in addition to the society's official projects. For example, you may belong to a county genealogical society and decide to join with a few members to write a history of the pioneers who settled a particular township within the county. If each member of the team shares the fruits of his or her research, you can cover three or four times more ground than you can by yourself.

Family and surname associations

In addition to geographically based associations, you can find groups tied to particular names or family groups. Typically, they are referred to as — you've probably already guessed — surname or family associations or research groups.

Family associations also frequently sponsor projects that coordinate the efforts of several researchers. These projects may focus on the family or surname in a specific geographic area or point in time, or they may attempt to collect information about every individual possessing the surname throughout time and then place the information in a shared database.

You can find family and surname associations through comprehensive genealogy sites (listed in The *Genealogy Online For Dummies* Internet Directory in this book), general Internet search engines (also listed in this book's directory section), or sites specializing in associations.

If a family or surname association isn't currently working on a project that interests you, by all means suggest a project that does interest you (as long as the project is relevant to the association as a whole).

Reuniting with Your Family (Family Reunions as a Research Occasion)

We strongly recommend that you interview relatives to glean information about your ancestors, to use as leads in finding records, and to enhance your genealogy. In fact, we started driving home this point in Chapter 1. Well, what better way to gather information from relatives than by attending a family reunion?

Family reunions can add a lot to your research because you find many relatives all in one place and typically most are eager to visit. A reunion is an efficient way to collect stories, photographs, databases (if others in the family research and keep their records in their computers), and even copies of records. You might even find some people interested in researching the family along with you. And a family reunion can be great fun, too.

When you attend your next family reunion, be sure to take along your notebook, list of interview questions (see Chapter 1 if you haven't developed your list yet), and camera. You can take some printed charts from your genealogical database, too — we bet that lots of your relatives will be interested in seeing them.

Rent-A-Researcher

There may come a time when you've exhausted all the research avenues directly available to you and you need help that family, friends, and society members can't give you. Maybe all the records you need to get past a research "brick wall" are in a distant place, or maybe you have too many other obligations and not enough time to research personally. You needn't fret. Professional researchers are happy to help you.

Professional researchers are people you pay a fee to dig around and find information for you. They will retrieve specific records that you identify or they will prepare an entire report on a family line using all of the types of resources available. And, as you might expect, the amount that you pay depends on the level of service that you require. Professional researchers are especially helpful when you need records from locations to which you cannot travel conveniently.

When looking for a professional researcher, you want to find someone who is reputable and experienced in the area in which you need help. Here's a list of questions you may want to ask when shopping around for a professional researcher:

- Is the researcher certified or accredited and, if so, by what organization?
- How many years experience does he have researching?
- What is his educational background?
- Does the researcher have any professional affiliations? In other words, does he belong to any professional genealogical organizations and, if so, which ones?
- What foreign languages does the researcher speak fluently?
- What records and resources does he have access to?

✔ What is the professional researcher's experience in the area where you need help? For example, if you need help interviewing distant relatives in a foreign country, has he conducted interviews in the past? Or if you need records pertaining to a particular ethnic or religious group, does he have experience researching those types of records?

✔ How does the researcher charge for his services — by the record, by the hour, or by the project? What methods of payment does he accept? What is the researcher's policy on refunds or dissatisfaction with his services?

✔ How many other projects is the researcher working on presently and what kinds of projects? How much time will he devote to your research project? When will he report his results?

✔ Does the researcher have references you can contact?

One way to find professional researchers is to look for them on comprehensive genealogy sites. Another is to consult an online directory of researchers, such as the Association of Professional Genealogists (www.apgen.org) directory or genealogyPro (www.genealogypro.com).

Follow these steps to check the genealogyPro directory:

1. **Using your Web browser, go to the genealogyPro site at** www.genealogyPro.com.

   Note: For more information on using a browser, see Appendix A.

2. **Click the link from the list in the right column of the page for the geographic area you're interested in.**

   For example, we're interested in finding someone to do research in England, so we click the England and Wales link. This link takes us to a page with links to particular researchers or research companies doing work in England and Wales and includes a brief description of each researcher's area of concentration.

3. **Click the link for a researcher who — based on the brief description posted — sounds promising.**

   In our example, clicking the link for Britfinders takes us to a page listing the company's address, phone number, e-mail address, Web page URL, qualifications, services, and fees.

When you find a professional researcher who looks promising, make your initial contact. Be sure to be as specific as possible about your needs. That helps the researcher pinpoint exactly what he or she needs to do, and makes it easier to calculate how much it will cost you.

> ✔ **What association sites (both family and geographical) are interested in my information?** See Chapters 4 and 6 for association sites.
>
> ✔ **What general sites (such as query sites and GEDCOM collections) are interested in my information?** See Chapters 4 and 6 for some examples of these sites.

You may want to use all available Internet resources to let people know about your information, including mailing lists, newsgroups, and Web sites.

For example, April has information on a McSwain family. She knows that they lived in Madison, Estill, Jessamine, and Nicholas counties in Kentucky. To identify sites where she may be able to post this information, she looked for one-name study pages on the surname *McSwain,* personal pages that have connections to the McSwain family, and any mailing lists dedicated to discussing the family. She also tried to find sites for each of the four counties in Kentucky that the McSwains resided in. Then she searched for family societies or county genealogical or historical societies in Kentucky that look for information on their past inhabitants. Finally, she looked for general-query sites and GEDCOM repositories (more about GEDCOM later in this chapter) that may accept her information.

Contacting your target audience

After you write down the names and addresses of sites that probably attract an audience that you want to target, you need to notify them. Create a brief but detailed e-mail message to make your announcement. When you submit your message, look at the format required by each resource that you're contacting. For example, the soc.genealogy.surnames newsgroups have a specific format for subject lines (for examples, see Chapter 4). Some *query sites* (places where you can post genealogical questions to get help from other researchers) also have specific formats, so you may need to modify your message for each of these sites. (For more information about query sites and posting queries, see Chapter 4.)

Here's a sample message to give you some ideas:

```
MCSWAIN, 1810-1910, KY, USA
I have information on the family of William McSwain of
Kentucky. William was born in 1802, married Elizabeth Hisle
in March 1827, and had the following children:
Thomas, Mary, Joseph, Sarah, Susan, Margaret, Elizabeth,
Nancy, and James.
```

Most people understand that you're willing to share information on the family if you post something to a site, so you probably don't need to say that within your message. Remember, people are more likely to read your message if it has a short-but-descriptive subject line, text that is brief and to the point, and contains enough information for the readers to determine whether your information can help them (or whether they have information that can assist you).

Exporting Your Information

Suppose you contact others who are interested in your information. What's the best way to share your information with them? Certainly, you can type everything up, print it, and send it to them. Or you can export a copy of your genealogy database file — which the recipients can then import into their databases and run as many reports as they want — and save a few trees in the process.

GEDCOM files

Most genealogical databases subscribe to a common standard for exporting their information called *Genealogical Data Communication,* or GEDCOM. (Beware that some genealogical databases deviate from the standard a little — making things somewhat confusing.)

A *GEDCOM file* is a text file that contains your genealogical information with a set of tags that tells the genealogical database importing the information where to place it within its structure. For a little history and more information about GEDCOM, see Chapter 9. Figure 11-1 shows an example of a GEDCOM file.

You may be asking, *Why is GEDCOM important?* It can save you time and energy in the process of sharing information. The next time someone asks you to send them your data, you can export your genealogy data into a GEDCOM file and send it to them instead of typing it up or saving a copy of your entire database.

Making a GEDCOM file using Family Tree Maker, a program on the CD-ROM that accompanies this book, is easy. (For installation instructions, see Appendix C.) To export information from Family Tree Maker to GEDCOM, try this:

1. **Open Family Tree Maker.**

   Usually, you can open your software by double-clicking the icon for that program or by going to the Programs (or All Programs) menu from the Start button and selecting the particular program.

```
helm-old_90.GED - Notepad
File  Edit  Format  View  Help
0 @I0904@ INDI
1 NAME Samuel Clayton /Abell/, Jr.
1 SEX M
1 BIRT
2 DATE 16 MAR 1844
2 PLAC Cedar Creek, Nelson Co., KY
1 DEAT
2 DATE 27 JUL 1923
2 PLAC Wapella, Dewitt Co., IL
1 _FA1
2 DATE 1850
2 PLAC Census - Larue Co., KY
1 _FA2
2 DATE 1860
2 PLAC Census - Larue Co., KY (listed as Clayton)
1 _FA3
2 DATE 1870
2 PLAC Census - Larue Co., KY
1 _FA4
2 DATE 1880
2 PLAC Census - Larue Co., KY
1 FAMS @F0358@
1 FAMS @F0356@
1 FAMC @F0359@
1 NOTE @NI0904@
0 @NI0904@ NOTE
1 CONC Records of Samuel's Civil War Service contained in the Compiled Service
1 CONC Records of Volunteer Union Soldiers who Servied in Organizations from
1 CONC Kentucky.  Samuel enlisted as a private in Co. F, 37th Kentucky Infantry
1 CONC at 16 years of age on August 3, 1863 (not consisted with birth date).
1 CONC Recorded as present for duty on October 31, 1863; November and December
1 CONC 1863; Januaryand February 1864; March and April 1864; May and June 1864;
1 CONC and July and August 1864.  Mustered out as a corporal on December 29,
1 CONC 1864 in Louisville, KY.  One author mentioned that Samuel's grandfather
1 CONC was Robert Abell.  The author said Samuel first enrolled in the Union
1 CONC Army at Camp Pope on November 20, 1861 and gave his age as 18. He was a
1 CONC private in Company C, 15th Kentucky Infantry.  He apparently deserted at
1 CONC Crab Orchard, Kentucky on October 20, 1862.  He was last heard from while
1 CONC at Hodgensville on February 15, 1863.  He apparently enrolled again in
1 CONC the Union Army at Glasgow, KY on August 3, 1863 and was a private in
1 CONC Company F, 37th KY INF.  He was promoted to 8th Corporal.  He was
1 CONC honorably discharged and mustered out at Louisville on December 29, 1864.
```

Figure 11-1:
An example of a GEDCOM file displayed in the Windows Notepad program.

2. **Use the default database that appears, or choose File⇨Open Family File to open another database.**

3. **After you open the database for which you want to create a GEDCOM file, choose File⇨Copy/Export Family File.**

   The New Family File dialog box appears. This dialog box enables you to enter a name for the file and choose the format to save the file in. (You'll want to choose GEDCOM as the file format.)

4. **Type the new name for your GEDCOM file in the File Name field, move your cursor to the Save as Type field and select GEDCOM (*.GED) as the format, and then click Save.**

   The Export to GEDCOM dialog box appears, as shown in Figure 11-2. This dialog box enables you to set up the GEDCOM file in a specific format.

5. **In the Destination field, choose the destination software program to which you want to export the file.**

   If you don't know which program the other person with whom you're sharing the GEDCOM uses, choose the Family Tree Maker setting.

Figure 11-2:
The Export
to GEDCOM
window in
Family Tree
Maker.

6. In the GEDCOM field, choose the version of GEDCOM to which you're exporting.

Most genealogical software is compatible with the most recent version of GEDCOM, so you're usually safe to keep the default setting. If you know that the person to whom you're sending your GEDCOM uses older software that supports an older version of GEDCOM, you can change the output settings to accommodate that person.

7. In the Character Set field, choose ANSI (which is the default).

8. If you have a preference for how the GEDCOM output is formatted, check or uncheck the Indent Records and Abbreviate Tags check boxes.

You can choose to have the records indented on your GEDCOM output instead of having all the coded lines in a straight list, flush-left in the file (refer to Figure 11-1 for an example of the flush-left GEDCOM). Indenting the records makes reading through the GEDCOM a little easier when you open it in a word processor. However, it sometimes presents problems when importing the GEDCOM into another genealogical software program. Family Tree Maker indents lines based on the number code for the line. For example, all 1s are flush left, 2s are indented once, and 3s are indented twice.

XML: GEDCOM's successor?

Although GEDCOM was originally designed to help researchers exchange information with each other while using various genealogical software programs, it isn't necessarily the best way to present information on the World Wide Web. Currently, efforts are underway to create a better way to display and identify genealogical information on the Web. Eventually, these efforts could produce the successor to GEDCOM.

One of the possible successors to GEDCOM is *eXtensible Markup Language,* more commonly recognized by the acronym, *XML.* XML is similar to HyperText Markup Language (HTML) in that it uses tags to describe information. However, the purpose of XML is different than HTML. HTML was designed to tell a Web browser, such as Netscape or Internet Explorer, how to arrange text and graphics on a page. XML is designed not only to display information, but also to describe the information.

An early version of XML for the genealogical community was *GedML* developed by Michael Kay. GedML uses XML tags to describe genealogical data on the Web, much like GEDCOM does for genealogical software. Here's an example of information provided in a GEDCOM file and its GedML equivalent:

GEDCOM:

```
0 @I0904@ INDI
1 NAME Samuel Clayton /ABELL/
1 SEX M
1 BIRT
2 DATE 16 Mar 1844
2 PLAC Nelson County, KY
1 FAMS @F0397@
```

GedML:

```
<INDI ID="I0904">
<NAME> Samuel Clayton
     <S>ABELL</S></NAME>
<SEX>M</SEX>
<EVEN EV='BIRT'>
<DATE>16 Mar 1844</DATE>
<PLAC> Nelson County, KY</PLAC>
     </EVEN>
<FAMS REF="F397"/>
</INDI>
```

XML, whether it's GedML or some other XML structure, promises an enhancement of the searchability of genealogical documents on the Web. Right now, it's difficult for genealogically focused search engines to identify what's genealogical in nature and what's not (for more on genealogically focused search engines, see Chapter 4). Also, tags allow search engines to determine whether a particular data element is a name or a place.

XML also provides an efficient way to link genealogical data between Web sites, gives users more control over how particular text is displayed (such as notes), and allows genealogists to place information directly on the Web without using a program to convert databases or GEDCOM files to HTML.

For more information on GedML, see users. breathe.com/mhkay/gedml/.

Likewise, you can have the GEDCOM tags abbreviated rather than written in their entirety. For example, the tag *Header* would be *Head* and *Address* would be *Addr*.

9. **After you complete all the required boxes and are satisfied with the options that you selected, click OK.**

   When you click OK, a bar appears across the screen showing the progress of the export, with the message "Exporting Individuals" listed above it.

After the GEDCOM file's created on your hard drive, you can open it in a word processor (such as WordPad) and review it to ensure that the information is formatted the way you want it. Also, reviewing the file in a word processor is a good idea so you can ensure that you included no information on living persons. After you're satisfied with the file, you can cut and paste it into an e-mail message or send it as an attachment using your e-mail program.

Reports

GEDCOM is a great option when two individuals have genealogical software that supports the standard. But what about all those people who are new to genealogy and haven't invested in software yet? How do you send them information that they can use? One option is to generate reports through your genealogical software, export them into your word processor, and then print copies to mail (or attach copies of the word-processing file to e-mail messages).

Chapter 3 gives step-by-step instructions for entering all your detailed family information into Family Tree Maker. (A basic version of this genealogical software is included on the CD-ROM accompanying this book.) The process for exporting a report should be similar for most genealogical software. The following steps show you specifically how to export a report from Family Tree Maker to a word processor:

1. **Open Family Tree Maker.**

   Usually, you can open your software by double-clicking the icon for that program or by going to the Programs (or All Programs) menu from the Start button and selecting the particular program.

   Note: If you aren't sure how to open your software, consult the user's manual.

2. **Choose View⇨Index of Individuals.**

   This action brings up a box that lists all the individuals entered in your database in alphabetical order.

3. **Scroll through the index and select the person for whom you want to generate a chart/report by double-clicking the name or highlighting the name and clicking OK.**

   This action takes you to the Family Page for the person you select.

   For example, if Matthew wants to generate a report for his ancestor Samuel Abell IV, he highlights Samuel's name in the index and clicks OK.

4. **Place your cursor in the person's name field.**

   Move your cursor into the Husband, Wife, or Children field to select the exact person that you want to generate a chart/report on.

   Likewise, Matthew moves the cursor into the name field for Samuel Abell IV.

5. **Click the appropriate button for the chart/report that you want (in the button bar at the top of the Family Tree Maker screen), or choose View⇨[*Type of tree or report*].**

   Buttons in the button bar correspond to Ancestor Tree, Descendant Tree, Hourglass Tree, All-in-One Tree, Outline Descendant Tree, Genealogy Report, and Family Group Sheet. Or, if you're using the drop-down menu, the charts/reports appear as All-in-One Tree, Ancestor Tree, Descendant Tree, Hourglass Tree, Outline Descendant Tree, Family Group Sheet, Genealogy Report, and Kinship Report. (You can generate other reports using Family Tree Maker, but these are the most common types and the five that we discuss in this chapter.)

   Family Tree Maker generates the requested chart/report for the person you select.

   For our example, if Matthew wants to generate an outline of Samuel Abell's descendants, he clicks the Outline button or uses the View menu to choose an Outline Descendant Tree. Family Tree Maker then generates an Outline chart on-screen.

6. **Choose Edit⇨Copy Outline Descendant Tree.**

   This places a copy of the report on the Windows Clipboard, which enables you to paste it into any Windows application that supports cutting and pasting information.

   Matthew copies the Outline Descendant Tree to the clipboard.

7. **Open WordPad (or any other word processor), and choose Edit⇨Paste.**

   This action places the Outline Descendant report into your word processor. You can now edit the report just as if you had typed the report into the program itself (see Figure 11-3).

   After he pastes the Samuel Abell Outline chart into WordPad, Matthew can review and edit it to ensure that it has all the information that he wants to include when sharing it with others. He can also double-check the chart to ensure that it doesn't include any information on living persons.

```
Untitled - Notepad
File  Edit  Format  View  Help
Descendants of Peter Abell
        1       Peter Abell       1740 - 1785
..              +Lucy {Carman}   1745 - 1811
.......         2    Jeannott (Jenneh) Abell
...........          +Samuel Abell   - 1863
................        3    Nathan Abell
................        3    Jesse Abell
................        3    Edmund Abell, Judge
................        3    Hannibal Abell
................        3    Mary Elizabeth Abell
................        3    Peter Abell      1809 - 1901
....................         +Caroline (or Ann) Read
....................         *2nd wife of Peter Abell:
....................         +Mary Ann Waring
....................         4    Robert Abell
....................         4    Peter Abell
....................         4    Sheldon M. Abell
....................         4    Anna Gibson Abell
....................         4    Philip Abell
....................         4    Janet Abell
....................         4    Zadock Abell     1851 -
....................          .     +Etta May Roy
....................         4    Lyman David Barber Abell     1859 -
....................               +Sally Lambert
....................         5    Emma Texas Abell        1885 -
....................               +Grover C. Ginger
................        3    Washington Abell      1809 - 1872
................             +Eleanor B. Overall   1814 -
................             4    Hannibal Abell  1835 - 1840
................             4    John O. Abell   1837 - 1838
................             4    James M. Abell  1839 - 1872
................              .     +Catharine G. Proctor
................             4    Matilda Abell   1841 -
................                   +Francis M. Culver
................             4    Gabriel Watham Abell    1844 - 1911
................                   +Louise Hughey
................             5    Clara Abell
................              .     +Fincher
................             4    Jesse Lee Abell 1847 - 1919
................                   +Elizabeth Laura Fort
................             5    Samuel Abell     1881 -
```

Figure 11-3:
A descendant report shown in Notepad.

When your Outline report is in a word-processing file, you can activate your favorite e-mail program and send the file to the individual who requested information. If the report is long, you can include it with your e-mail as an attachment. If the report is short, you can simply cut and paste it into the text of your e-mail message.

If You Post It, They Will Come

Instead of sending information to several different individuals, consider placing your information at a site where people can access it at their convenience. One option is to post your information on a Web site. (See Chapter 12 for more information.) But you have some other options if you're not ready to take the Web-designing plunge.

One option is to find others who are working on the same surnames or geographical areas and who already have Web pages, and ask them to post your information on their sites. Don't be offended if they decline — most Internet accounts have specific storage limits, and they may not have room for your information.

A second option is to submit your information to a general site that collects GEDCOM files. Examples of these sites include

- **Ancestry World Tree:** www.ancestry.com/share/awt/main.htm
- **GenServ:** www.genserv.com
- **My-GED.com:** www.my-ged.com
- **WorldConnect:** worldconnect.rootsweb.com

Citing Your Sources

We can't stress enough the importance of citing your sources when sharing information — online or through traditional means. Be sure to include references that reflect where you obtained your information; that's just as important when you share your information as it is when you research it. Not only does referencing provide the other person with leads to possible additional information, but it also gives you a place to return and double-check your facts if someone challenges your facts. Sometimes, after exchanging information with another researcher, you both notice that you have conflicting data about a particular ancestor. Knowing where to turn to double-check the facts (and, with any luck, find out who has the correct information) can save you time and embarrassment.

Here are some examples of ways to cite online sources of information:

- **E-mail messages:** Matthew Helm, [<mhelm@tbox.com> or 111 Main Street, Anyplace, Anystate 11111]. "Looking for George Helm," Message to April Helm, 12 January 2004. [Message cites vital records in Helm's possession.]

- **Newsgroups:** Matthew Helm, [<mhelm@tbox.com> or 111 Main Street, Anyplace, Anystate 11111]. "Computing in Genealogy" in soc.genealogy.computing, 12 January 2004.

- **Web sites:** Matthew Helm, [<mhelm@tbox.com> or 111 Main Street, Anyplace, Anystate 11111]. "Helm's Genealogy Toolbox. "<genealogy.tbox.com> January 2004. [This site contains numerous links to other genealogical resources on the Internet. On January 12, located and checked links on Abell family, found two that were promising.] (Of course, with a note like the preceding one in brackets, you expect that your next two citations are the two Web sites that looked promising. For each site, you should provide notes stating exactly what you did or did not find.)

Although most genealogical software programs now enable you to store source information and citations along with your data, many still don't export the source information automatically. For that reason, double-check any reports or GEDCOMs you generate to see whether your source information is included before sharing them with other researchers. If the information isn't included, create a new GEDCOM file that includes sources.

Mandatory Lecture on Privacy

We couldn't sleep at night if we didn't give you the mandatory lecture on maintaining the privacy of living individuals when you share your genealogical information.

In the rush to get genealogical information posted on the Internet, people sometimes forget that portions of the information in their databases, and thus in their GEDCOM files, are considered private.

Why worry about privacy? Let us count (a few of) the reasons . . .

We've heard horror stories about Social Security numbers of living individuals ending up in GEDCOM files that are available on the Internet. We've also heard of people who didn't know that their biological parents weren't married (to each other, anyway) and found out through an online database, and so forth. Private detectives and other people who search for information on living persons frequently use genealogical databases to track people. For these reasons, it is illegal in some states and countries to share information about living persons on the Internet without first getting each person's written permission to do so. To avoid an invasion of privacy and any legal problems that could arise from you sharing your information, you should always clean out (exclude) any information on living individuals from your GEDCOM file before you give it to anyone.

More and more genealogists are now aware of the privacy implications of online research and sharing. As a result, some have designed programs to clean out information on living individuals from GEDCOM files. One such piece of freeware, GEDClean, is available on the CD-ROM that accompanies this book, as well as from www.raynorshyn.com/gedclean/Compare.html. Even if you use software to clean a file, be sure to double-check the data in the file to ensure that the software catches everything and that you *don't* share any information on living people.

Chapter 12

Creating a Place to Call Home

. . . .

In This Chapter

▶ Finding a home for your home page

▶ Getting to know HTML

▶ Using genealogical software utilities

▶ Enhancing your Web pages with photographs

. . . .

So you've loaded your genealogical database with information about your relatives and ancestors, and you've shared data with others by e-mail. Now you're ready to create and post your own home page (Web site). In this chapter, we explore where you can post a simple site and how to do so. This chapter gives you the basics on creating a home on the Internet where your information can reside and accept visitors.

If you're looking for really detailed information about creating a full-blown and fancy Web site, or about beginning and advanced HTML programming, then you're looking in the wrong place. Genealogy and basic computer use in pursuit of genealogy is the focus of this book — not Web-site creation or HTML programming. This chapter covers the very basics to get you started. For more information about HTML, we recommend that you check out these other *For Dummies* books (all published by Wiley Publishing, Inc.): *Creating Web Pages For Dummies*, 6th Edition, by Bud E. Smith and Arthur Bebak; *The Internet For Dummies*, 9th Edition, by John R. Levine, Carol Baroudi, and Margaret Levine Young; and *HTML 4 For Dummies*, 4th Edition, by Ed Tittel and Natanya Pitts.

Home Sweet Home

Before you can build your home page, you need to find a home (that is, a *host*) for it. Although you can design a basic home page on your own computer using no more than a word processor, others won't be able to see it until you put the page on a Web server on the Internet. A *Web server* is a computer that's connected directly to the Internet that serves up Web pages when you request them using your computer's Web browser.

Commercial Internet service providers

If you subscribe to a commercial *Internet service provider* (ISP) like America Online, EarthLink, or MSN, or if you subscribe to a local provider, then you may already have a home for your Web pages. Most commercial ISPs include a specific space allocation for user home pages in their memberships, as well as some tools to help you build your site. Check your membership agreement to see whether you have space. Then you can follow the ISP's instructions for creating your Web site (using the service's page builder or editor) or for getting your independently created Web pages from your computer to the ISP's server. (If you didn't keep a copy of your membership agreement, don't fret! Most ISPs have an informational Web page that you can get to from your ISP's main page; the informational page reviews membership benefits.) You may as well take advantage of this service if you're already paying for it.

If your particular membership level doesn't include Web space, but the ISP has other membership levels that do, then hold off on bumping up your membership level. You can take advantage of some free Web-hosting services that may save you money. Keep reading . . .

Free Web-hosting services

There are some Web sites that give you free space for your home page provided that you agree to their rules and restrictions. We can safely bet that you won't have any problems using one of these freebies, because the terms (such as no pornography, nudity, or explicit language allowed) are genealogist-friendly.

If you decide to take advantage of Web space, remember that the companies providing the space must pay their bills. Often they can make space available free to individuals by charging advertisers for banners and other advertisements. In such cases, the Web host reserves the right to require that you leave these advertisements on your home page. If you don't like the idea of an advertisement on your home page, or if you have strong objections to one of the companies that advertises with the site that gives you free space, then you should find a fee-based Web space for your home page.

For a list of places where you can get a free Web page, check out the Yahoo! Free Web Site Hosting Providers page at

```
dir.yahoo.com/Business_and_Economy/Business_to_Business/
Communications_and_Networking/Internet_and_World_Wide_Web/
Network_Service_Providers/Hosting/Web_Site_Hosting/Free_
Hosting/
```

or try the WebHostDirectory site at `www.webhostdir.com/`. We don't have enough room in this book to provide information about each of the companies or services listed at either of these sites (after all, this is a book about genealogy — not Web pages), so we focus on a couple of services that have been around for awhile.

Tripod

`www.tripod.lycos.com`

Tripod provides 20MB of free space for your Web pages and 1GB of monthly *bandwidth* (which refers, in this case, to the amount of traffic you can receive to your site), as well as access to tools to help you build your Web pages.

Here's how you find out more about (and join) Tripod.

1. **Browse on over to** `www.tripod.lycos.com` **and then click the <u>Find the Perfect Fit</u> link on the right side of the Tripod homepage.**

   This takes you to the Compare All Subscription Plans page where you can do a quick comparison of all that Tripod has to offer.

2. **Click the <u>Sign Up</u> link above or below the Free column.**

   The Choose a Membership Plan page pops up.

3. **Click the <u>Try Tripod for FREE!</u> link at the lower left of the page.**

4. **Complete the online membership application.**

   The online form asks you to provide a member name and password, as well as your title, name, mailing address with zip code, country of residence, birth date, e-mail address, and phone number. It also asks about educational level and occupation, although you are not required to complete these fields in order to sign up. You can also choose to identify some of your hobbies, activities, or interests, and identify which registration offers you'd like to receive (if any).

5. **Upon completing the form and reading the consent statement, click the I Agree button.**

   After you submit the registration form, Tripod takes you to the Confirmation page, where you can click the <u>Activate Your Account and Start Building</u> link to begin to build your Web site using various tools. If you already need to update any registration information that you provided, you can click the Registration Information link to do so.

Yahoo! GeoCities

`geocities.yahoo.com/ps/learn2/HowItWorks4_Free.html`

GeoCities provides 15MB of free space, a free e-mail account, 3GB of bandwidth per month, and wizards to help you build your Web pages. If you're a new user to Yahoo! GeoCities, click the Sign Up link and complete the resulting form. You're asked to provide an ID or member name and password, as well as your birth date, e-mail address, language that will be used for the page content, Zip code, gender, occupation, and industry. You also have the opportunity to sign up for mailings. After you complete the form, click the Submit This Form button. Yahoo! GeoCities gives you a Confirmation Web page where you can click the Build Your Web Site Now link. This Web page shows you how to create your site using the available tools.

RootsWeb.com

`accounts.rootsweb.com/`

RootsWeb.com is a genealogical site that offers homes to many projects, societies, and individuals who want to post family history related material on the Web. It is a division of MyFamily.com and sister site to Ancestry.com. RootsWeb.com has been around for several years and is quite well known in the genealogical community. Its reputation makes it a good place to post your Web site. Conveniently, it offers free space if you're posting acceptable material. To apply for free space, you first must read and agree to the RootsWeb agreement for a Freepages Web space account. Then you complete an online form, which includes a justification as to what you plan to use the Web space for, and then click the Submit button. One catch to getting free space at RootsWeb.com is that you must wait three to five days for your request for space to be processed.

Do You Speak HTML?

HyperText Markup Language (or HTML) is the language of the World Wide Web. HTML is a code in which text documents are written so Web browsers can read and interpret those documents, converting them into graphical images and text that you can see through the browser. HTML is a relatively easy language to learn, and many genealogists who post Web pages are self-taught. If you prefer not to read about it and teach yourself by experimenting, there are sure to be classes as well as other resources in your area that could teach you the basics of HTML. Check with a local community college for structured classes, local genealogical societies for any workshops focusing on designing and posting Web pages, or the World Wide Web itself for online courses. Chapter 14 provides a few sites you can use to find online courses and other tools to help you build your Web site.

For more information about the World Wide Web and Web browsers, take a look at Appendix A.

Here are a couple of things to remember about HTML:

✔ You write HTML as a text document using a text editor, an HTML editor, or a word processor, and you save it as a text document (with the file name extension of `htm` or `html`).

✔ You use a Web browser to interpret HTML documents as graphical and text pages on the Internet.

What does HTML look like?

To get an idea of what HTML looks like — both as the text document and as the converted graphical image — take a look at some extremely simple HTML tags that April created for a Web page called My Favorite Abe. Figure 12-1 shows the Web page that's created by the tags.

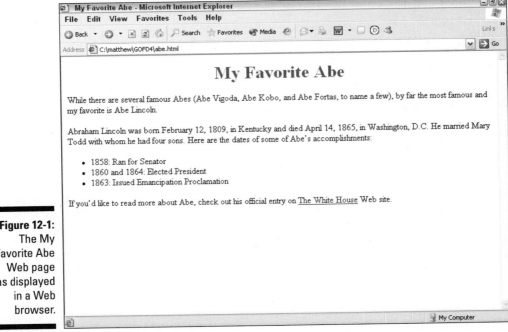

Figure 12-1:
The My Favorite Abe Web page as displayed in a Web browser.

Here's what the HTML codes (also called tags) look like:

```
<HTML>

<HEAD>
<TITLE>My Favorite Abe</TITLE>
</HEAD>
<BODY BGCOLOR = "White" ALINK = "Blue" VLINK = "Gray">
<H1><FONT COLOR = "Green"><CENTER>My Favorite
        Abe</CENTER></FONT></H1>
While there are several famous Abes (Abe Vigoda, Abe Kobo,
        and Abe Fortas, to name a few), by far the most
        famous is Abe Lincoln.<P>
Abraham Lincoln was born February 12, 1809, in Kentucky and
        died April 14, 1865, in Washington, D.C. He
        married Mary Todd with whom he had four sons. Here
        are the dates of some of Abe's accomplishments:
<UL>
<LI>1858: Ran for Senator
<LI>1860 and 1864: Elected President
<LI>1863: Issued Emancipation Proclamation
</UL><P>
If you'd like to read more about Abe, check out his official
        entry on
<A HREF =
        "http://www.whitehouse.gov/history/presidents/al16
        .html"> The White House</A> Web site.
</BODY>
</HTML>
```

The tags are placed within angle brackets, like this: `<BODY>`. These tags tell the browser how to interpret the text that follows and whether to actually show that text on the Web page. Just as you have to tell the browser when to begin interpreting text in a certain manner, you also have to tell it when to stop. This ending command consists of an open bracket, a front slash, the tag word, and a close bracket, like this: `</BODY>`.

For example:

```
<TITLE>My Favorite Abe</TITLE>
```

In this line, the `<TITLE>` tag tells the browser where to begin treating text as a title and `</TITLE>` also tells it where to end that treatment. Think of HTML tags as on and off commands where `< >` indicates *on* and `</ >` indicates *off.*

Some basic tags for writing your own HTML

If you've been reading along systematically in this chapter, you know that just preceding this section is an example of what HTML codes or tags look like. But what are the tags themselves? HTML involves too many tags to do justice here when the main point is to create and post a basic genealogical Web page. We really only have space here to cover just a few of the many tags.

If you're interested in more advanced HTML programming, Chapter 14 provides a couple of Web sites to visit. For an even more detailed read, check out *HTML 4 For Dummies*, 4th Edition, by Ed Tittel and Natanya Pitts. Or if you're looking for more information than we can offer here but not quite as much detail as a straight-HTML book offers, then we recommend that you check out *Creating Web Pages For Dummies*, 6th Edition, by Bud E. Smith and Arthur Bebak.

Take a look at Table 12-1 for some basic tags and their functions. For each tag identified, the *off* (or ending) command would be the same word in brackets preceded by a / (slash symbol). (We explore a few exceptions to the off-command rule in Table 12-2.) You must turn off tags in the reverse order that you turned them on. For example, if you use the tags <HTML><HEAD>, then you close them with </HEAD></HTML>.

Table 12-1 explains what some common HTML tags tell Web browsers to do.

Table 12-1		Tag, You're It!
Tag	*What It Means*	*What It Tells the Browser*
<HTML>	HTML	This text document is written in HTML and should be interpreted as such.
<HEAD>	Head element	The following text is the header of the document. (This is where you put the title and any descriptive information.)
<TITLE>	Title	The following text is the title of the Web page. (It appears in the title bar at the top of your browser.)
<BODY>	Body	The body or main part of the document. (Here you put all pertinent information that you want to appear on your Web page.)

(continued)

Table 12-1 *(continued)*

Tag	What It Means	What It Tells the Browser
`<H1>`	Heading	Denotes a heading for the page or section of text and the size that it should be. (Headings come in six levels: `<H1>`, `<H2>`, `<H3>`, `<H4>`, `<H5>`, and `<H6>`. `<H1>` is the largest print, and `<H6>` is the smallest.)
`<CENTER>`	Center	Center the following text on the page or within a table cell or column.
`<B>`	Bold	Bold the following text.
`<I>`	Italicize	Italicize the following text.
`<U>`	Underline	Underline the following text.
`<A HREF= "URL">`	A hypertext link	The following text is a link to another reference page/site and should take people there when they click it. (The URL for the other site goes in the quotation marks; the off command for this code is simply `</A>`.)
`<FONT COLOR= "(color)">`	Font color	The following text should be a particular color. (The color, written in either code or plain English, goes in the quotation marks; the off command is `</FONT>`.)
`<FONT SIZE= "(number)">`	Font size	The following text should be a particular size. (The size goes in the quotation marks; the off command is `</FONT>`.)
`<FONT FACE= "(font name)">`	Font face	The following text should be printed in a particular font or typeface. (The font or typeface name goes in the quotation marks; the off command is `</FONT>`.)
`<OL>`	Ordered list	The following is a numbered list. (Use this code with `<LI>`, identified in Table 12-2. The off command is `</OL>`.)
`<UL>`	Unordered list	The following is going to be a bulleted list. (Use this code with `<LI>`, identified in Table 12-2. The off command is `</UL>`.)

You don't necessarily have to close all HTML tags. Table 12-2 shows codes that are exceptions to the off-command rule. You don't have to use a </ > code to tell the browser when to stop interpreting something.

Table 12-2	Closing-Tag Exceptions	
Tag	*What It Means*	*What It Tells the Browser*
`<P>`	Paragraph break	Skip a line and begin a new paragraph.
` `	Line break	End a line here, then go to the next line to begin the next command or line of text.
`<LI>`	List item	This is a new item to identify on its own line in a list.
`<IMG SRC "image URL">`	Image source	Picks up a graphical image from a URL to insert here. (The URL or address of the graphical file goes between the quotation marks.)
`<HR>`	Horizontal rule	Puts a horizontal line across the page here to divide up the page.
`<BODYBGCOLOR= "(color)">`	Body background	The background color of the document should be a particular color. (The color, written in either code or plain English, goes in the quotation marks.)
`<ALINK COLOR= "(color)">`	Active link color	Colors each link on the page a certain color until it's visited by people who load the page into their browsers. (The color, written in either code or plain English, goes in the quotation marks.)
`<VLINK COLOR= "(color)">`	Visited link color	The color that each link on the page becomes after the person clicked through to the link and then returns to the page. (The color, written in either code or plain English, goes in the quotation marks.)

You probably noticed that we use all uppercase letters in our coding, but that's just our own preference. You can use lowercase, uppercase, or a combination of both when programming in HTML. We prefer all-uppercase so we can more easily identify where the codes are when we need to edit an HTML document. We also like to skip lines between commands so we can more easily look through the HTML document to see how we coded it.

Writing some HTML

Using the basic codes we provide in the preceding section, you can design and write a simple but functional Web site based on the My Favorite Abe Web page. To make the process easier, you can use your word processor to copy the codes for the site as they appear, simply substituting your own ancestor's information where Abe's personal information appears. (Of course, you probably want to change the title of the Web page, too, so it indicates that it contains information about one of your ancestors instead of Mr. Lincoln.) After you finish, save the file in plain-text format with an HTML extension (.htm or .html). Save the file to your hard drive or to a floppy disk. (When you're ready to make your real home page, save the file to your hard drive and then upload it to the Web server that will host your site. Although you may be able to save your page directly to the Web server, be sure to keep a backup copy of the file on your own machine or on a floppy disk.)

Want to see what the page looks like through a browser's eyes? Try this:

1. **Launch your Web browser.**

   Usually, you can open the browser by double-clicking its icon or by using the Start menu to get to your programs. You don't necessarily have to be online to look at your Web page, so don't worry about going through all the steps for signing onto your Internet service provider account. Just open the browser.

2. **Use your browser's Open Page command to open the document.**

   Most browsers have an Open Page command in the File menu. When you click Open Page, a dialog box appears, asking you which file you want to open. Type the name of the file in which you saved your HTML document (or use the Browse feature to search for your document) and then hit Enter or click the OK button.

Does anything look funny — say, everything past a certain point is all bold, all italicized, or in a huge font? If so, go back and double-check your coding to make sure that you turned off all the codes. To refresh your memory about turning off codes, see "What does HTML look like?" earlier in this chapter, and read everything from there to here.

Using an HTML editor

An *HTML editor* is a program that walks you through HTML programming so you don't have to learn all the codes and remember to turn them on and off. Some editors use text that you've already written in your word processor, while others have you type text directly into the editor. To tell the editor how particular text should appear on a Web page (such as the format it should take — title, body of text, a list, and so on), you click an icon or drop-down menu option, and the editor applies the necessary codes.

The CD-ROM that accompanies this book has a popular HTML editor called Macromedia HomeSite. We recommend that you install it on your computer and practice with it, using instructions provided in Appendix C.

Using tutorials or online HTML editors

Some sites that host Web pages for free have online HTML editors and tutorials you can use (also for free) if you sign up for a Web site with them. Likewise, many commercial Internet service providers (such as America Online and MSN) have HTML editors in the form of wizards or templates that help you design your Web pages. The tutorials and editors walk you through designing your Web page, prompting you to select the items you want on your page, even reminding you to save your page at appropriate times. Then they write the actual HTML tags for your page. Follow the instructions for using the editors that are provided by the free hosting service or Internet service provider.

A Little Help from Some Genealogical Software Utilities

After figuring out how to write some HTML or to use HTML editors to code documents for you, you're ready to design your home page. Before you do so, however, decide exactly what you want your home page to contain. In Chapter 11, for example, we look at how to share GEDCOM data online without using the World Wide Web. Of course, you'd probably like to share your GEDCOM file on your own home page — so this section explains how to get your GEDCOM file ready for sharing on the Web, and shows you how to format it without manually converting your GEDCOM to HTML. (For more information about GEDCOM, see Chapter 9.)

First and foremost, make sure that your GEDCOM file is ready to share with others. By this, we mean that it's free from any information that could land you in the doghouse with any of your relatives — close or distant! (For more about ensuring that your GEDCOM file has no information about living individuals, head to Chapter 11. You can also take a look at this chapter's sidebars, "Privacy" and "Copyrights.")

Some genealogical software programs enable you to indicate whether you want information on each relative included in reports and GEDCOMs. Other programs don't allow you to do this. You can imagine what a hassle it is to sort through a GEDCOM file line by line, deleting information on living relatives when you have several hundred individuals (or more!) in your database. To alleviate the necessity of this task, one of our fellow genealogists developed a helpful little program called *GEDClean*.

GEDClean is a freeware utility that searches through your GEDCOM file and removes any information about living persons for you. The utility then saves the cleaned GEDCOM for you to use with other genealogical utilities designed to help you put your information on the Web. You can download a free copy at www.raynorshyn.com/gedclean/. Here's how to use the utility:

1. **Install and open the GEDClean program that you downloaded from**

   www.raynorshyn.com/gedclean/

   A yellow window pops up with the three steps for GEDClean.

2. **Click Step 1: Select the Name of Your GEDCOM File.**

   You see a dialog box asking you to specify the GEDCOM file that you want to use GEDClean on.

3. **Choose the GEDCOM file that you created in Chapter 11 (or another GEDCOM that you have readily available). Click OK.**

   This step brings you back to the yellow window, and the name and directory path of your GEDCOM file should appear under Step 1.

4. **Click Step 2: Select Individuals to Exclude from Your GEDCOM File.**

   You see a dialog box asking what you want to do to exclude living individuals from your GEDCOM. You can use an existing file that identifies all living persons whose data is in your GEDCOM file. You can have GEDClean scan your GEDCOM file looking for anyone with a specific note that indicates that the person is alive. Or you can have GEDClean scan your entire GEDCOM file and look for anyone who may possibly be alive.

   Unless you have an existing file that states who should be excluded, or you've somehow marked your GEDCOM file to reflect living individuals, you should choose Option 3 and have GEDClean scan the whole GEDCOM looking for people who may be alive.

5. Click Option 3: Analyze GEDCOM and then click OK.

For each person that GEDClean finds with no vital information (primarily birth date or death date), you get an Unknown Status window, asking what you want to do with that person's data.

6. If GEDClean prompts you with an Unknown Status window, type either living **(details are excluded in the cleaned GEDCOM) or** not living **(details are included).**

Be forewarned that if you have a lot of people in your database (thus in your GEDCOM file), the process of responding to each window for Unknown Status can be a little time-consuming. However, making sure that you exclude information on any living relatives is well worth the effort!

7. Click Step 3: Clean the GEDCOM File.

GEDClean runs through the GEDCOM file and removes information on those people you indicated are alive. The utility then saves your original GEDCOM file under a new name (with the extension .old) and saves the cleaned GEDCOM file under your original GEDCOM file name.

8. Choose File⇨Exit to exit GEDClean.

When you have a GEDCOM file that is free of information about all living persons, you're ready to prepare your GEDCOM file for the Web. You can choose from several programs to help you convert your GEDCOM to HTML. (We identify a few of these programs — and their Web addresses — in The *Genealogy Online For Dummies* Internet Directory in this book.) GED2HTML may be the most commonly known GEDCOM-to-HTML converter available, and it's available for downloading at www.gendex.com/ged2html. Here's how to use it with your cleaned GEDCOM file:

1. Open the GED2HTML program that you downloaded from

www.gendex.com/ged2html

A dialog box asks you to enter the location of your GEDCOM file. (You can browse if you can't remember the path name for the GEDCOM file.)

2. Type the path for your GEDCOM file and then click OK.

A typical path looks like this: c:\my documents\ helm.ged

GED2HTML runs a program using your GEDCOM file. You can watch it going through the file in a black window that appears.

3. After the program is done, press Enter to close the program window.

GED2HTML saves the output HTML files in a folder (appropriately called HTML) in the same directory where the GED2HTML program is saved.

Privacy

Sometimes, we genealogists get so caught up in dealing with the records of deceased persons that we forget one basic fact: Much of the information we've collected and put in our databases pertains to *living individuals*. In our haste to share our information with others online, we often create our GEDCOM files and reports and then ship them off to recipients without thinking twice about whether we may offend someone or invade his or her privacy by including personal information. We need to be more careful.

Well, okay, why *shouldn't* you include everything you know about your relatives?

✔ **You may invade someone's right to privacy:** Your relatives may not want you to share personal information about them with others, and they may not have given you permission to do so.

✔ **Genealogists aren't the only people who visit genealogical Internet sites:** For example, private detectives are known to lurk about, watching for information that may help their cases. Estranged spouses may visit sites looking for a way to track down their former partners. Also, people with less-than-honorable intentions may visit a genealogical Web site looking for potential scam or abuse victims. And some information, such as your mother's maiden name, may help the unscrupulous carry out fraud.

When sharing genealogical information, your safest bet is to include only the data that pertains to people who have long been deceased — unless you've obtained written consent from living persons to share information about them. By *long been deceased,* we mean deceased for more than ten years — although the time frame could be longer depending on the sensitivity of the information. You may also want to keep in mind that the U.S. Government standard dictates that no record covered under the Privacy Act is released until it's at least 72 years old.

4. **Open your Web browser.**

   Usually you can open the browser by double-clicking its icon or by using the Start menu (in Windows 95 or higher) to get to your programs.

5. **Use your browser's Open Page command to open any of the HTML output files.**

   Most browsers have an Open Page command in the File menu. When you choose Open Page, a dialog box appears, asking you which file you want to open. Browse to the directory where GED2HTML put your HTML output. Select an HTML document to look at.

   After seeing what your output looks like and reviewing it to make sure it doesn't contain any information that shouldn't be posted, you're ready to add it to your Web site (or link to it as its own Web page).

6. **Follow any instructions from your Web host, and upload your GED2HTML files to your Web server. Put any links to those files on your home page so you can share your GEDCOM information online.**

For example, suppose GED2HTML saved an HTML-coded index of all of the people in your GEDCOM to a file called `persons.html`. After uploading or copying this file to your Web host's server, you can use a link command such as

```
<A HREF = "[directory path]/persons.html">
```

from your main home page to this index of persons to share it on the Web.

Deciding Which Treasures to Include

Although the content of genealogical Web pages with lots of textual information about ancestors or geographic areas may be very helpful, all-text pages won't attract the attention of your visitors. Even we get tired of sorting through and reading endless narratives on Web sites; we like to see things that personalize a Web site and are fun to look at. Graphics, icons, and photographs are ideal for this purpose. A couple of nice-looking, strategically placed photos of ancestors make a site feel more like a home.

If you have some photographs that have been scanned and saved as .jpg or .gif images, you can post them on your Web site. Just make sure that a copy of the .jpg or .gif file is uploaded to your Web host's server in a directory that you can point to with HTML codes on your home page. By using the `<IMG SRC = " ">` code, you can tell browsers where to go to pick up that image or photograph. (Be sure to type the filename for that image exactly as it appears on your hard drive or other resource.)

Just as you should be careful about posting factual information about living relatives, be careful about posting photos of them. If you want to use an image that has living relatives in it, get their permission before doing so. Some people are very sensitive about having their pictures posted on the Web. Also, use common sense and taste in selecting pictures for your page. Although a photo of little Susie at age 3 wearing a lampshade and dancing around in a tutu may be cute, a photo of Uncle Ed at age 63 doing the same thing may not be so endearing!

Copyrights

Copyright is the controlling right that a person or corporation owns over the duplication and distribution of a work that the person or corporation created. Although facts themselves can't be copyrighted, *works in which facts are contained* can be. Although the fact that your grandma was born on January 1, 1900, can't be copyrighted by anyone, a report that contains this information and was created by Aunt Lola may be. If you intend to include a significant portion of Aunt Lola's report in your own document, you need to secure permission from her to use the information.

With regard to copyright and the Internet, remember that just because you found some information on a Web site (or other Internet resource) does not mean that it's not copyrighted. If the Web site contains original material along with facts, it is copyrighted to the person who created it — regardless of whether the site has a copyright notice on it!

To protect yourself from infringing on someone's copyright and possibly ending up in a legal battle, you should do the following:

✔ Never copy another person's Web page, e-mail, or other Internet creation (such as graphics) without his or her written consent.

✔ Never print out an article, story, report, or other material to share with your family, friends, genealogical or historical society, class, or anyone else without the creator's written consent.

✔ Always assume that a resource is copyrighted.

✔ Always cite sources of the information in your genealogy and on your Web pages.

✔ Always *link* to other Web pages rather than copying their content on your own Web site.

If you don't understand what copyright is or you have questions about it, be sure to check out the U.S. Copyright Office's Home Page at lcweb.loc.gov/copyright/. Two U.S. Copyright Office pages of particular interest at the site are Copyright Basics and Frequently Asked Questions (FAQs).

Part V
The Part of Tens

The 5th Wave   By Rich Tennant

©RICHTENNANT

"That's strange – according to this copy of your birth certificate I got for Tommy's genealogy project, you're not Queen of the Universe and Master of all Men."

In this part . . .

Ah, The Part of Tens — a staple of the *For Dummies* books. Use these chapters as quick references when you're looking for the following:

- ✔ Online databases to search for records and information
- ✔ Some things to ponder when designing your own genealogical Web pages
- ✔ Places to visit when you need a bit of help with your research
- ✔ Tips for making the most of your research

Chapter 13

Ten Handy Databases

In This Chapter

▶ Discovering online databases with useful data

▶ Finding databases that can provide research hints

*T*hroughout the book, we talk about different online databases that are available. Here's a list of some databases that we think you may find useful in your research. Each database entry in this chapter has a brief description of what the database contains and how you may use it to further your research goals.

Social Security Death Index

www.ancestry.com/search/rectype/vital/ssdi/main.htm

The Social Security Death Index is a listing of individuals whose deaths were reported to the Social Security Administration since 1962. Currently, this database contains more than 70 million records. The information that is available here includes name, birth date, death date, last residence, last benefit, Social Security number, and the state of issue of the deceased's Social Security card. With this information, you can request a copy of the Social Security card application that provides more information on the individual. This database is a good resource when you try to fill in the gaps of missing information on individuals after the 1930 Census. There are a few different online sources for the SSDI — the most up-to-date copy seems to be at Ancestry.com, so that's the Web address we provide above. Some of the others are listed here:

- ✔ Family Finder Search page at

    www.genealogy.com/ifftop.html

- ✔ FamilySearch at

    www.familysearch.org/Eng/Search/frameset_search.asp?PAGE=ssdi/

    search_ssdi.asp

American Family Immigration History Center

www.ellisisland.org/search/passSearch.asp

The American Family Immigration History Center (AFIHC) holds a collection of immigrant arrival records for those who entered the United States through Ellis Island and the Port of New York between 1892 and 1924. The online site contains a passenger-list database of information such as the name of the passenger, residence, arrival date, age upon arrival, gender, marital status, ship name, and port of departure.

FamilySearch: Family History Library Catalog

www.familysearch.org/eng/Library/FHLC/frameset_fhlc.asp

In Chapter 4, we highlight several features of the FamilySearch site. One that we don't talk about is the Family History Library Catalog. This catalog lists over 3 million microfilms and 300,000 books in the Family History Library collection. This is a good resource for finding family histories that are already completed on branches of your family.

National Archives and Records Administration Archival Research Catalog

www.archives.gov/research_room/arc/

To do research in the United States, it's a good idea to know what federal records can help your search. The National Archives and Records Administration Archival Research Catalog (ARC) database houses descriptions of over 245,000 items. You can query the system through a basic-search or advanced-search interface. Microfilm publications can be searched via another interface at

www.nara.gov/cgi-bin/starfinder/0?path=micfilm.
txt&id=mfilm&pass=&OK=OK

Bureau of Land Management, General Land Office Records

www.glorecords.blm.gov

This site contains the images of over 2 million land records issued between 1820 and 1908. Within the next few years, serial patents issued after 1908 until the mid-1960s will be added to the site. You can view the land patent images here in a variety of ways, including GIF images, TIFF images, and Adobe Acrobat (PDF) files.

ProQuest Genealogy and Local History Online

www.heritagequestonline.com/prod/genealogy/books

Part of the HeritageQuest Online subscription site, the Genealogy and Local History Online collection contains over 25,000 digitized family and local histories. Each work is fully indexed and can be searched under the three main categories of people, places, and publications. Although HeritageQuest Online is available primarily to institutions, the information can also be accessed by individuals through the subscription Genealogy.com Family and Local Histories collection (www.genealogy.com/hqosub.html).

Alexandria Digital Library Gazetteer Server

testbed.alexandria.ucsb.edu/gazclient/index.jsp

Looking for a particular place in the world? The Alexandria Digital Library Gazetteer contains over 4 million features throughout the world. You can search by place name and define what feature type that you're looking for (buildings, cities, drainage basins, landmarks, parks, and rivers, for example). You can also limit the area searched by clicking a map to define the search area.

HyperHistory Online

www.hyperhistory.com/online_n2/History_n2/a.html

Although it's not a genealogical database per se, HyperHistory Online contains some interesting resources for genealogists who want to see what historical events occurred during their ancestors' lives. The site contains over 2,000 maps, charts, and articles recounting 3,000 years of world history. It's divided into four topical areas, including People, History, Events, and Maps. The People area contains lifelines of individuals from 1000 B.C. to A.D. 1996. Historical timelines are available from before 1000 B.C. to A.D. 1998. The Event index covers significant occurrences in science, culture, and politics between A.D. 1791 and A.D. 1999. The Map section contains several maps covering ancient times to the twentieth century.

National Union Catalog of Manuscript Collections

lcweb.loc.gov/coll/nucmc/

Sometimes it's difficult to find materials in archives and manuscript repositories because their catalogs are not always readily available. These institutions often have family histories and Bibles, journals, personal papers, and political papers. The purpose of the National Union Catalog of Manuscript Collections (NUCMC), which is maintained by the Library of Congress, is to provide you with access to a listing of collections of archives and repositories that don't have their own publicly accessible catalogs.

Topozone

www.topozone.com

Location, and the terrain surrounding it, often played an important role in the lives of our ancestors. Although we may not be able to see maps of the terrain as it existed a hundred years ago, we can see modern-day topographic maps produced by the United States Geological Survey for the entire United States. To find a map, just type a place name in the search field (or you can search by latitude or longitude), select a state (if known), and you're off to the races. The Results page of the search lists the place name, county, state, type of feature, elevation, USGS quad, latitude, and longitude. Clicking the place name brings up the appropriate topographical map.

Chapter 14

Ten Things to Remember When Designing Your Genealogical Web Site

You've probably seen them: Web sites that look like the maintainers simply plugged their surnames in specified spots and maybe changed the background color of the page. Typically, such pages don't contain much information of value to anyone — they're simply lists of surnames with no context and maybe lists of links to some of the better-known genealogical Web sites. Some might say that these sites are clones. We agree. You don't want your genealogical Web site to look just like everyone else's, and neither do you want it to contain almost exactly the same information. You want yours to be unique and useful to other genealogists so a lot of people will visit your site and recommend it to others. So what can you do to avoid the genealogical Web-site rut that many genealogists find themselves in? Here we offer a few ideas and places to get help.

Be Unique — Don't Copy Other Web Sites

Please, please, please tell us that you want to set your home page apart from all other genealogical Web sites! You don't really have to be told not to copy other sites, right? But when you design your site, the pressure is on, and coming up with ideas for textual and graphical content can be pretty hard sometimes. We understand that this pressure can make it awfully tempting for you to take ideas from other Web sites that you like. Although you can certainly look to other sites for ideas on formatting and types of content, don't copy them! Web sites are copyrighted by the person(s) who created them — even if they don't display a copyright notice — and you can get in trouble for copying them. (See Chapter 12 for more information about copyrights.)

The other reason you shouldn't copy other Web sites is that you want your page to attract as many visitors as possible — and in order to do this, you need to offer something unique that makes it worth people's time to stop by. After all, if your site has the same old information as another site, people have no particular need to visit your page. For example, because several comprehensive genealogical sites already exist, posting a Web site that merely has links to other genealogical pages doesn't make much sense. Likewise, if you're thinking about making a one-name study site on a surname for which four or five one-name study sites already exist, you may want to focus your home page on another surname you're researching.

Be creative. Look around and see what existing genealogical Web sites offer, and then seek to fill the void — pick a unique topic, name, or location that doesn't have much coverage (or better yet, one that doesn't have any coverage at all). If you really want to post a surname site, think about making a site for your surname in a particular state or country. Or think about posting some transcribed records that would benefit genealogists who are researching ancestors from a particular county.

Include the Surnames That You're Researching and Provide Your Contact Information

If the purpose of your Web site is not only to share your collection of genealogical information but to get information from others as well, then be sure to include a list of the names you're researching. And don't be stingy with information. We encourage you to share at least a little information about your ancestors with those surnames. Just a list of surnames alone isn't going to be very helpful to visitors to your site, particularly if any of the surnames on your list are common — Smith, Johnson, Jones, Martin, and so forth. An online version of the information contained in your GEDCOM (a text file that contains the contents of your genealogical database, created using GED2HTML or another similar program — see Chapter 12 for more information) will do because it includes an index of surnames that people can look through, and also has information about your ancestors with those surnames. Also be sure to include your name and e-mail address so that people know how to get in touch with you to share data.

Make It Attractive Without Being Too Flashy

Choose your colors and graphics wisely! Although using some color and graphics (including photographs) helps your Web site stand out and makes it more personal, be careful about using too much color or too many graphics. By *too much color,* we mean backgrounds that are so bright that they almost blind your visitors (or make the rest of the site hard to look at), or backgrounds that drown out the colors of your links. You want your site to be appealing to others as well as to you; before using neon pink or lime green, stop and think about how others may react.

The more graphics you use and the larger they are, the longer a computer takes to load them. (And animated graphics are even worse! Not only do they take a long time to load, but they can make your visitors dizzy and disoriented if you have several graphics moving in different directions at the same time.) Graphics files aren't the only factor that affects how quickly computers load files: the amount of bandwidth of your Internet connection and the amount of space available on your hard drive also affect download time. Waiting for a page to load that has more graphics than useful text content is frustrating. You can pretty much bet that people won't wait around, so concentrate on making your page as user-friendly as possible from the beginning. Use graphics tastefully and sparingly.

If you have a large amount of family photos that you really want to share, put each on its own page and then provide links to the photo pages from your home page. This way, visitors who aren't interested in seeing any of the photos don't have to wait for the images to load on their computers just to view the other contents of your site, and visitors who are only interested in a particular image don't have to wait for all the other photos to load.

The "Where to Go for Help" section later in this chapter identifies some online resources that lead you to sites with Web-safe colors and graphics that you can download and use on your Web site.

Be Careful What You Post

Be careful and thoughtful when designing your Web site and posting information contributed by others. Don't post any information that could hurt or offend someone. Respect the privacy of others and post information only on people who have been deceased for many years. (Twenty-five years is a good conservative figure to use when in doubt.) Even then, be cautious about telling old family stories that may affect people who are still alive. (For more information about privacy, see Chapters 11 and 12.)

Always Cite Your Sources

We can't stress this enough! Always cite your sources when you put genealogical narrative on your Web site, or when you post information from records that you've collected or people you've interviewed. That way, people who visit your page and get data from it know exactly where you got the information and can follow up on it if they need or want to. (Also, by citing your sources, you keep yourself out of trouble because others may have provided the information to you, and they deserve the credit for the research.)

Not All Web Browsers Are Created Equal

World Wide Web browsers interpret HTML documents differently depending on who created the software. Also, some Web browsers have HTML tags that are specific to the browser. So, although you may create a Web site that looks great using Microsoft Internet Explorer, it may look off-center or somewhat different when using Netscape Navigator or Opera. Because of this problem, try not to use tags that are specific to any one browser when you create your Web site. For that matter, whenever possible, test your page in several browsers before posting it for public access. Better yet, use a testing service that allows the "experts" to look at your page and give you feedback. The Yahoo! HTML Validation and Checkers page at

```
dir.yahoo.com/Computers_and_Internet/Data_Formats/HTML/
Validation_and_Checkers/
```

provides a decent list of programs that check your Web site and notify you about broken links. To find out more about browsers, see Appendix A.

Check and Recheck Your Links

If you include links on your home page to other Web sites that you've designed or sites maintained by someone else, double-check the links when you post your pages. Make sure that the links work properly so that visitors to your site don't have problems navigating around sites that you recommend or that support your home page. A lot of genealogical Web sites tend to be transient — the maintainers move them for one reason or another, or take them down entirely — so you should also check back periodically (once a month or so) to make sure that the links still work.

If you have a lot of links on your Web site and you don't have the time to check every single one yourself (which is a common scenario), look to the Yahoo! HTML Validation and Checkers page at

```
dir.yahoo.com/Computers_and_Internet/Data_Formats/HTML/
Validation_and_Checkers/
```

It links to a list of programs that check your Web site and notify you about broken links.

Market Your Genealogical Web Site

After you put together your Web site and post it on your provider's server, you need to let people know that it exists so they can stop by and visit your site. How do you do this? We recommend that you follow some of the same tips in Chapter 4 for marketing the research that you've done on your surnames (using mailing lists if the site deals with particular surnames or geographic areas). In particular, one of the best ways to promote your Web site is to register it with several comprehensive genealogical Web sites that receive a lot of traffic from people looking for genealogy-related pages.

Also, most of the major search engines have links to registration or submission pages within their sites that enable you to submit your URL. Of course, in the interest of saving time, you can visit Add Me Site Submission at

```
www.addme.com/submission.htm
```

which forwards your Web site information to up to 14 search engines for free.

Helping Others Is Its Own Reward

Don't go overboard patting your own back — you know, promoting your home page on the actual home page for the sake of receiving awards from other sites, magazines, societies, or other sources. Post your genealogical home page with the intent of helping other genealogists and encouraging a sharing genealogical community. If you use the majority of your page to advertise your awards and beg people to vote for your site in popularity contests, you lose a lot of valuable space where you can post information that's useful to genealogists. And you may lose credibility with your visitors causing them to turn away — which defeats the purpose of self-promotion in the first place.

Now, we're not saying that you shouldn't acknowledge awards that your site receives if it has good and sound genealogical content. We recognize that it's good business to give a little traffic back to the sites, magazines, societies, or other sources that send visitors your way by awarding your page some honor. We're simply saying that you can acknowledge the honors you receive in a tasteful and humble manner. You don't have to plaster all the graphics for every single award across the top of your page. Rather, you can set up a separate Web page for awards and provide a link from your home page so that those who are interested in seeing your honors can go to that page.

Where to Go for Help

Chapter 12 tells you how to create a simple Web site and discusses some HTML editors that are available from Web hosts. But these resources may not even begin to cover all the wonderful things that you intend to do with your Web site. Maybe you want to learn more about how to do fancier things with your Web site. If this is the case, you should check out community colleges in your area or workshops offered by local libraries or genealogical societies. Community colleges and workshops often offer classes or sessions on how to make a Web site, walking you through the basics of HTML — what the tags are, how to use them, and how to post a Web site.

If the thought of attending a structured class gives you hives or just makes you roll your eyes, you can learn more about HTML and Web-site design in other ways. You can teach yourself; many books and online sites are out there to help you. In fact, Wiley Publishing, Inc. offers several *For Dummies* books you may want to consider: *HTML 4 For Dummies,* 4th Edition, by Ed Tittel and Natanya Pitts; *Creating Web Pages For Dummies,* 6th Edition, by Bud Smith and Arthur Bebak; *Web Design For Dummies,* by Lisa Lopuck; and *Building a Web Site For Dummies*, by David Crowder and Rhonda Crowder. The following online sites have links to many resources for designing and programming Web pages, in addition to resources that have colors, backgrounds, graphics, and other Web-site enhancements that you can download:

✔ **Yahoo!'s World Wide Web: Beginner's Guides:**

`dir.yahoo.com/Computers_and_Internet/Internet/World_Wide_Web/Beginner_s_Guides/`

✔ **CNET's Builder.com: Web Design Library:**

`builder.com.com`

✔ **Web Building Tutorial:**

`www.w3schools.com/site/default.asp`

Chapter 15

Ten Sites That Offer Help

Do census records make you feel senseless? Panicked at the idea of using the Soundex? Just plain confused about where to start? These ten sites may relieve some of the anxiety you feel toward researching your genealogy.

Ancestors

byubroadcasting.org/ancestors/

Ancestors — a unique multi-part television series about genealogy — has a companion Web site that contains several resources for beginners. The site has information on various types of records and sources that you collect as a genealogist, tips from other researchers, and a resource guide with locations of genealogy resources in each state. If you're interested in watching the two series, you can find a television schedule for the second series and information about ordering copies of the first series on video.

Ancestry.com Learning Center

www.ancestry.com/library/archive.asp

While Ancestry.com is well known for its collection of databases and digitized images, perhaps equally of value is its little known collection of articles, columns, and other online resources to assist genealogists. The Learning Center contains over 7,500 articles (taken from *Ancestry* magazine, *Genealogical Computing,* and online columnists) divided into categories that include How-To, Family origins, Technology, Organizations, and many other topics.

Ancestry.com also offers 19 online courses that you can take for a fee. Each course consists of four weeks of lessons with experienced genealogists. In order to provide a more in-depth learning experience, the site has partnered with Vermont College to provide seminars where you can earn continuing-education credit for learning about family-history research.

Genealogy Helplist

helplist.org

Looking for genealogical help in a specific geographical area? The Genealogy Helplist may be able to answer some of your questions. The Helplist is a group of volunteers who assist other researchers by looking up items at libraries, archives, and other institutions near them. The site contains links to helplists for more than 20 countries, as well as the 50 states.

GEN-NEWBIE-L

www.rootsweb.com/~newbie

This is the home page for the GEN-NEWBIE-L mailing list. This mailing list is a forum for individuals who are new to computers and genealogy and are look-ing for a place to discuss a variety of topics in a comfortable environment.

To subscribe to the GEN-NEWBIE-L mailing list, follow these steps:

1. **Open your favorite e-mail program and start a new e-mail message.**

2. **Type** Gen-Newbie-L-request@rootsweb.com **in the Address line.**

3. **Leave the Subject line blank and type only the word** subscribe **in the body of your message. Also make sure that you turn off any signature lines present in your email.**

4. **Send your e-mail message.**

Soon you receive a confirmation message with additional details on unsub-scribing from the mailing list (if you want to do so down the road) and other administrative items. If you have questions about the mailing list, consult the home page for help. For more information about using e-mail, see Appendix A.

National Genealogical Society

www.ngsgenealogy.org

The National Genealogical Society has more than 17,000 members nation-wide. At its Web site, you can find information on the society's home-study genealogy course, starting your genealogy research, research services, the society's library catalog, and conferences. The site also has information about membership — no surprise there — and does a good job of keeping visitors abreast of genealogical news and events. There's even a "bookstore," which actually carries a lot more than just books on its virtual shelves.

The Present Meets the Past: Genealogy Instruction for Beginners, Teenagers, and Kids

home.earthlink.net/~howardorjeff/instruct.htm

This site offers basic information for starting your genealogical research. Sections of the site include instructions on where to begin, a list of questions to ask relatives, where to go for information, and what you need in your "research kit." Of special interest are two sections for children and teenagers who want to begin researching their family trees.

ROOTS-L

www.rootsweb.com/roots-l

This is the home page for the ROOTS-L mailing list. If you're looking for an all-purpose mailing list on genealogy, ROOTS-L may be for you. ROOTS-L is the oldest and largest genealogical mailing list, with more than 10,000 subscribers. List members discuss all types of genealogical issues. On the mailing list's companion Web page, you can find subscription information, help files, a searchable archive of past ROOTS-L messages, and a brief history of the list.

To subscribe to the list, follow these steps:

1. **Open your favorite e-mail program and start a new e-mail message.**

2. **Type** ROOTS-L-request@rootsweb.com **in the Address line.**

3. **Leave the Subject line blank and type only the word** subscribe **in the body of your message.**

4. **Send your e-mail message.**

Soon, you receive a confirmation message with additional details on unsubscribing from the mailing list (if that becomes necessary) and other administrative items. (Check out Appendix A for more on using e-mail.)

Getting Started in Genealogy and Family History

www.genuki.org.uk/gs/

The GENUKI (U.K. and Ireland Genealogy) Web site provides a list of helpful hints for starting out in genealogical research. The extensive list covers these elements: deciding the aim of your research, using Family History Centers, joining a genealogical society, tracing immigrants, and organizing your information. You also find a list of reference materials — should you want to read more about the topics GENUKI discusses.

About Genealogy: The Family Tree and Genealogy Research Guide

genealogy.about.com

If you are looking for information on a wide-range of genealogical topics, hop on over to the About Genealogy site. The site is frequently updated with new material and has a large archive of past articles that are categorized by subject. General subjects included are surnames, genealogy records, genealogy how-to, and genealogy tools. Articles are also organized by country, state, and ethnicity. In addition to articles, the site has forums (great places for posting queries), chat rooms, and a sign-up form for its e-mail newsletter.

Chapter 16

Ten Tips for Genealogical Smooth Sailing

....

In This Chapter

▶ Enhancing your genealogical research

▶ Avoiding pitfalls

....

*Y*ou want to make optimal use of your time when researching your genealogy — online and offline. Being time-efficient means planning well and keeping organized notes so that bad leads don't distract you. Making the most of your time also means staying motivated when and if a bad lead does distract you. Your genealogy research is worth continuing. This chapter offers some tips to help you plan, organize, and execute your research.

Start with What You Know

Sure, this concept seems basic, but it's worth repeating: When you begin researching your genealogy, start with what you know — information about yourself and your immediate family. Then work your way back in time, using information from relatives and copies of records that you obtain. Putting together the puzzle is much easier if you have some pieces first. If you start directly with your great-great-grandpa and all you know about him is his name, you're going to get frustrated very early in the process — especially if great-great-grandpa has a relatively common name like John Sanders or William Martin! Can you imagine trying to track down records on *all* the John Sanderses or William Martins who turn up in one year's census? (We believe in thoroughly covering the basics, so if you want to hear this again, go to Chapter 1.)

Get Organized

The better organized you are, the more success you're likely to have with your research efforts. If you know ahead of time where you stand in researching your family lines, you can identify rather quickly which records or other materials you need to find about a particular surname, location, or time frame. Knowing your gaps in information enables you to get right down to the nitty-gritty of researching instead of spending the first hour or two of your research rehashing where you left off last time.

To help yourself get organized, keep a *research log* — a record of when and where you searched for information. For example, if you ran a Google (www.google.com) search on the name Emaline Crump on January 1, 2004, and found ten pages that you wanted to visit, record that in your research log. Also record when you visited those pages and whether they provided any useful information to you. That way, next time you're online researching your Crump ancestors, you know that you already ran a Google search and visited the particular resulting pages, so you don't have to do it again. (Of course, you may want to check back in the future and run the search again to see whether any *new* Crump-related sites turn up. Again, your research log can come in handy because it can remind you of whether you've already visited some of the resulting sites.)

You can print a copy of a research log at the Church of Jesus Christ of Latter-day Saints site at

www.lds.org/images/howdoibeg/Research_Log.html

A couple of other options are to create your own research log with a plain old notebook or a spreadsheet on your handy-dandy computer, or to use an already-prepared form that comes with your genealogical database (if available).

Always Get Proof

Unfortunately, not all researchers take the same amount of care when gathering sources and presenting the fruits of their research. So it's not a good idea to trust everything that other researchers print or post.

Even when using primary sources, evaluate the information that you find on each record. If the information does not add up, it is possible that the record could be wrong. If you suspect this is the case, it's a good idea to find another record that can help clear up the inconsistency.

If you assume that everything you hear or read is true, you're likely to get distracted frequently by bad leads. You could end up tracing an entire branch of a family that you're not even related to. And just think of all the lost time you could have spent working on your family line!

Always Cite Your Sources

We can't say this enough — always cite your sources. In other chapters (Chapter 11, for example), we explore why citing your sources is a smart thing to do when sharing your genealogical information with others. We also touch on the importance of citing sources for your own research — so important, in fact, that we reiterate the point here. Make sure you know where, when, and how you obtained a particular piece of information about your ancestors just in case you ever need to verify the information or get another copy of the record. Doing so saves you a lot of grief. It also brings you greater respect from others for your efforts.

Focus, Focus, Focus

If you're trying to remember all your ancestors in all your family lines and research them all at the same time, you're bound to get confused and burnt out! Focus on one or two branches at a time. Even better — focus on one or two people within a branch at a time. By maintaining a tight focus, you can still find information on other relatives in that branch of the family and collect records and data that pertain to them — but you're able to do so without driving yourself crazy.

Share Your Information

One of the best ways to facilitate getting genealogical information from others is to share some information first. Although most genealogists are rather generous people to begin with, some still believe in protecting their discoveries like closely guarded treasures — it's "every man for himself" in their minds. However, after they realize that you want to *give* information as well as receive it, some of them lighten up and are much more willing to share with you. By sharing information, you can save each other time and energy, as well as begin to coordinate your research in a manner that benefits both of you.

Sharing information is one area where the Internet has proven to be an invaluable resource for genealogists. It provides easy access for unconditional and conditional sharing of information among genealogists. Those of you who are willing to share your knowledge can go online and post information to your heart's content. And in return, simply ask the researchers who benefit from your site to share their findings with you. And for those of you who are a little more apprehensive about sharing your knowledge, you can post messages describing what you're looking for and state that you're willing to share what you have with anyone who can help you.

Join a Society or Research Group

You've probably heard the phrase "Two heads are better than one," right? Well, this theory holds true for genealogy. Joining a society or a research group enables you to combine research efforts with others who are interested in a particular surname or geographic location, so that together you save time and energy obtaining documents that benefit everyone. A society or research group also provides you with a support group to which you can turn when you begin to get discouraged or whenever you want to share a triumph.

You can find genealogical societies and research groups in several ways. Check out your favorite comprehensive genealogical site (see The *Genealogy Online For Dummies* Internet Directory in this book for a list) and look under both the category that lists societies and the place category for the location where you live. Or, if you're interested in finding a society in the United States, take a look at the Federation of Genealogical Societies home page at www.fgs.org (which identifies member societies by location) or the USGenWeb Project at www.usgenweb.org (which links to state pages that identify resources for the state and its counties).

Attend a Conference or Workshop

Conferences and workshops that are hosted by genealogical societies can be a great resource for you. They can help you get organized, learn how to research a particular place or look for specific records, and motivate you to keep plugging along with your research even if you have days when you feel like you haven't accomplished a thing. Conferences and workshops also enable you to meet other researchers with whom you have something in common, whether it's researching a specific surname or geographic location, or just research in general. Being in the company of someone with whom you can share your genealogical successes and failures is always nice.

Typically, conferences and workshops offer sessions that instruct you on various traditional researching topics like the following:

- Using local libraries and archives
- Finding and using land records
- Obtaining vital records
- Converting Soundex codes and using the census
- Publishing a genealogical report or book

More and more workshops offer computer-based sessions like the following:

- Using genealogical software
- Designing and posting your own genealogical Web page
- Joining online societies and mailing lists
- Presenting overviews of the Internet's genealogical offerings
- Using a computer in general

You can use your trusty computer and Internet connection to find genealogical and historical conferences and workshops in your area. The Federation of Genealogical Societies (`www.fgs.org/fgs-calendar.asp`) provides information about conferences coming up within the next couple of months. For events in the United Kingdom, look at the GENEVA: The GENUKI calendar of Genealogical Events and Activities (`users.ox.ac.uk/~malcolm/genuki/geneva/`). You can also use these sites to get the word out about a conference or workshop that you're helping to plan!

Attend a Family Reunion

Family reunions enable you to visit relatives you haven't seen in a long time and to meet new relatives you never would have known. While we cover family reunions in more detail in Chapter 10, we want to reiterate here that reunions are a wonderful opportunity to build your genealogical base by just chatting with relatives about old family stories, ancestors, and the like. Although a reunion doesn't feel like a formal interview, it can give you much of the same information that you would receive if you sat down and formally interviewed each of the people in attendance. Taking along a tape recorder or video camera is a good idea because you don't have to worry about writing down everything your relatives say right at that moment — you can just sit back and enjoy talking with your family. Plus, your genealogy records are greatly enhanced by audio or video. (Just make sure that, when you're going to tape a conversation, you have the permission of the relatives you plan to record and that you set aside *lots* of time later on to transcribe the tapes.)

Family reunions also offer you the opportunity to share what you know about the family and exchange genealogical records and reports. If you know ahead of time that several of your relatives are also into genealogical research, you can better plan with them what records, pictures, reports, and other resources to bring. If you're not sure that any of your relatives are into genealogical research, we recommend that you take a notebook with some printed reports and maybe a narrative family history or genealogy (if you've already put one together) that you can share. Remember, your work doesn't have to be complete (in fact, it probably won't be) or perfect in grammar for others to enjoy seeing what you've collected.

To find out about family reunions, watch the family association and one-name study Web sites of the surnames that you're researching. Typically, this type of Web site has sections set up for reunion announcements. Also, see the Reunions Magazine site at

```
www.reunionsmag.com
```

Planning a reunion can often be a challenging experience. Fortunately, software is available to help you with all the details. Family Reunion Organizer by Formalsoft is just such a program. You can find a demo copy of the software on the CD accompanying this book, or at the software's Web site:

```
family-reunion.com/organizer/
```

Don't Give Up

You're going to have days where you spend hours at the library or archives — or on the Internet — with no research success whatsoever (or so you may think). Don't let those days get you down, and certainly don't give up! Instead of thinking about what you didn't learn about your ancestors on such days, think in terms of what you *did* learn — that your ancestors were not in that record for that particular place at that particular time. By checking that record, you eliminated one more item on your to-do list. So the next time you get ready to research, you know exactly where *not* to look for more information.

Appendix A

Going Online

● ●

*B*efore we talk about what you need to go online and how to do it, we want to explain what we mean by *online*. We use the term *online* to refer to gaining access to and using the Internet. So what is the Internet?

The *Internet* is a system of computer networks joined together by high-speed data lines called *backbones*. The Internet began as a smaller system of regional networks, called ARPANET, sponsored and used by the United States military in the 1960s. Over time, other government agencies and colleges and universities that were conducting research for the government were added to the network. Eventually, as personal computers became common, the Internet sprang forward in public awareness and became accessible to the average person through Internet service providers (which we talk about later in this appendix, in the "Getting an Internet Service Provider" section).

This appendix covers the computer equipment that you need to access the Internet, finding an Internet service provider to provide the access, and the types of resources you find on the Internet after you're on it. Of course, the primary focus of this book is genealogy online — not the Internet and computer use in general — so we just touch on the types of Internet resources available. In some cases, we provide examples and details to help you when you come across some common situations in your online genealogical research (situations like sending e-mail, joining mailing lists, and using newsgroups). And because we don't want to leave you in a lurch if you're trying to learn all you can about every Internet resource, we include some references to other books that may interest you if you want to know more about a particular aspect of the Net.

Is Your Computer Ready to Go Online?

If your computer is relatively new, it most likely came loaded with the hardware and software that you need to access and effectively get around on the Internet. However, if you purchased your computer several years ago, you may have to add a piece of hardware or software before you can access and use the Internet. In general, you need to have a base system that meets the same requirements as those for running genealogical software (see Chapter 9 for more information), plus a modem and some communications software.

Modem on up

A *modem* is a piece of equipment that enables your computer to talk to other computers through a telephone line. A modem can be internal (meaning inside your computer) or external (meaning you plug it into your computer). A modem transmits information to and from your computer at a speed that's measured by the total number of characters, or *bits,* that it can send or receive per second. The higher the number of bits — the faster the modem. Most Internet service providers support modem speeds of up to 56,000 bits per second (bps). (For more on Internet service providers, see "Getting an Internet Service Provider," later in this appendix.)

To use a modem to access the Internet and talk with other computers, you need communications software that tells the modem what to do and also interprets information coming back to your computer. The exact kind of software that you need depends on your modem and your Internet service provider (ISP). Check with your ISP to determine exactly what you need and how to get it, and then double-check the owner's manual for your modem to ensure that the software is compatible with your modem. Most commercial ISPs (such as America Online, AT&T WorldNet, and EarthLink) give you free copies of the software that you need to access and use the many online resources they offer.

Don't forget a telephone line

In addition to a computer equipped with a modem, you need a telephone line to access the Internet (that is, unless you have a *broadband* provider that supplies a Digital Subscriber Line (DSL) line or cable line). Using a jack-to-phone telephone cord, connect your modem to the wall jack so the modem can use the telephone line to dial out and communicate with other computers. (Generally the modular plug you use to hook the phone cord into your modem is on the back of your external modem or on the back of your computer if you have an internal modem.) Your modem calls your Internet service provider and gains access to the Internet for you.

You don't necessarily have to have a second telephone line in your house to access the Internet. You can use your regular line and phone number. However, you may want to think about a few things:

✔ If you subscribe to a call-waiting service, be aware that call waiting can interrupt an online session, which can be very frustrating. When a waiting call rings through, your computer gets very confused, and the consequences can be far from fun. If you have call waiting, we recommend that you follow your communications software instructions (or your phone company's instructions) for blocking it while you're online.

✔ If you spend long periods of time online (which is extremely easy to do when you get into genealogical research and have running dialogs with other researchers), you may want to remind your relatives and friends that your computer sometimes uses that phone line to access the Internet. Letting them know that the line will be tied up saves them frustration and worry if they're trying to reach you and continually get a busy signal.

✔ If you have several phones hooked up on the line, remember to tell others in the household you're going to be online. When someone picks up an extension in the home, it can cut off your Internet connection.

Getting an Internet Service Provider

When you're looking for an Internet service provider (ISP), you can choose among several types of access:

✔ Work or school

✔ Direct connection

✔ Commercial online service providers (local, national, or international)

✔ Freenets

Some services are free, while others charge a monthly fee to give you access to more resources and even some specialized resources. So how do you choose? Review all the available options in your area and determine which one offers the most of what you need.

Access from work or school

If you work in an office or attend a school that has an Internet connection, you may already have access to some or all the resources available on the Internet, particularly e-mail and the World Wide Web. Whether you're allowed to use that access for personal, genealogical research depends on your company or school, of course. Many offices have reasonable policies against using company equipment and time for personal purposes, so be sure that you know your company's policy before embarking on your genealogical pursuits online at work. If you work in an office that doesn't permit personal use of the Internet, you're in the same boat as the majority of the population, and you'll have to get Internet access from your home.

Direct connection to the Internet

Traditionally, direct connection to the Internet was just that — an Internet line came directly into your home, and your computer was hooked directly into it. Because the line coming into your home was dedicated just to the Internet, you didn't need to worry about keeping a phone line available or a modem to use that phone line. Typically, if you had a direct connection, you had a computer that was running at all times and may have been acting as a *server* (a computer that makes information on its drives available for access by other computers). This server ran programs that knew where to route visitors to your computer, and also let you onto the Internet to look at other sites and use other resources. For most online genealogists, however, the expense and technical knowledge that it took to maintain a dedicated Internet line at home made having one unrealistic.

Today, you have several options for direct connections to the Internet within the home. The options that are available depend on what services are offered in your particular area. Increasingly, three types of connections are making their way into homes: cable, Digital Subscriber Line (DSL), and satellite connections.

Cable connections are offered by cable television outfits as well as by some telecommunication companies. These connections use cable that's similar to cable TV. The cable hooks into a cable modem, which is then connected to your computer. This connection is "always on" — meaning that you do not have to use a phone line to dial into an ISP. The quality of the cable connection depends on how many people in your area are online at the same time as you — if the field is crowded at any particular time, your connection speed is likely to drop. In some ways, cable modems are the modern equivalent of the old telephone "party lines."

A *Digital Subscriber Line (DSL)* is an Internet-access service that's usually offered by telephone companies. These lines use the capacity of traditional phone lines to connect to the Internet. The speed of these lines depends on how far you're located from the central telephone office. The farther away you are, the slower your connection. Unlike cable connections, however, the total capacity of a DSL line is available to you — the line isn't shared by multiple people.

The newest technology that enables you to have a direct connection involves accessing the Internet through a *satellite*. A few companies offer Internet connections using satellite dishes, which are similar to the digital dishes some people use to receive television channels. Although this technology is not fully implemented yet, these connections are expected to offer close-to-cable-modem speed and will probably suffer from the similar traffic constraints.

Commercial Internet service providers

Chances are, names like America Online, AT&T WorldNet, EarthLink, and MSN pop into your mind when we say *commercial Internet service providers.* Although these are four of the better-known providers, many more are available. Taking a look around to find the service that best meets your needs is worth your time. Commercial Internet service providers are companies or organizations that provide subscribers dial-up access to the Internet. Their scope can be international, national, or local. Commercial ISPs offer varying services, but typically all provide e-mail and Internet access. Most major providers also have special interest groups and forums that members can participate in, as well as access to newsgroups. Many now offer space where you can post your own Web site. (For more information about designing and posting Web sites, see Chapters 12 and 14.)

Just because your aunt, brother, or best friend uses a particular commercial ISP doesn't necessarily mean that the same service is the best one for you. After all, you may have different needs. Your aunt may live in a metropolitan area where the provider has several telephone-access numbers, but you may live in a rural community or isolated area where the provider doesn't have a local telephone access number, and you'd get stuck with long-distance charges if you used the same provider. Or your brother may subscribe to a provider that gives him only e-mail access, but you want to browse the Internet and keep abreast of the genealogy newsgroups. Because your needs may be different, we recommend that you ask several questions when considering any ISP, whether it's a national, international, or local provider:

- ✔ What services — e-mail, Internet access, space for a Web site, *FTP (File Transfer Protocol,* a way to transfer files from your computer to another, or vice versa, over the Internet), newsgroups, and so on — does the ISP provide?

- ✔ Does the ISP provide the software you need for accessing its system? Can you use your own software if you prefer?

- ✔ What is the ISP's pricing policy? Does it have a set rate for unlimited access, or does it have a tiered system where you pay for a set number of hours of access per month, and then get charged a certain amount for each hour that you go over?

- ✔ Does the provider have local telephone access numbers available in the area where you live? If not, does it have free 1-800 telephone-access numbers you can use? If so, do you have to pay extra for access to them? (*Access numbers* are the phone numbers your modem calls to log you in to the ISP's servers so you can get online.)

- ✔ If your subscription includes space for a Web site, does the ISP provide support services to help you set up your home page?

✔ How does the ISP handle customer support? Do you have to post an e-mail message and, if so, how quickly does it respond? Do you have to call a long-distance telephone number to speak to a customer service representative? What are the provider's hours of customer support?

Shop around to see who gives you the better deal and can best address your Internet needs — a local ISP or one of the national or international providers. You can find a local ISP a few different ways. You can look in your local phone directory or the newspaper, ask your friends and coworkers, or go to the directory Web site at `www.thelist.com`, which has listings of ISPs by area code. And to help you comparison shop, here are the names and Web addresses (Web addresses are technically known as *Uniform Resource Locators,* or *URLs*) for several better-known commercial online services. (Keep in mind that these aren't the only major providers available — they're just a sampling.)

✔ **America Online (AOL):** `www.newaol.com`

✔ **AT&T WorldNet:** `download.att.net/dbsitelet/index.html?ATT762NET1`

✔ **EarthLink:** `www.earthlink.net`

✔ **Microsoft Network (MSN):** `join.msn.com/?pgmarket=en-us&page=dept/dialup`

Freenets

Freenets are Internet service providers that are locally based and offer access to people in the community either free of charge or for a minimal charge. (Yes, it is a contradiction to say that there may be a minimal charge for a freenet — which is why you also hear freenets called *community networks* these days.) Some freenets can give free access to individuals because they have corporate sponsorship, and others are associated with educational institutions. Freenets are rather hard to find and may limit the types of service available. To see if a freenet is in your area, flip through your local phone directory or watch the newspaper. You may also want to ask at the local library or use a friend's or relative's Internet access to check out the directory Web site at `www.thelist.com`, which identifies ISPs by area code.

Types of Internet Resources

When you prepare to go online, knowing the types of Internet resources available to you is helpful. By reviewing what the resources are and what they're called, you become more familiar with some terms that you may encounter on the Internet after you go online.

E-mail

Electronic mail — commonly called *e-mail* — is just what it sounds like: mail (or, if you prefer, messages) sent from one person to another electronically over the Internet. Because you can communicate with others worldwide on any given topic (surname, geographic location, types of records, and so on), e-mail is the best Internet tool when it comes to online genealogical research.

How you get an e-mail program varies. If you subscribe to a commercial ISP, the communications software that the ISP provides should include e-mail software. An e-mail program may have come with your computer when you bought it, or your World Wide Web browser may have one. You can also purchase an e-mail program or download one off the Internet. Regardless of how you get your e-mail software, most work generally the same way.

To use your e-mail software, install the program following the instructions provided with the software.

Sending e-mail

When you want to send a message, follow these general steps:

1. **Open your e-mail program.**

   You generally do this by double-clicking the program's icon (the icon varies depending on the program you use) or by using your Start program menu.

2. **Click the button that lets you create a new message. (Or you can usually use a drop-down menu to tell the software that you want to create a new message.)**

3. **In the To field, type the e-mail address for the message's recipient.**

   The protocol for an e-mail address is this: [*user name*]@[*name of the person's ISP*]. For example, April's e-mail address is: ahelm@tbox. com (ahelm is her user name, and tbox.com is her ISP through which she gets her e-mail messages).

4. **In the Subject field, type a brief note stating what the message is about.**

5. **In the message box, type the message that you want to send to the other person.**

6. **After you finish your message, click the Send button or use a drop-down menu to tell the software to send the message.**

Receiving and reading e-mail

When you install your e-mail program, you're prompted with questions or dialog boxes to finish configuring your computer and ISP account to receive e-mail. Contact your ISP if you have problems setting the configurations. After you set the configurations, e-mail that others send to you automatically arrives in your inbox, which sits on your ISP account and is accessible whenever you access the Internet. After you log on to your ISP and open your e-mail inbox, you can read any messages that you receive by double-clicking the message line in the Inbox or highlighting the message that you want to read and clicking the Open button.

Check out Chapters 4 and 10 for more information on using e-mail for particular genealogical purposes and to learn about *netiquette* (guidelines for communicating effectively and politely with e-mail).

Finding e-mail addresses for other people

You're probably asking, "Whom can I e-mail?" You can e-mail anyone with an e-mail address. So where can you get addresses for other genealogical researchers? For the most part, you get e-mail addresses from people when they contact you or when they post a message to a mailing list, post a query, or put up a Web site. However, sometimes you may be looking for a particular person's e-mail address and can't find it (whether you've lost it or never had it), which is when online directories come in pretty handy.

An *online directory* is just that — a listing of names and addresses (e-mail and/or regular mail, depending on the directory) that you can access and search on the Internet. Most directories are accessible on the World Wide Web (we cover the World Wide Web in more detail later). Here's how to use an online directory to look for a particular person's e-mail address:

1. **Open your World Wide Web browser.**

   You generally do this by double-clicking the program's icon or using the Start program menu.

2. **In your browser's URL field, type the Yahoo! People Search Web address** (people.yahoo.com).

   The Yahoo! People Search page comes up.

3. **In the First Name field, type the person's first name (if you know it).**

   For this example, we look for April in the People Search directory. In the First Name field, we type **April**.

4. **In the Last Name field, type the person's last name.**

   We type **Helm**.

5. **In the Search For section, click the Email Address radio button.**

This restricts the Yahoo! People Search so that it looks only for e-mail addresses, not traditional mailing addresses.

6. **Click Search.**

Yahoo! executes the search and brings up an E-mail Basic Search Results page showing any matches that it found or informing you that it doesn't find anyone with that name. For each match, the Search Results page provides the person's name, e-mail address, and location. Each name is a link to more information. For our example, one of April's e-mail addresses came up as the first match.

Directories like Yahoo! People Search are great when you're trying to track down the e-mail addresses for just a few people you want to contact. However, online directories do have their limitations. If you're searching for someone who has a common name — say, John Martin or Elizabeth Smith — you're in for a challenge when you use an online directory. You need to know a little bit more about people with common names to effectively search for their e-mail addresses. Information such as where they live is helpful. Although Yahoo! provides only the country of the person's e-mail address, other online directories provide full address information.

Another twist to online directories that you may encounter is that they can turn up more than one e-mail address for the same person. If you'd run a search on Matthew's name instead of April's in the steps above, three or four of the many Matthew Helms who showed up on the results page would have been the Matthew you were looking for. (The reason for this is that Matthew has three or four different e-mail accounts.)

Mailing lists

Mailing lists are closely related to e-mail in that they involve e-mailing other people, but you e-mail others en masse instead of one-on-one. (You may hear mailing lists referred to as *listservs,* although technically Listserv is a software program for managing mailing lists and not a mailing list itself.) Mailing lists are formed by groups of people who share common interests. In terms of genealogical research, the common interest may be a specific surname, locality, or ethnic group.

We discuss mailing lists and posting queries to them in Chapter 4, along with an example of how to subscribe to a mailing list. In general, to subscribe to a mailing list, all you have to do is send an e-mail message to a designated e-mail address and put the word **subscribe** in the subject line.

Telnet

Telnet is a text-based program that enables you to use your computer to log on to another computer and view files or documents made available there for public access. You can't download the files, and you can't upload your files to the other computer, either. To log on to another computer, you need a telnet client (software) or a World Wide Web browser (such as Netscape Navigator and Microsoft Internet Explorer) that launches a telnet client. (For more on browsers, see the "World Wide Web" section later in this appendix.)

As the World Wide Web has become more popular, telnet has started to fall by the wayside. Most of the remaining telnet sites of interest to genealogists are library card catalogs. You can usually link to and view even those card catalogs that haven't moved to the World Wide Web by using your Web browser.

File Transfer Protocol

File Transfer Protocol (FTP) is a way to transfer files from your computer to another (or vice versa) over the Internet. You must have software that enables you to transfer files over the Internet, and you can only use it to log on to other computers that allow FTP access. After you log on to a computer that allows FTP access, you can download files that are available for FTP or, in some instances, upload your own file to that computer.

How you get to an FTP site on another computer to log on and download or upload files depends on the other site and the FTP software that you use. The general gist of it is this: Using your software, you tell your computer to transfer files into the other computer. The other computer asks you to log in (you must provide a password), and then gives you access to the FTP files that you're allowed to download. If, for some reason, you aren't authorized to transfer files into the other computer, your attempt is rejected. A lot of computer systems allow you to download things *anonymously,* meaning you can log in to a machine that you don't know the password for by simply typing **anonymous** for the user name and typing in your e-mail address as the password.

Some World Wide Web pages have FTP files available for downloading directly from the Web pages. All you have to do is click the link to the file, and your computer asks where you want the file to be saved.

Gopher

Gopher was developed at the University of Minnesota as a way to hierarchically categorize data on the Internet. Gopher uses a series of text-based menus through which you can browse. You click menu choices to get to other levels of information and eventually to the particular file or document that you're looking for. Gopher was popular before the World Wide Web and has, for the most part, been replaced by Web sites.

You can access Gopher sites in several different ways. You can use a Gopher client (or software) or your World Wide Web browser. (Actually, because you can use your Web browser, Gopher software has become largely obsolete these days.) Depending on which way you decide to go, your instructions for getting to Gopher sites vary. However, the method for navigating within a Gopher site is the same: Clicking menu choices takes you to submenus, down through the hierarchy.

Newsgroups

Newsgroups are places to post messages of interest to groups of people at large. Newsgroups are similar to mailing lists in that you use e-mail to send a message that many people can read. However, instead of the message being sent individually to everyone on a mailing list, the message is posted to a news server, which in turn copies the message to other news servers. The other news servers wait for people who are interested in the topic to request the latest postings.

Newsgroups are subdivided into hierarchies. Each hierarchy has a top-level label such as soc or alt. Beneath the top level is a second hierarchy, followed by a third level, and so on.

In general, you have a few ways to get to the newsgroups or the messages posted to them:

- ✔ If your Internet service provider (ISP) has a news feed, you can use a news reader configured to pick up the news feed and connect you to its news server. If you use Netscape Navigator or Internet Explorer, a news-reader is built in. (To use this method of access, we recommend consulting the manual or other instructions provided by your individual ISP to configure your news reader. Your ISP will tell you what your specific news-server settings should be.)

- ✔ If your Internet service provider doesn't have a news feed or you don't have the software necessary to access it, you can get to some newsgroups through the World Wide Web. (One such site is Google Groups at groups.google.com.) We prefer to access newsgroups through the Web because it's easy and requires only a World Wide Web browser. For more on browsers, see the "World Wide Web" section later in this appendix. To find out how to access and use Google Groups, keep reading.

- ✔ If the newsgroup is *gatewayed* with a mailing list (traffic from the newsgroup is relayed to a mailing list and vice versa), you can receive the messages posted to the newsgroup through that mailing list.

Here's how to access a newsgroup and read it through the World Wide Web:

1. **Open your World Wide Web browser.**

    You usually do this by double-clicking the program's icon or using the Start program menu.

2. **In your browser's URL field, type the Web address for Google Groups** (groups.google.com).

3. **Click the soc link.**

    This takes you to a page with a list of the soc newsgroups, including soc.genealogy.

4. **Select the soc.genealogy link.**

    A page listing all the soc.genealogy newsgroups pops up. From here, you can select any of these to explore the messages posted to that particular group.

World Wide Web

The *World Wide Web* is a system for viewing and using multimedia documents on the Internet. The documents that you view on the Web are written in a code called *Hypertext Markup Language* (HTML) that is translated into graphical pages (which may have sound and motion attached) by software called a *Web browser*. (For general information about features of a browser and how to use one, see the section "Web browsers" in this appendix. For more on HTML, take a look at Chapter 12.)

The pages of the multimedia documents usually have hypertext links that you can click to get to other sites. You can navigate the Web by typing the address of a Web site — also called a *Uniform Resource Locator* (URL) — in the appropriate field of your browser and pressing Enter, or by clicking the links on a page to get to other pages.

Although you hear the Web referred to *as* the Internet, the Web is *not* the Internet. The Web is a resource *on* the Internet; it doesn't make up the whole Internet all by itself. (Other sections of this appendix explain various Internet resources in addition to the Web.)

Web browsers

Several different Web browser programs are available. You can download some browsers for free off the Internet; others come loaded on your computer with software packages; some you buy separately; and still others come with your subscription to an Internet service provider. Most offer similar standard navigation features, and almost all are easy to use.

The two most popular browsers are Netscape Navigator and Microsoft Internet Explorer. Here are some of the common features of these two browsers and how to use those features:

- Each browser has a field in which you enter the address, or URL, to get to a Web page. Navigator calls its address field *Location* or *Netsite,* and Internet Explorer calls its field *Address.*

- The Stop button halts a page that's loading into your browser.

- The Back button on the button bar takes you back to the previous page. Similarly, the Forward button takes you forward to the site that you were viewing before you hit the Back button.

- The Reload button (Navigator) and the Refresh button (Internet Explorer) reload the page that you're looking at. If any changes to the page occurred while you were online, reloading or refreshing the page picks up those changes and reflects them.

- Clicking the Print button prints a copy of the page that you're looking at. If the Web page is too long to fit on one regular sheet of paper, the browser tells the printer where to split the Web page to print on multiple sheets of paper.

- *Bookmarks* (Navigator) and *Favorites* (Internet Explorer) give you a shortcut list to pages that the software manufacturers think you may be interested in or looking for. Additionally, you can add your own bookmarks or favorites for your frequently visited sites by choosing Bookmarks⇨Add Bookmark in Navigator or Favorites⇨Add to Favorites in Internet Explorer.

- Both programs have Help drop-down menus that offer more information on using the browser and its features.

Search engines

Search engines are programs that search large indexes of information gathered by robots sent out to *catalog* (sort and record) resources on the Internet. (*Robots* are programs that travel throughout the Internet and collect information on the various sites and resources that they run across.) You can access the information contained in search engines through an *interface* (an online form or page).

Some of the better-known search engines are

- **Google:** www.google.com
- **Lycos:** www.lycos.com

  ✔ **AltaVista:** www.altavista.com

  ✔ **HotBot:** www.hotbot.com

  ✔ **Excite:** www.excite.com

Although each search engine has its own variations, all of them function similarly. All search engines have an interface with a form in which you enter keywords to search for in the search engine's index. Each search engine then runs a search of its index, returning its findings to you with links directly to the pages where the search engine's robot identified the keywords.

Chat rooms

Chat rooms are Internet sites where you can log on and participate in conversations in real time (or with just a few seconds delay). Although you may not encounter and use chat rooms a lot in your genealogical research, we did want you to know that they exist.

A few chat rooms discuss genealogy specifically. Typically, the genealogy chat rooms (or in some cases, sessions that are pre-arranged) are hosted by or are available through the commercial Internet service providers (particularly America Online) or the Internet Relay Chat (IRC) network.

The IRC hosts several areas (called *channels*) where you can find discussions about genealogy. To access and use a chat channel on IRC, you have to use chat software.

In addition to chat rooms, there are other ways to communicate with researchers "in real time." Products such as AOL/Netscape Instant Messaging and ICQ allow researchers to communicate with each other. For more information on AOL/Netscape Instant Messaging, see wp.netscape.com/aim/index_ie5.html. Information on ICQ can be found at web.icq.com.

Appendix B

What Does This Mean? (A Glossary of Terms)

Abstract: A brief overview or summary of what a document or Web site contains.

Ahnentafel: A well-known genealogical numbering system. Ahnentafel is a method of numbering that has a mathematical relationship between parents and children. The word itself means *ancestor* and *table* in German; also referred to as the *Sosa-Stradonitz System* of numbering.

Albumen print: A type of photograph that was produced on a thin piece of paper coated with albumen and silver nitrate and usually mounted on cardboard; typically taken between 1858 and 1910.

Ambrotype: A type of photograph that was printed on thin glass and usually had a black backing; typically taken between 1858 and 1866.

America Online: A popular commercial Internet service provider.

Ancestor: A person from whom you are descended.

Ancestor chart: A chart that runs horizontally across a page and identifies a primary person (including that person's name, date and place of birth, date and place of marriage, and date and place of death), his/her parents, and then each of their parents, and so on until the chart runs off the page. Usually called a *Pedigree chart.*

Ancestral file: A database created and maintained by the Church of Jesus Christ of Latter-day Saints, with millions of names available in Family Group Sheets and Pedigree charts; part of the FamilySearch collection of CD-ROMs, which are accessible at Family History Centers. See also *Family History Center* and *Family History Library.*

Archive: A physical location where historical documents and records are stored.

AT&T WorldNet: A popular commercial Internet service provider.

Automoderator: A computer program that determines whether a post to a newsgroup is appropriate, and if so, posts it to the newsgroup.

Backbones: High-speed data lines that support the Internet.

Bandwidth: The capacity that a particular phone line or other networking cable has to carry traffic to and from the Internet or computer network.

Banns: See *marriage banns.*

Baptismal certificate: A certificate issued by a church at the time of baptism; sometimes used to approximate a birth date in the absence of a birth certificate.

Bibliography: A list of books or other materials that were used in research; also a list of books or other materials that are available on a particular topic.

Biographical sketch: A brief written account of a person's life.

Biography: A detailed written account of a person's life.

Birth certificate: A legal record stating when and where a person was born.

Bookmark: A method for saving links to your favorite Web sites within your Web browser so you can easily return to them.

Bounce: When e-mail doesn't reach the intended party for whatever reason and is returned to the sender.

Bounty land: Federal land given to a person in exchange for military service or some other civic service.

Browser: See *World Wide Web browser.*

Bureau of Refugees, Freedmen, and Abandoned Lands: Established in 1865, the bureau had programs to assist ex-slaves after the American Civil War. Also called *Freedman's Bureau.*

Cabinet card: A larger version of the carte-de-visite photograph; typically taken between 1865 and 1906.

Cable connection: Direct access to the Internet using cable lines.

Cache: A directory on your computer where your Web browser stores information about Web pages and images it has downloaded. Using the cache, the browser can load that page faster if you visit it again within a specified period.

Canon Code: A code that explains the bloodline relationship in legal terms by identifying how many degrees of separation (or steps) exist between two people related by blood. Canon law counts only the number of steps from the nearest common ancestor of both relatives.

Carte-de-visite: A type of photograph that was a small paper print mounted on a card; collections were usually bound together in photo albums. Typically taken between 1858 and 1891.

CD-ROM: Acronym for Compact Disc-Read Only Memory; used in your computer's compact disc drive. A CD-ROM stores large amounts of information (including multimedia) that can be retrieved by your computer.

Census: The counting of a population undertaken by a government.

Census index: A listing of people who are included in particular census records, along with references indicating where you can find the actual census records.

Census return: The record/form on which census information is collected. Also called a *census schedule.*

Census schedule: Another term for a *census return* form.

Channel: An area within Internet Relay Chat where you can find discussions on particular topics, including genealogy.

Charter: A formal or informal document that defines the scope of a newsgroup.

Chat room: An Internet site where you can log in and participate in real-time conversations.

Cite: To name the source of some information and provide reference to the original source.

Civil Code: A code that explains the bloodline relationship in legal terms by identifying how many *degrees of separation* (or kinship steps) exist between two people related by blood; civil law counts each step between two relatives as a degree.

Civil records: Government documents that contain information on the civic duties of your ancestors, proceedings of municipal governments, or any other records of your ancestors' interaction with the government; often found in local and state archives or courthouses.

Civil registration: Primary record of a vital event in life: birth, death, or marriage; for the most part, originals are kept by local governments. Also called *vital records* in the United States and Canada.

Commercial Internet service provider: A company or organization that supplies access to the Internet for a fee.

Community network: An Internet service provider that's locally based and offers access to people in the community (usually free of charge). Also called *freenet.*

Comprehensive genealogical site: A Web site that identifies a large number of other genealogical sites containing information on a number of families, locations, or a variety of other genealogy-related subjects.

Cookies: Pieces of information that are sent to your computer by other computers when you visit certain Web pages. Generally, cookies are used for navigation purposes or by commercial sites that want to rotate banner advertisements for you so you don't get tired of the same old advertisement.

Copyright: Copyright is the exclusive right of a creator to reproduce, prepare derivative works, distribute, perform, display, sell, lend, or rent his/her creations.

County clerk: The clerk of the county court that records or maintains records of transactions and events in that county. Sometimes called the *county recorder.*

Cyberspace: A slang term for the Internet.

Daguerreotype: A type of photograph that required a long exposure time and was taken on silver-plated copper; typically taken between 1839 and 1860.

Database: A collection of information that is entered, organized, stored, and used on a computer.

Death certificate: A legal record stating when and where a person died.

Declaration of intent: A sworn statement by a person who intends to become a naturalized citizen of the United States.

Deed: A document that records the transfer of ownership of a piece of property or land.

Descendant: A person who descended from a particular ancestor.

Descendant chart: A chart that contains information about an ancestor and spouse (or particular spouses if there was more than one), their children and their spouses, grandchildren and spouses, and so on down the family line; usually formatted vertically on a page like a list.

Dial-up connection: A method of connecting to the Internet wherein your computer uses a telephone line to call in to an *Internet service provider.*

Digest mode: An option for receiving postings to some mailing lists in which several messages are batched together and sent to you instead of each message being sent separately.

Digital camera: A camera that captures images to computer memory instead of to film, and then downloads the images to your computer.

Digital Subscriber Line (DSL): Direct access to the Internet using specialized phone lines. This service is faster than a dial-up connection, which uses traditional phone lines.

Digitized record: A copy or image of a record that has been made using electronic means.

Direct connection: Direct access to the Internet from your home. There are four ways in which you can have a direct connection: You can access the Internet through an Internet line that comes directly into your home or business and is hooked up to your computer(s); a cable connection; a Digital Subscriber Line (DSL); or a satellite connection.

Directory: A collection of information about individuals who live in a particular place.

Download: Getting a file (information or a program) to your computer from another computer.

EarthLink: A popular commercial Internet service provider.

Electronic mail: Messages sent from one person to another electronically over the Internet. Also called *e-mail.*

E-mail: Short for *electronic mail.*

Emigrant: A person who leaves or moves away from one country to settle in another country.

Emoticons: Graphics created by combinations of keys on the keyboard to express an emotion within a message.

Enumeration district: The area assigned to a particular enumerator of the census.

Enumerator: A person who collected details on individuals during a census.

Estate: The assets and liabilities of a person who dies.

Family association: An organized group of individuals who are researching the same family.

Family association site: A Web site that's designed and posted by an organization devoted to researching a particular family.

Family Group Sheet: A summary of a particular family, including biographical information about a husband, wife, and their children.

Family history: The written account of a family's existence over time.

Family History Center: Local branches of the *Family History Library.*

Family History Library: The Church of Jesus Christ of Latter-day Saints' main library in Salt Lake City, Utah. The Family History Library has the world's largest collection of genealogical holdings, including print sources and microfilmed records, as well as records and other information shared by genealogical researchers worldwide.

Family History Library Catalog: A listing of records (books, films, microfiche, CDs, cassette tapes, videos, and microfilms) available at the Family History Library in Salt Lake City, Utah; part of the FamilySearch collection of CD-ROMs, which are accessible at Family History Centers.

Family Outline report: A list of the descendants of a particular ancestor.

FamilySearch: A collection of information compiled by the Church of Jesus Christ of Latter-day Saints; it includes the Ancestral File, Family History Library Catalog, International Genealogical Index, Military Index, Social Security Death Index, and Scottish Church Records.

FAQ: Acronym for Frequently Asked Questions.

FHC: Acronym for Family History Center.

FHL: Acronym for Family History Library.

File Transfer Protocol: A way to transfer files from your computer to another, or vice versa, over the Internet. Also called *FTP.*

Flame: A verbal (written) attack online.

Forum: A subject-specific area where members post messages and files.

Fraternal order: A service club or organization of persons.

Freedman's Bureau: Abbreviated name for the Bureau of Refugees, Freedmen, and Abandoned Lands.

Freedman's Savings and Trust Company: Established in 1865, this was a bank for ex-slaves.

Freenet: An Internet service provider that's locally based and offers access to people in the community free of charge. Also called *community network.*

Freeware: Software that you usually obtain and use for free by downloading it off the Internet.

Frequently Asked Questions: A Web page or message posted to a mailing list or newsgroup that explains answers to the most-asked questions to the particular Web site, mailing list, or newsgroup. Usually serves as a starting point for people new to a site or resource.

FTP: Acronym for File Transfer Protocol.

Gateway: Computer(s) that forward messages and route data between networks.

Gatewayed: When traffic from a newsgroup is relayed to a related mailing list and vice versa.

Gazetteer: Geographical dictionary that provides information about places.

GEDCOM: Acronym for GEnealogical Data COMmunication.

Genealogical database: Software in which you enter, store, and use information about ancestors, descendants, and others relevant to your genealogy.

Genealogical Data Communication: The standard file format for exporting and importing information between genealogical databases; intended to make data translatable between different genealogical software programs so you can share your family information easily. Also called GEDCOM.

Genealogically focused search engine: A program that indexes the full text of Web sites that are of interest and value to genealogists, and allows you to search the index for particular keywords.

GENDEX: An index of online genealogical databases that comply with the GEDCOM converted to HTML indexing format.

Genealogical society: An organized group that attempts to preserve documents and history for the area in which the society is located; often a genealogical society has a second purpose, which is to help its members research their ancestors.

Genealogy: The study of *ancestors, descendants,* and family origins.

Geographic-specific Web site: A Web site that has information pertaining to a particular locality (town, county, state, country, or other area).

Glass-plate negative: A type of photograph made from light-sensitive silver bromide immersed in gelatin; typically taken between 1848 and 1930.

Gopher: A computer protocol (developed at the University of Minnesota) that offers a way to categorize data on the Internet by using a series of text-based, hierarchical menus through which you can browse and click.

Helm Online Family Tree Research Cycle: A five-phase research model that explains the ongoing process of genealogical research.

Henry System: A widely used and accepted genealogical numbering system, it assigns a particular sequence of numbers to the children of a family's progenitor and to subsequent generations.

Hierarchy: In terms of a newsgroup, a hierarchy is the major grouping to which a newsgroup belongs; for example, `soc.genealogy.computing` belongs to the `soc` hierarchy.

Historical society: An organized group that attempts to preserve documents and history for the area in which the society is located.

Home page: The entry point for a World Wide Web site.

HTML: Acronym for HyperText Markup Language.

HyperText Markup Language: The programming language of the World Wide Web. HTML is a code that's translated into graphical pages by software called a World Wide Web browser.

IGI: Acronym for International Genealogical Index.

Immigrant: A person who moves into or settles in a country.

Immigration record: A record of the entry of a person into a specific country where he or she was not native-born or naturalized.

Index: A list of some sort. An index can be a list of Web sites, types of records, and so on.

Interface: An online form or page.

Interlibrary loan: A system in which one library loans a book or other material to another library for a person to borrow or use.

International Genealogical Index: A list of births and marriages of deceased individuals reflected in records collected by the Church of Jesus Christ of Latter-day Saints. The International Genealogical Index (also called IGI) is part of the FamilySearch collection of CD-ROMs, accessible at Family History Centers.

Internet: A system of computer networks joined together by high-speed data lines called *backbones*.

Internet Relay Chat: A network providing channels (or areas) where you can find real-time discussions about genealogy and participate using chat software. Also called *IRC*.

Internet service provider: A company or other organization that provides people with access to the Internet through a direct connection or dial-up connection. Also called *ISP*.

Intestate: The estate status of a person who died without leaving a valid will.

IRC: Acronym for Internet Relay Chat.

ISP: Acronym for Internet service provider.

Kinship report: A list of family members and how they relate directly to one particular individual in your database; usually kinship reports include the Civil Code and Canon Code for the relationship to the individual.

Land grant: Permission to purchase land or a gift of land in exchange for military service or other civic service.

Land patent: A document that conveyed the title of a piece of land to a new owner after that person met required conditions to own the land.

Land record: A document recording the sale or exchange of land; most land records are maintained at a local level where the property is located.

Listowner: A person who oversees a mailing list.

Listserv: A software program for managing electronic mailing lists.

Lurking: Reading messages that others post to a mailing list or newsgroup without posting any messages of your own.

Maiden name: The surname with which a woman is born; sometimes reflected as *née* on records and documents.

Mail mode: The method for mailing lists in which each message is sent to you separately as it's posted.

Mailing list: An e-mail exchange forum that consists of a group of people who share common interests; e-mail messages posted to the list come directly to your e-mail in full-format (mail mode) or digest mode; the list consists of the names of everyone who joins the group. When you want to send a message to the group, you post it to a single e-mail address that subsequently delivers the message to everyone on the list.

Manumission papers: Documents granting slaves their freedom.

Marriage banns: A proclamation made in front of a church congregation expressing one's intent to marry.

Marriage bond: A financial contract guaranteeing that a marriage was going to take place; usually posted by the groom and another person (often the father or brother of the bride).

Marriage certificate: A legal document certifying the union of two individuals.

Marriage license: A document granting permission to marry from a civil or ecclesiastical authority.

Maternal: Relating to the mother's side of the family.

Microfiche: A clear sheet that contains tiny images of documents, records, books, and so on; you must read it with a microfiche reader or other magnifying equipment.

Microfilm: A roll of clear film that contains tiny images of documents, records, books, and so forth; you must read it with a microfilm reader.

Microsoft Network: A popular commercial Internet service provider. Also called MSN.

Military Index: A list of those killed in the Korean and Vietnam Wars; part of the FamilySearch collection of CD-ROMs, which are accessible at Family History Centers.

Modem: A piece of equipment that allows your computer to talk to other computers through a telephone or cable line; modems can be internal (inside your computer) or external (plugged into one of your computer's serial ports or card).

Moderator: A person who determines whether a post to a newsgroup or mailing list is appropriate, and if so, posts it.

Mortgage: Legal agreement to repay money borrowed with real property as collateral.

MSN: Acronym for Microsoft Network.

MSN TV: An Internet receiver containing a small computer with limited functions that hooks directly into your television set and enables you to connect to the MSN TV Internet service provider for access to e-mail, the World Wide Web, and newsgroups.

Muster record: A type of military pay record reflecting who was present with a military unit at a particular time and place.

Naturalization: The official process of becoming a citizen or subject of a particular country in a manner other than birth in that country.

Naturalization record: The legal document proving one is a naturalized citizen.

Netiquette: Simple guidelines for communicating effectively and politely on the Internet.

Newbie: A person who is new to the Internet.

Newsgroup: A place to post messages of a particular focus so groups of people at large can read them online; messages are posted to a news server which, in turn, copies the messages to other news servers.

News reader: Software needed for reading messages posted to a newsgroup.

News server: One or more computers that replicate newsgroups over the Internet.

Notebook computer: A compact computer that's portable.

Obituary: An account of one's death that usually appears in a newspaper or other type of media.

One-name study: A page on the World Wide Web that focuses on research involving one particular surname regardless of the geographic location in which it appears.

Online: Gaining access to and using the Internet or something that is available through the Internet.

Orphan: An infant or child whose parents are both deceased. In some earlier times and places, a child was considered an orphan if his/her father had died but the mother was still living.

Palmtop: A hand-sized computer that is portable and can contain some of the same programs housed on desktop computers.

Passenger list: Listing of the names of passengers who traveled from one country to another on a particular ship.

Paternal: Relating to the father's side of the family.

Pedigree chart: A chart that runs horizontally across a page, identifying a primary person (including that person's name, date and place of birth, date and place of marriage, and date and place of death), his/her parents, and then each of their parents, and so on until the chart runs off the page. Sometimes called an *ancestor chart.*

Pension record: A type of military record reflecting the amount of a pension that the government paid to an individual who served in the military; pension records also showed the amount of pension paid to the widow or orphan(s) of such an individual.

Personal Web page: A page on the World Wide Web that was designed and posted by an individual or family.

Petition for land: An application that your ancestor may have filed for a land grant.

Plat map: A map of lots within a tract of land, usually showing the owners' names. Also spelled "platte map."

Platinum print: A type of photograph with a matte surface that appeared to be embedded in the paper. Images were often highlighted with artistic chalk, giving the photo a hand-drawn quality; typically taken between 1880 and 1930.

Primary source: A document, oral account, photograph, or any other item that was created at the time a certain event occurred; information for the record was supplied by a witness to the event.

Probate: Settlement of one's estate after death.

Probate records: Types of court records that deal with the settling of an estate upon one's death. Probate records include contested wills and will readings; often the file contains testimonies and the ruling.

Professional researcher: A person who will research your genealogy — particular family lines — or obtain copies of documents for you for a fee.

Progenitor: The farthest-back ancestor you know about in a particular family line.

Query: A research question that you post to a particular Web site, mailing list, or newsgroup so that other researchers can help you solve your genealogical research problems/challenges.

Research groups: A group of people who coordinate their research and share resources to achieve success.

Robot: A program that travels throughout the Internet and collects information about sites and resources that it comes across. Also called a *spider.*

Roots Surname List: A list of surnames, their associated dates, and locations accompanied by the contact information for persons researching those surnames that is maintained by RootsWeb.com. Also called *RSL.*

RSL: Acronym for Roots Surname List.

Satellite connection: Direct access to the Internet using a satellite dish and signals.

Scanner: A device that captures digital images of photographs and documents into your computer.

Search engine: A program that searches either a large index of information generated by robots or a particular Web site.

Secondary source: A document, oral account, or any other record that was created after an event took place or for which information was supplied by someone who was not an eyewitness to the event.

Server: A computer that makes information available for access by other computers.

Service record: A type of military record that chronicles the military career of an individual.

Shareware: Software that you can try before you pay to license and use it permanently; usually you download shareware off the Internet.

Shotgun approach: A bad idea; the process of sending mass e-mails to anyone you find with your surname through one of the online white pages sites.

Signature file: A file that you can create and attach to the bottom of your e-mail messages that gives your name, contact information, surnames that you're researching, or anything else you want to convey to others.

Site: One or more World Wide Web pages; also called a *Web site.*

Snail mail: Mail delivered by hand — such as U.S. Mail.

Social Security Death Index: An index of those persons for whom Social Security death claims were filed with the United States government. Although there are a few records in the index that pre-date 1962, most date from 1962 to the present.

Sosa-Stradonitz System: See *ahnentafel*.

Sound card: An internal computer device that enables you to hear the audio features of software or audio files that you download off the Internet.

Soundex: A system of indexing the U.S. federal census that groups names that sound alike but are spelled differently; the Soundex code for a name includes a letter followed by three numbers.

Source: Any person or material (book, document, record, periodical, and so on) that provides information for your research.

Spam: Unsolicited junk e-mail that tries to sell you something or offers a service.

Spider: A program that travels throughout the Internet and collects information about sites and resources it comes across. Also called a *robot*.

Stereographic card: A type of photograph that was paired and rendered a three-dimensional effect when used with a viewer; developed in the 1850s.

Surname: A last name or family name.

Survey: Detailed drawing and legal description of the boundaries of a land parcel.

Tax record: A record of any tax paid, including property, inheritance, and church taxes; most taxes were collected at the local level, but some of the records have now been turned over to government archives.

Telnet: A text-based program that allows you to log in to another computer and view files or documents that are available for public access; you need telnet-client software to use telnet.

Thread: A group of messages with a common subject on a newsgroup.

Tintype: A type of photograph that was made on a metal sheet; the image was often coated with a varnish. Typically taken between 1858 and 1910.

Tiny tafel: A compact way to show the relationships within a family database. Tiny tafel provides a Soundex code for a *surname* and the dates and locations where that surname may be found according to the database.

Toggling: The process of flipping back and forth between open programs on your computer by using the Alt and Tab keys in Windows or the Application Switcher in Macintosh.

Tract book: A book describing the lots within a township or other geographic area.

Transcribed record: A copy of the content of a record that has been duplicated word for word.

Uniform Resource Locator: A standard online address provided for resources on the World Wide Web; also called *URL.*

URL: Acronym for Uniform Resource Locator.

U.S. Colored Troops database: An online database of information on more than 230,000 soldiers of African descent who served in the U.S. Colored Troops; part of the Civil War Soldiers and Sailors System sponsored by the National Park Service.

Video-capture board: A device that enables your computer to grab images from your video camera or VCR.

Vital record: Primary record of a vital event in life — birth, death, or marriage; for the most part, local governments keep the originals. Often called *civil registrations* outside the United States.

Warrant: A certificate to receive land when your ancestor's petition for a land grant was approved.

Webmaster: A person responsible for creating and maintaining a particular Web site.

Web site: One or more World Wide Web pages created by an individual or organization; also called a *site.*

Will: A legal document that explains how a person wishes his/her estate to be settled or distributed upon death.

Witness: One who attests that he/she saw an event.

World Wide Web: A system for viewing and using multimedia documents on the Internet; Web documents are created in HyperText Markup Language (HTML) and are read by World Wide Web browser programs.

World Wide Web browser: Software that enables you to view HTML documents on the Internet.

World Wide Web page: A multimedia document that is created in HTML and is viewable on the Internet with the use of a World Wide Web browser.

XML: A specialized computer code, similar to HTML, that uses tags to describe information. The broader purpose of XML is not only to display information, but also to describe the information.

Zip disk: A computer disk that you use with an Iomega Zip drive; stores up to 250MB of data.

Appendix C

About the CD

*H*ere's some of what you can find on the *Genealogy Online For Dummies,* 4th Edition, CD-ROM:

- ✔ Family Tree Maker for Windows, a trial version of the popular genealogy database
- ✔ Homesite 5.5, an evaluation copy of the popular HTML editor
- ✔ World Place Finder, a gazetteer geared to genealogists

System Requirements

Make sure your computer meets *at least* the following minimum system requirements. If your computer doesn't match up to most of these requirements, you may have problems using the contents of the CD:

- ✔ A PC with a Pentium or faster processor, or a Mac OS computer with a 68040 or faster processor.
- ✔ Microsoft Windows 98 or later, or Mac OS system software 7.55 or later.
- ✔ At least 32MB of total RAM installed on your computer. For best performance, we recommend at least 64MB of RAM installed.
- ✔ At least 500MB of hard-drive space available to install all the software from this CD. (You need less space if you don't install every program.)
- ✔ A CD-ROM drive — double-speed (2x) or faster.
- ✔ A sound card for PCs. (Mac OS computers have built-in sound support.)
- ✔ A monitor capable of displaying at least 256 colors or grayscale.
- ✔ A modem with a speed of at least 33,600 bps (56K recommended).

If you need more information on the basics, check out *PCs For Dummies,* 9th Edition, by Dan Gookin; *Macs For Dummies,* 7th Edition, by David Pogue; and *iMac For Dummies,* 2nd Edition, by David Pogue (all published by Wiley Publishing, Inc.).

Using the CD with Microsoft Windows

If your system is built around a PC that runs Microsoft Windows, here's the scoop on using the CD:

1. **Insert the CD into your computer's CD-ROM drive.**

2. **Open your browser.**

   If you don't have a browser, we include Microsoft Internet Explorer and Netscape Communicator on the CD-ROM. They can be found in the Programs folders at the root of the CD.

3. **Click Start⇨Run.**

4. **In the dialog box that appears, type** D:\START.HTM.

   Replace *D* with the proper drive letter if your CD-ROM drive uses a different letter. (If you don't know the letter, see how your CD-ROM drive is listed under My Computer.)

5. **Read through the license agreement, nod your head and smile, and click the Accept button if you want to use the CD.**

   After you click Accept, you jump to the Main Menu.

   This action displays the file that walks you through the content of the CD.

6. **To navigate within the interface, simply click any topic of interest to go to an explanation of the files on the CD and how to use or install them.**

7. **To install the software from the CD, simply click the software name.**

   You see two options — the option to run or open the file from the current location or the option to save the file to your hard drive. Choose to run or open the file from its current location, and the installation procedure continues. After you are done with the interface, simply close your browser as usual.

To run some of the programs, you may need to keep the CD inside your CD-ROM drive. This is a Good Thing. Otherwise the installed program would have required you to install a very large chunk of the program to your hard drive, which would have kept you from installing other software.

How to Use the CD Using the Mac OS

To install the items from the CD to your Macintosh's hard drive, follow these steps:

1. **Insert the CD into your computer's CD-ROM drive.**

   In a moment, an icon representing the CD you just inserted appears on your Mac desktop. The icon may look like a CD-ROM.

2. **Double click the CD icon to show the CD's contents.**

3. **In the window that appears, double-click the START.HTM icon.**

4. **Read through the license agreement, nod your head and smile, and click the Accept button if you want to use the CD — after you click Accept, you jump to the Main Menu.**

   This action displays the file that walks you through the content of the CD.

5. **To navigate within the interface, simply click any topic of interest to be taken to an explanation of the files on the CD and how to use or install them.**

6. **To install the software from the CD, simply click the software name.**

   After you're done with the interface, simply close your browser as usual.

What You Get on the CD

Here's a summary of the software on this CD.

Genealogy programs

Ancestral Quest 2002
For Windows. Demo version.

Ancestral Quest is a Windows program for storing and organizing your genealogical findings. Included on this disc is the demonstration version of the program. Detailed information about the software is available at www.ancquest.com/.

AniMap Plus 2.5
For Windows. Demo version.

This is a demonstration version of the AniMap & SiteFinder program. AniMap is an interactive historical atlas that helps you track your family's movements and county-boundary changes over time. Information about the full program is available at www.goldbug.com/AniMap.html.

Clooz 1.23
For Windows. Demo version.

Clooz is an "electronic filing cabinet" that allows you to organize and store the many records you gather during your genealogical search. You can learn more about the many features of the program at www.clooz.com.

Family Tree Maker
For Windows. Trial version.

Genealogy.com provides a limited Version 9.0 of its popular genealogical database called Family Tree Maker. The program is easy to use and enables you to produce a variety of charts and reports, as well as record information on an unlimited number of people. The only limitation of this version is that you are not able to use the FamilyFinder Index functionality that is standard with the full Version 9.0. To find more information about the most recent version of Family Tree Maker and how to upgrade to it, visit www.familytreemaker.com.

GEDMark
For Windows. Demo version.

GEDMark is a utility that writes author information to GEDCOM files so that users of a file know who created it. For more information, see www.progenysoftware.com/gedmark.html.

Genelines 2.0
For Windows. Demo version.

This is a demonstration version of Genelines 2.0, a charting utility for files produced by Family Tree Maker and Personal Ancestral File, as well as GEDCOM files. Genelines produces five types of historical bar charts, including the individual geneline, comparative geneline, pedigree, direct descendant, and family group. For more information, see Progeny Software's site at www.progenysoftware.com.

Geneweaver 1.1
For Windows. Demo version.

Geneweaver is a program that helps you track the medical history of your family. More information on the program can be found at `www.geneweaveronline.com`.

Legacy Family Tree 5.0
For Windows. Full version.

The Millennia Corporation has provided a fully functional, basic version of its genealogical database software, called Legacy Family Tree. It stores data on an unlimited number of people and produces various charts and reports. For a detailed list of features and information about upgrading to the newest version of Legacy Family Tree, check out `www.legacyfamilytree.com/`.

Reunion 8
For Mac. Demo version.

This is the demonstration version of the popular genealogical program for Macintosh. It allows you to document, store, and display information about your family. The demo version limits you to information about 35 people. If you find that you like Reunion after using the demo, you can purchase the full version. For more information about Reunion, visit its Web site at `www.leisterpro.com/`.

RootsMagic
For Windows. Demo version.

RootsMagic is a new genealogical database program designed by the creator of the popular Family Origins program. The demonstration version of the program allows you to enter up to 50 individuals. More information on this program is found at `www.rootsmagic.com`.

World Place Finder
For Windows. Demo version.

World Place Finder is a gazetteer with more than 3.3 million towns and cities from around the world. It also includes churches and cemeteries in the United States. Not only can it be used to find places, it will also check the contents of your GEDCOM file for misspelled or incomplete place names. For more information, see `www.progenysoftware.com/placefinder.html`.

Other utilities

Acrobat Reader

For Windows and Mac. Evaluation version.

Acrobat Reader 6.0, from Adobe Systems, is a free program that lets you view and print Portable Document Format, or PDF, files. The PDF format is used by many programs that you find on the Internet for storing documentation because it supports the use of such stylish elements as assorted fonts and colorful graphics. You can also get more information by visiting the Adobe Systems Web site (www.adobe.com).

HomeSite

For Windows. Evaluation version.

HomeSite 5.5, from Allaire, is a popular shareware HTML editor for Windows. If you're interested in creating your own Web site, this program makes creating and editing documents with HTML (the programming language used to make a Web page) a breeze. Get more information on HomeSite at www.macromedia.com/software/homesite/.

Photoshop Elements 2.0

For Windows. Evaluation version.

Photoshop Elements is a multipurpose graphics tool for Windows. This program lets you view images in virtually any graphics format that you're likely to encounter on the Internet. In addition, it lets you edit and crop images, convert images from one file format to another, and even create pictures from scratch — all of which can be useful in helping to create your own Web pages. Visit the program's Web site at www.adobe.com/products/photoshopel/main.html for more information.

WinZip 8.1

For Windows. Shareware version.

WinZip 8.1, from Nico Mak Computing, is an invaluable file compression and decompression Windows shareware utility. Many files that you find on the Internet are compressed — or shrunken in size via special programming tricks — both to save storage space and to cut down on the amount of time that they require to be downloaded. You may also occasionally receive compressed files (ZIP files) as e-mail attachments. After you have a compressed file on your hard drive, you can use WinZip to decompress it and make it useable again. To learn even more about WinZip, visit the program's Web site (www.winzip.com).

Distinguishing Between Freeware and Shareware

Freeware is a program that its creator makes available for public use on a free-of-charge basis. Usually, you download freeware off the Internet, (although some exceptions exist in which you can get freeware on CD-ROM), and it doesn't require that you register your copy. You can use freeware for as long as you like with no obligations.

Shareware is another story. Shareware isn't free — it is commercial software that you're allowed to use on a trial basis for no charge. After the trial period is over, you must decide whether to keep it and pay for it or delete it from your computer. If you decide to buy the shareware, you should follow the registration instructions that come with it.

Using the Directory Links

The *Genealogy Online For Dummies* Internet Directory in this book provides many URLs for sites that we recommend you visit to get an idea of what is available in various categories. Rather than make you flip page by page through the directory to find these URLs, we thought we'd save you some time and paper cuts! We put links to all sites identified in the directory here! Isn't that convenient? Here's what you need to do to use these links:

1. **With the CD-ROM in your drive, launch your Web browser.**

2. **Choose File⇨Open (or Open⇨File, depending on your browser).**

   An Open dialog box appears.

3. **If you're using Windows, type** D:\LINKS\LINKS.HTM **in the Open text box. (If your CD-ROM drive isn't D, be sure to use the correct letter for your drive.)**

   If you're using Mac OS, use the Open dialog box to display the contents of the CD-ROM. Select the Links.htm file from the Links folder and press Return or Enter.

4. **Click the link for any site that you want to visit.**

   This opens a second browser window that takes you to the Web site that you selected. The links page remains open in the original browser window so you can toggle back to it to select another link.

If You've Got Problems (Of the CD Kind)

We tried our best to compile programs that work on most computers with the minimum system requirements. Alas — your computer may differ, and some programs may not work properly for some reason.

The two likeliest problems are that you don't have enough memory (RAM) for the programs that you want to use, or you have other programs running that are affecting installation or running of a program. If you get error messages like Not enough memory or Setup cannot continue, try one or more of these methods and then try using the software again:

✔ **Turn off any anti-virus software that you have on your computer.** Installers sometimes mimic virus activity and may make your computer incorrectly believe that a virus is infecting it.

✔ **Close all running programs.** The more programs you're running, the less memory is available to other programs.

✔ **Have your local computer store add more RAM to your computer.** This is, admittedly, a drastic and somewhat expensive step. However, if you have a Windows 95 PC or a Mac OS computer with a PowerPC chip, adding more memory can really help the speed of your computer and allow more programs to run at the same time.

If you still have trouble with installing the items from the CD, please call the Customer Service phone number: 800-762-2974 (outside the U.S.: 317-572-3993).

Index

• C •

• E •

• T •

Wiley Publishing, Inc., End-User License Agreement

READ THIS. You should carefully read these terms and conditions before opening the software packet(s) included with this book "Book". This is a license agreement "Agreement" between you and Wiley Publishing, Inc. "WPI". By opening the accompanying software packet(s), you acknowledge that you have read and accept the following terms and conditions. If you do not agree and do not want to be bound by such terms and conditions, promptly return the Book and the unopened software packet(s) to the place you obtained them for a full refund.

1. **License Grant.** WPI grants to you (either an individual or entity) a nonexclusive license to use one copy of the enclosed software program(s) (collectively, the "Software") solely for your own personal or business purposes on a single computer (whether a standard computer or a workstation component of a multi-user network). The Software is in use on a computer when it is loaded into temporary memory (RAM) or installed into permanent memory (hard disk, CD-ROM, or other storage device). WPI reserves all rights not expressly granted herein.

2. **Ownership.** WPI is the owner of all right, title, and interest, including copyright, in and to the compilation of the Software recorded on the disk(s) or CD-ROM "Software Media". Copyright to the individual programs recorded on the Software Media is owned by the author or other authorized copyright owner of each program. Ownership of the Software and all proprietary rights relating thereto remain with WPI and its licensers.

3. **Restrictions on Use and Transfer.**

   (a) You may only (i) make one copy of the Software for backup or archival purposes, or (ii) transfer the Software to a single hard disk, provided that you keep the original for backup or archival purposes. You may not (i) rent or lease the Software, (ii) copy or reproduce the Software through a LAN or other network system or through any computer subscriber system or bulletin-board system, or (iii) modify, adapt, or create derivative works based on the Software.

   (b) You may not reverse engineer, decompile, or disassemble the Software. You may transfer the Software and user documentation on a permanent basis, provided that the transferee agrees to accept the terms and conditions of this Agreement and you retain no copies. If the Software is an update or has been updated, any transfer must include the most recent update and all prior versions.

4. **Restrictions on Use of Individual Programs.** You must follow the individual requirements and restrictions detailed for each individual program in the About the CD-ROM appendix of this Book. These limitations are also contained in the individual license agreements recorded on the Software Media. These limitations may include a requirement that after using the program for a specified period of time, the user must pay a registration fee or discontinue use. By opening the Software packet(s), you will be agreeing to abide by the licenses and restrictions for these individual programs that are detailed in the About the CD-ROM appendix and on the Software Media. None of the material on this Software Media or listed in this Book may ever be redistributed, in original or modified form, for commercial purposes.

5. **Limited Warranty.**

   (a) WPI warrants that the Software and Software Media are free from defects in materials and workmanship under normal use for a period of sixty (60) days from the date of purchase of this Book. If WPI receives notification within the warranty period of defects in materials or workmanship, WPI will replace the defective Software Media.

   (b) WPI AND THE AUTHOR(S) OF THE BOOK DISCLAIM ALL OTHER WARRANTIES, EXPRESS OR IMPLIED, INCLUDING WITHOUT LIMITATION IMPLIED WARRANTIES OF MER-CHANTABILITY AND FITNESS FOR A PARTICULAR PURPOSE, WITH RESPECT TO THE SOFTWARE, THE PROGRAMS, THE SOURCE CODE CONTAINED THEREIN, AND/OR THE TECHNIQUES DESCRIBED IN THIS BOOK. WPI DOES NOT WARRANT THAT THE FUNC-TIONS CONTAINED IN THE SOFTWARE WILL MEET YOUR REQUIREMENTS OR THAT THE OPERATION OF THE SOFTWARE WILL BE ERROR FREE.

   (c) This limited warranty gives you specific legal rights, and you may have other rights that vary from jurisdiction to jurisdiction.

6. **Remedies.**

   (a) WPI's entire liability and your exclusive remedy for defects in materials and workman-ship shall be limited to replacement of the Software Media, which may be returned to WPI with a copy of your receipt at the following address: Software Media Fulfillment Department, Attn.: *Genealogy Online For Dummies,* 4th Edition, Wiley Publishing, Inc., 10475 Crosspoint Blvd., Indianapolis, IN 46256, or call 1-800-762-2974. Please allow four to six weeks for delivery. This Limited Warranty is void if failure of the Software Media has resulted from accident, abuse, or misapplication. Any replacement Software Media will be warranted for the remainder of the original warranty period or thirty (30) days, whichever is longer.

   (b) In no event shall WPI or the author be liable for any damages whatsoever (including without limitation damages for loss of business profits, business interruption, loss of business information, or any other pecuniary loss) arising from the use of or inability to use the Book or the Software, even if WPI has been advised of the possibility of such damages.

   (c) Because some jurisdictions do not allow the exclusion or limitation of liability for conse-quential or incidental damages, the above limitation or exclusion may not apply to you.

7. **U.S. Government Restricted Rights.** Use, duplication, or disclosure of the Software for or on behalf of the United States of America, its agencies and/or instrumentalities "U.S. Government" is subject to restrictions as stated in paragraph (c)(1)(ii) of the Rights in Technical Data and Computer Software clause of DFARS 252.227-7013, or subparagraphs (c)(1) and (2) of the Commercial Computer Software - Restricted Rights clause at FAR 52.227-19, and in similar clauses in the NASA FAR supplement, as applicable.

8. **General.** This Agreement constitutes the entire understanding of the parties and revokes and supersedes all prior agreements, oral or written, between them and may not be modified or amended except in a writing signed by both parties hereto that specifically refers to this Agreement. This Agreement shall take precedence over any other documents that may be in conflict herewith. If any one or more provisions contained in this Agreement are held by any court or tribunal to be invalid, illegal, or otherwise unenforceable, each and every other pro-vision shall remain in full force and effect.

FOR DUMMIES®

The easy way to get more done and have more fun

PERSONAL FINANCE & BUSINESS

Investing
0-7645-2431-3

Home Buying
0-7645-5331-3

Grant Writing
0-7645-5307-0

Also available:

Accounting For Dummies
(0-7645-5314-3)

Business Plans Kit For Dummies
(0-7645-5365-8)

Managing For Dummies
(1-5688-4858-7)

Mutual Funds For Dummies
(0-7645-5329-1)

QuickBooks All-in-One Desk Reference For Dummies
(0-7645-1963-8)

Resumes For Dummies
(0-7645-5471-9)

Small Business Kit For Dummies
(0-7645-5093-4)

Starting an eBay Business For Dummies
(0-7645-1547-0)

Taxes For Dummies 2003
(0-7645-5475-1)

HOME, GARDEN, FOOD & WINE

Feng Shui
0-7645-5295-3

Gardening
0-7645-5130-2

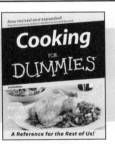

Cooking
0-7645-5250-3

Also available:

Bartending For Dummies
(0-7645-5051-9)

Christmas Cooking For Dummies
(0-7645-5407-7)

Cookies For Dummies
(0-7645-5390-9)

Diabetes Cookbook For Dummies
(0-7645-5230-9)

Grilling For Dummies
(0-7645-5076-4)

Home Maintenance For Dummies
(0-7645-5215-5)

Slow Cookers For Dummies
(0-7645-5240-6)

Wine For Dummies
(0-7645-5114-0)

FITNESS, SPORTS, HOBBIES & PETS

Fitness
0-7645-5167-1

Golf
0-7645-5146-9

Guitar
0-7645-5106-X

Also available:

Cats For Dummies
(0-7645-5275-9)

Chess For Dummies
(0-7645-5003-9)

Dog Training For Dummies
(0-7645-5286-4)

Labrador Retrievers For Dummies
(0-7645-5281-3)

Martial Arts For Dummies
(0-7645-5358-5)

Piano For Dummies
(0-7645-5105-1)

Pilates For Dummies
(0-7645-5397-6)

Power Yoga For Dummies
(0-7645-5342-9)

Puppies For Dummies
(0-7645-5255-4)

Quilting For Dummies
(0-7645-5118-3)

Rock Guitar For Dummies
(0-7645-5356-9)

Weight Training For Dummies
(0-7645-5168-X)

Available wherever books are sold.
Go to www.dummies.com or call 1-877-762-2974 to order direct

WILEY

FOR DUMMIES®

A world of resources to help you grow

TRAVEL

0-7645-5453-0

0-7645-5438-7

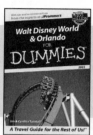

0-7645-5444-1

Also available:

America's National Parks For Dummies
(0-7645-6204-5)

Caribbean For Dummies
(0-7645-5445-X)

Cruise Vacations For
Dummies 2003
(0-7645-5459-X)

Europe For Dummies
(0-7645-5456-5)

Ireland For Dummies
(0-7645-6199-5)

France For Dummies
(0-7645-6292-4)

Las Vegas For Dummies
(0-7645-5448-4)

London For Dummies
(0-7645-5416-6)

Mexico's Beach Resorts
For Dummies
(0-7645-6262-2)

Paris For Dummies
(0-7645-5494-8)

RV Vacations For Dummies
(0-7645-5443-3)

EDUCATION & TEST PREPARATION

0-7645-5194-9

0-7645-5325-9

0-7645-5249-X

Also available:

The ACT For Dummies
(0-7645-5210-4)

Chemistry For Dummies
(0-7645-5430-1)

English Grammar For
Dummies
(0-7645-5322-4)

French For Dummies
(0-7645-5193-0)

GMAT For Dummies
(0-7645-5251-1)

Inglés Para Dummies
(0-7645-5427-1)

Italian For Dummies
(0-7645-5196-5)

Research Papers For Dummies
(0-7645-5426-3)

SAT I For Dummies
(0-7645-5472-7)

U.S. History For Dummies
(0-7645-5249-X)

World History For Dummies
(0-7645-5242-2)

HEALTH, SELF-HELP & SPIRITUALITY

0-7645-5154-X

0-7645-5302-X

0-7645-5418-2

Also available:

The Bible For Dummies
(0-7645-5296-1)

Controlling Cholesterol
For Dummies
(0-7645-5440-9)

Dating For Dummies
(0-7645-5072-1)

Dieting For Dummies
(0-7645-5126-4)

High Blood Pressure For
Dummies
(0-7645-5424-7)

Judaism For Dummies
(0-7645-5299-6)

Menopause For Dummies
(0-7645-5458-1)

Nutrition For Dummies
(0-7645-5180-9)

Potty Training For Dummies
(0-7645-5417-4)

Pregnancy For Dummies
(0-7645-5074-8)

Rekindling Romance For
Dummies
(0-7645-5303-8)

Religion For Dummies
(0-7645-5264-3)

Available wherever books are sold. Go to www.dummies.com or call 1-877-762-2974 to order direct

FOR DUMMIES®

Plain-English solutions for everyday challenges

HOME & BUSINESS COMPUTER BASICS

0-7645-0838-5

0-7645-1663-9

0-7645-1548-9

Also available:

Excel 2002 All-in-One Desk Reference For Dummies (0-7645-1794-5)

Office XP 9-in-1 Desk Reference For Dummies (0-7645-0819-9)

PCs All-in-One Desk Reference For Dummies (0-7645-0791-5)

Troubleshooting Your PC For Dummies (0-7645-1669-8)

Upgrading & Fixing PCs For Dummies (0-7645-1665-5)

Windows XP For Dummies (0-7645-0893-8)

Windows XP For Dummies Quick Reference (0-7645-0897-0)

Word 2002 For Dummies (0-7645-0839-3)

INTERNET & DIGITAL MEDIA

0-7645-0894-6

0-7645-1642-6

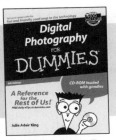

0-7645-1664-7

Also available:

CD and DVD Recording For Dummies (0-7645-1627-2)

Digital Photography All-in-One Desk Reference For Dummies (0-7645-1800-3)

eBay For Dummies (0-7645-1642-6)

Genealogy Online For Dummies (0-7645-0807-5)

Internet All-in-One Desk Reference For Dummies (0-7645-1659-0)

Internet For Dummies Quick Reference (0-7645-1645-0)

Internet Privacy For Dummies (0-7645-0846-6)

Paint Shop Pro For Dummies (0-7645-2440-2)

Photo Retouching & Restoration For Dummies (0-7645-1662-0)

Photoshop Elements For Dummies (0-7645-1675-2)

Scanners For Dummies (0-7645-0783-4)

Get smart! Visit www.dummies.com

- **Find listings of even more Dummies titles**
- **Browse online articles, excerpts, and how-to's**
- **Sign up for daily or weekly e-mail tips**
- **Check out Dummies fitness videos and other products**
- **Order from our online bookstore**

Available wherever books are sold. Go to www.dummies.com or call 1-877-762-2974 to order direct

FOR DUMMIES®

Helping you expand your horizons and realize your potential

GRAPHICS & WEB SITE DEVELOPMENT

0-7645-1651-5

0-7645-1643-4

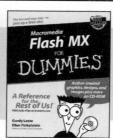

0-7645-0895-4

Also available:

Adobe Acrobat 5 PDF For Dummies (0-7645-1652-3)

ASP.NET For Dummies (0-7645-0866-0)

ColdFusion MX For Dummies (0-7645-1672-8)

Dreamweaver MX For Dummies (0-7645-1630-2)

FrontPage 2002 For Dummies (0-7645-0821-0)

HTML 4 For Dummies (0-7645-0723-0)

Illustrator 10 For Dummies (0-7645-3636-2)

PowerPoint 2002 For Dummies (0-7645-0817-2)

Web Design For Dummies (0-7645-0823-7)

PROGRAMMING & DATABASES

0-7645-0746-X

0-7645-1626-4

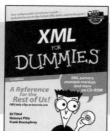

0-7645-1657-4

Also available:

Access 2002 For Dummies (0-7645-0818-0)

Beginning Programming For Dummies (0-7645-0835-0)

Crystal Reports 9 For Dummies (0-7645-1641-8)

Java & XML For Dummies (0-7645-1658-2)

Java 2 For Dummies (0-7645-0765-6)

JavaScript For Dummies (0-7645-0633-1

Oracle9i For Dummies (0-7645-0880-6)

Perl For Dummies (0-7645-0776-1)

PHP and MySQL For Dummies (0-7645-1650-7)

SQL For Dummies (0-7645-0737-0)

Visual Basic .NET For Dummies (0-7645-0867-9)

LINUX, NETWORKING & CERTIFICATION

0-7645-1545-4

0-7645-1760-0

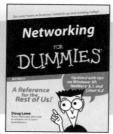

0-7645-0772-9

Also available:

A+ Certification For Dummies (0-7645-0812-1)

CCNP All-in-One Certification For Dummies (0-7645-1648-5)

Cisco Networking For Dummies (0-7645-1668-X)

CISSP For Dummies (0-7645-1670-1)

CIW Foundations For Dummies (0-7645-1635-3)

Firewalls For Dummies (0-7645-0884-9)

Home Networking For Dummies (0-7645-0857-1)

Red Hat Linux All-in-One Desk Reference For Dummies (0-7645-2442-9)

UNIX For Dummies (0-7645-0419-3)

Available wherever books are sold.
Go to www.dummies.com or call 1-877-762-2974 to order direct